CW00495364

My Life and L

Vol. 1

Frank Harris

Alpha Editions

This edition published in 2024

ISBN : 9789357967365

Design and Setting By
Alpha Editions
www.alphaedis.com
Email - info@alphaedis.com

As per information held with us this book is in Public Domain.
This book is a reproduction of an important historical work. Alpha Editions uses the best technology to reproduce historical work in the same manner it was first published to preserve its original nature. Any marks or number seen are left intentionally to preserve its true form.

FOREWORD

to

THE STORY OF "MY LIFE AND LOVES."

"Go, soul, the body's guest,

Upon a thankless errand:

Fear not to touch the best,

The Truth shall be thy warrant."

Sir Walter Raleigh.

Here in the blazing heat of an American August, amid the hurry and scurry of New York, I sit down to write my final declaration of Faith, as a preface or foreword to the Story of my Life. Ultimately it will be read in the spirit in which it has been written and I ask no better fortune. My journalism during the war and after the Armistice brought me prosecutions from the Federal Government. The authorities at Washington accused me of sedition and though the third Postmaster General, Ex-Governor Dockery, of Missouri who was chosen by the Department as the Judge, proclaimed my innocence and assured me I should not be prosecuted again, my magazine (Pearson's) was time and again held up in the post, and its circulation reduced thereby to one-third. I was brought to ruin by the illegal persecution of President Wilson and his Arch-Assistant Burleson, and was laughed at when I asked for compensation. The American Government, it appears, is too poor to pay for its dishonorable blunders.

I record the shameful fact for the benefit of those Rebels and Lovers of the Ideal who will surely find themselves in a similar plight in future emergencies. For myself I do not complain. On the whole I have received better treatment in life than the average man and more lovingkindness than I perhaps deserved. I make no plaint.

If America had not reduced me to penury I should probably not have written this book as boldly as the ideal demanded. At the last push of Fate (I am much nearer seventy than sixty) we are all apt to sacrifice something of Truth for the sake of kindly recognition by our fellows and a peaceful ending. Being that "wicked animal", as the French say, "who defends himself when he is attacked" I turn at length to bay, without any malice, I hope, but also without any fear such as might prompt compromise. I have always fought for the

Holy Spirit of Truth and have been, as Heine said he was, a brave soldier in the Liberation War of Humanity: now one fight more, the best and the last.

There are two main traditions of English writing: the one of perfect liberty, that of Chaucer and Shakespeare, completely outspoken, with a certain liking for lascivious details and witty smut, a man's speech: the other emasculated more and more by Puritanism and since the French Revolution, gelded to tamest propriety; for that upheaval brought the illiterate middle-class to power and insured the domination of girl-readers. Under Victoria, English prose literature became half childish, as in stories of "Little Mary", or at best provincial, as anyone may see who cares to compare the influence of Dickens, Thackeray and Reade in the world with the influence of Balzac, Flaubert and Zola.

Foreign masterpieces such as "Les Contes Drolatiques" and "L'Assommoir" were destroyed in London as obscene by a magistrate's order; even the Bible and Shakespeare were expurgated and all books dolled up to the prim decorum of the English Sunday-school. And America with unbecoming humility worsened the disgraceful, brainless example.

All my life, I have rebelled against this old maid's canon of deportment, and my revolt has grown stronger with advancing years.

In the "Foreword" to "The Man Shakespeare" I tried to show how the Puritanism that had gone out of our morals had gone into the language, enfeebling English thought and impoverishing English speech.

At long last I am going back to the old English tradition. I am determined to tell the truth about my pilgrimage through this world, the whole truth and nothing but the truth, about myself and others, and I shall try to be at least as kindly to others as to myself.

Bernard Shaw assures me that no one is good enough or bad enough to tell the naked truth about himself; but I am beyond good and evil in this respect.

French literature is there to give the cue and inspiration: it is the freest of all in discussing matters of sex and chiefly by reason of its constant preoccupation with all that pertains to passion and desire, it has become the world literature to men of all races.

"Women and Love", Edmond de Goncourt writes in his journal, "always constitute the subject of conversation wherever there is a meeting of intellectual people socially brought together by eating and drinking. Our talk at dinner was at first smutty (polissonne) and Tourgueneff listened to us with the open-mouthed wonder (l'étonnement un peu medusé) of a barbarian who only makes love (fait l'amour) very naturally (très naturellement)."

Whoever reads this passage carefully will understand the freedom I intend to use. But I shall not be tied down even to French conventions. Just as in painting, our knowledge of what the Chinese and Japanese have done, has altered our whole conception of the art, so the Hindoos and Burmese too have extended our understanding of the art of love. I remember going with Rodin through the British Museum and being surprised at the time he spent over the little idols and figures of the South Sea Islanders: "Some of them are trivial", he said, "but look at that, and that, and that—sheer masterpieces that anyone might be proud of—lovely things!"

Art has become coextensive with humanity, and some of my experiences with so-called savages may be of interest even to the most cultured Europeans.

I intend to tell what life has taught me, and if I begin at the A. B. C. of love, it is because I was brought up in Britain and the United States; I shall not stop there.

Of course I know the publication of such a book will at once justify the worst that my enemies have said about me. For forty years now I have championed nearly all the unpopular causes, and have thus made many enemies; now they will all be able to gratify their malice while taking credit for prevision. In itself the book is sure to disgust the "unco guid" and the mediocrities of every kind who have always been unfriendly to me. I have no doubt too, that many sincere lovers of literature who would be willing to accept such license as ordinary French writers use, will condemn me for going beyond this limit. Yet there are many reasons why I should use perfect freedom in this last book.

First of all, I made hideous blunders early in life and saw worse blunders made by other youths, out of sheer ignorance: I want to warn the young and impressionable against the shoals and hidden reefs of life's ocean and chart, so to speak, at the very beginning of the voyage when the danger is greatest, the 'unpath'd waters'.

On the other hand I have missed indescribable pleasures because the power to enjoy and to give delight is keenest early in life, while the understanding both of how to give and how to receive pleasure comes much later, when the faculties are already on the decline.

I used to illustrate the absurdity of our present system of educating the young by a quaint simile. "When training me to shoot", I said, "my earthly father gave me a little single-barreled gun, and when he saw that I had learned the mechanism and could be trusted, he gave me a double-barreled shot-gun. After some years I came into possession of a magazine gun which could shoot half a dozen times if necessary without reloading, my efficiency increasing with my knowledge."

My Creator, or Heavenly Father, on the other hand, when I was wholly without experience and had only just entered my teens, gave me, so to speak, a magazine gun of sex, and hardly had I learned its use and enjoyment when he took it away from me forever, and gave me in its place a double-barreled gun: after a few years, he took that away and gave me a single-barreled gun with which I was forced to content myself for the best part of my life.

Towards the end the old single-barrel began to show signs of wear and age: sometimes it would go off too soon, sometimes it missed fire and shamed me, do what I would.

I want to teach youths how to use their magazine gun of sex so that it may last for years, and when they come to the double-barrel, how to take such care that the good weapon will do them liege service right into their fifties, and the single-barrel will then give them pleasure up to three score years and ten.

Moreover, not only do I desire in this way to increase the sum of happiness in the world while decreasing the pains and disabilities of men, but I wish also to set an example and encourage other writers to continue the work that I am sure is beneficent, as well as enjoyable.

W. L. George in "A Novelist on Novels" writes: "If a novelist were to develop his characters evenly the three hundred page novel might extend to five hundred, the additional two hundred pages would be made up entirely of the sex preoccupations of the characters. There would be as many scenes in the bedroom as in the drawing-room, probably more, as more time is passed in the sleeping apartment. The additional two hundred pages would offer pictures of the sex side of the characters and would compel them to become alive: at present they often fail to come to life because they only develop, say five sides out of six.... Our literary characters are lop-sided because their ordinary traits are fully portrayed while their sex-life is cloaked, minimized or left out.... Therefore the characters in modern novels are all false. They are megalocephalous and emasculate. English women speak a great deal about sex.... It is a cruel position for the English novel. The novelist may discuss anything but the main preoccupation of life.... we are compelled to pad out with murder, theft and arson which as everybody knows, are perfectly moral things to write about."

Pure is the snow—till mixed with mire—

But never half so pure as fire.

There are graver reasons than any I have yet given why the truth should be told boldly. The time has come when those who are, as Shakespeare called them, "God's Spies" having learned the mystery of things, should be called to counsel, for the ordinary political guides have led mankind to disaster: blind leaders of the blind!

Over Niagara we have plunged, as Carlyle predicted, and as every one with vision must have foreseen and now like driftwood we move round and round the whirlpool impotently without knowing whither or why.

One thing certain: we deserve the misery into which we have fallen. The laws of this world are inexorable and don't cheat! Where, when, how have we gone astray? The malady is as wide as civilization which fortunately narrows the enquiry to time.

Ever since our conquest of natural forces began, towards the end of the eighteenth century, and material wealth increased by leaps and bounds, our conduct has deteriorated. Up to that time we had done the gospel of Christ mouth-honor at least; and had to some slight extent shown consideration if not love to our fellowmen: we did not give tithes to charity; but we did give petty doles till suddenly science appeared to reinforce our selfishness with a new message: progress comes through the blotting out of the unfit, we were told, and self-assertion was preached as a duty: the idea of the Superman came into life and the Will to Power and thereby Christ's teaching of love and pity and gentleness was thrust into the background.

At once we men gave ourselves over to wrong doing and our iniquity took monstrous forms.

The creed we professed and the creed we practised were poles apart. Never I believe in the world's history was there such confusion in man's thought about conduct, never were there so many different ideals put forward for his guidance. It is imperatively necessary for us to bring clearness into this muddle and see why we have gone wrong and where.

For the world-war is only the last of a series of diabolical acts which have shocked the conscience of humanity. The greatest crimes in recorded time have been committed during the last half century almost without protest by the most civilised nations, nations that still call themselves Christian. Whoever has watched human affairs in the last half century must acknowledge that our progress has been steadily hell-ward.

The hideous massacres and mutilations of tens of thousands of women and children in the Congo Free State without protest on the part of Great Britain who could have stopped it all with one word, is surely due to the same spirit that directed the abominable blockade (continued by both England and America long after the Armistice) which condemned hundreds and thousands of women and children of our own kith and kin to death by starvation. The unspeakable meanness and confessed fraud of the Peace of Versailles with its tragic consequences from Vladivostock to London and finally the shameless, dastardly war waged by all the Allies and by America on Russia, for money, show us that we have been assisting at the overthrow of morality itself and returning to the ethics of the wolf and the polity of the Thieves' Kitchen.

And our public acts as nations are paralleled by our treatment of our fellows within the community. For the small minority the pleasures of living have been increased in the most extraordinary way while the pains and sorrows of existence have been greatly mitigated, but the vast majority even of civilised peoples have hardly been admitted to any share in the benefits of our astounding material progress. The slums of our cities show the same spirit we have displayed in our treatment of the weaker races. It is no secret that over fifty per cent of English volunteers in the war were below the pigmy physical standard required and about one half of our American soldiers were morons with the intelligence of children under twelve years of age: "vae victis" has been our motto with the most appalling results. Clearly we have come to the end of a period and must take thought about the future.

The religion that directed or was supposed to direct our conduct for nineteen centuries has been finally discarded. Even the divine spirit of Jesus was thrown aside by Nietzsche as one throws the hatchet after the helve or to use the better German simile, the child was thrown out with the bath-water. The silly sex-morality of Paul has brought discredit upon the whole Gospel. Paul was impotent, boasted indeed that he had no sexual desires, wished that all men were even as he was in this respect, just as the fox in the fable who had lost his tail, wished that all other foxes should be mutilated in the same way in order to attain his perfection.

I often say that the Christian churches were offered two things: the spirit of Jesus and the idiotic morality of Paul, and they all rejected the highest inspiration and took to their hearts the incredibly base and stupid prohibition. Following Paul we have turned the Goddess of Love into a fiend and degraded the crowning impulse of our Being into a capital sin; yet everything high and ennobling in our nature springs directly out of the sexual instinct.

Grant Allan says rightly: "Its alliance is wholly with whatever is purest and most beautiful within us. To it we owe our love of bright colours, graceful form, melodious sound, rhythmic motion. To it we owe the evolution of music, of poetry, of romance, of belles lettres, of painting, of sculpture, of decorative art, of dramatic entertainment. To it we owe the entire existence of our aesthetic sense which in the last resort is a secondary sex-attribute.

From it springs the love of beauty, around it all beautiful arts circle as their centre. Its subtle aroma pervades all literature. And to it we owe the paternal, maternal and marital relations, the growth of the affections, the love of little pattering feet and baby laughter."

And this scientific statement is incomplete: not only is the sexual instinct the inspiring force of all art and literature; it is also our chief teacher of gentleness and tenderness, making lovingkindness an ideal and so warring against cruelty and harshness and that misjudging of our fellows which we men call justice. To my mind, cruelty is the one diabolic sin which must be wiped out of life and made impossible.

Paul's condemnation of the body and its desires is in direct contradiction to the gentle teaching of Jesus and is in itself idiotic. I reject Paulism as passionately as I accept the gospel of Christ. In regard to the body I go back to the Pagan ideals, to Eros and Aphrodite and

The fair humanities of old religions.

Paul and the Christian churches have dirtied desire, degraded women, debased procreation, vulgarized and vilified the best instinct in us.

"Priests in black gowns are going their rounds,

And binding with briars, my joys and desires."

And the worst of it all is that the highest function of man has been degraded by foul words so that it is almost impossible to write the body's hymn of joy as it should be written. The poets have been almost as guilty in this respect as the priests: Aristophanes and Rabelais are ribald, dirty: Boccaccio cynical while Ovid leers cold-bloodedly and Zola like Chaucer finds it difficult to suit language to his desires. Walt Whitman is better though often merely commonplace. The Bible is the best of all; but not frank enough even in the noble Song of Solomon which now and then by sheer imagination manages to convey the ineffable!

We are beginning to reject Puritanism and its unspeakable, brainless pruderies; but Catholicism is just as bad. Go to the Vatican Gallery and the great Church of St. Peter in Rome and you will find the fairest figures of ancient art clothed in painted tin, as if the most essential organs of the body were disgusting and had to be concealed.

I say the body is beautiful and must be lifted and dignified by our reverence: I love the body more than any Pagan of them all and I love the soul and her aspirations as well; for me the body and the soul are alike beautiful, all dedicate to Love and her worship.

I have no divided allegiance and what I preach today amid the scorn and hatred of men will be universally accepted tomorrow; for in my vision, too, a thousand years are as one day.

We must unite the soul of Paganism, the love of beauty and art and literature with the soul of Christianity and its human lovingkindness in a new synthesis which shall include all the sweet and gentle and noble impulses in us.

What we all need is more of the spirit of Jesus: we must learn at length with Shakespeare: "Pardon's the word for all!"

I want to set this Pagan-Christian ideal before men as the highest and most human too.

Now one word to my own people and their peculiar shortcomings. Anglo-Saxon domineering combativeness is the greatest danger to Humanity in the world today. Americans are proud of having blotted out the red Indian and stolen his possessions and of burning and torturing negroes in the sacred name of equality. At all costs we must get rid of our hypocrisies and falsehoods and see ourselves as we are—a domineering race, vengeful and brutal, as exemplified in Haiti; we must study the inevitable effects of our soulless, brainless selfishness as shown in the world-war.

The Germanic ideal which is also the English and American ideal, of the conquering male that despises all weaker and less intelligent races and is eager to enslave or annihilate them, must be set aside. A hundred years ago, there were only fifteen millions of English and American folk; today there are nearly two hundred millions and it is plain that in another century or so, they will be the most numerous, as they are already by far the most powerful, race on earth.

The most numerous folk hitherto, the Chinese, has set a good example by remaining within its own boundaries, but these conquering, colonizing Anglo-Saxons threaten to overrun the earth and destroy all other varieties of the species man. Even now we annihilate the Red Indian because he is not subservient, while we are content to degrade the negro who doesn't threaten our domination.

Is it wise to desire only one flower in this garden of a world? Is it wise to blot out the better varieties while preserving the inferior?

And the Anglo-Saxon ideal for the individual is even baser and more inept. Intent on satisfying his own conquering lust, he has compelled the female of the species to an unnatural chastity of thought and deed and word. He has thus made of his wife a meek, upper-servant or slave (die Hausfrau), who has hardly any intellectual interests and whose spiritual being only finds a narrow outlet in her mother-instincts. The daughter he has labored to degrade into the strangest sort of two-legged tame fowl ever imagined: she must seek a mate while concealing or denying all her strongest sex-feelings: in fine, she should be as cold-blooded as a frog and as wily and ruthless as an Apache on the war-path.

The ideal he has set before himself is confused and confusing: really he desires to be healthy and strong while gratifying all his sexual appetites. The highest type, however, the English gentleman, has pretty constantly in mind the individualistic ideal of what he calls an "all-round man", a man whose body and mind is harmoniously developed and brought to a comparatively high state of efficiency.

He has no inkling of the supreme truth that every man and woman possesses some small facet of the soul which reflects life in a peculiar way or, to use the language of religion, sees God as no other soul born into the world, can ever see Him.

It is the first duty of every individual to develop all his faculties of body, mind and spirit as completely and harmoniously as possible; but it is a still higher duty for each of us to develop our special faculty to the uttermost consistent with health; for only by so doing shall we attain to the highest self-consciousness or be able to repay our debt to humanity. No Anglo-Saxon, so far as I know, has ever advocated this ideal or dreamed of regarding it as a duty. In fact, no teacher so far has even thought of helping men and women to find out the particular power which constitutes their essence and inbeing and justifies their existence. And so nine men and women out of ten go through life without realising their own special nature: they cannot lose their souls for they have never found them.

For every son of Adam, for every daughter of Eve, this is the supreme defeat, the final disaster. Yet no one, so far as I know, has ever warned of the danger or spoken of this ideal.

That's why I love this book in spite of all its shortcomings and all its faults: it is the first book ever written to glorify the body and its passionate desires and the soul as well and its sacred, climbing sympathies.

Give and forgive, I always say, is the supreme lesson of life.

I only wish I had begun the book five years ago, before I had been half drowned in the brackish flood of old age and become conscious of failing memory; but notwithstanding this handicap, I have tried to write the book I have always wanted to read, the first chapter in the Bible of Humanity. And so I front this foreword with the lovely figure of Venus Queen, and I close it with the face of Christ as seen by Rubens when He forgave the adulterous woman.

Hearken to good counsel:

"Live out your whole free life, while yet on earth,
Seize the quick Present, prize your one sure boon:
Though brief, each day a golden sun has birth;
Though dim, the night is gemmed with stars and moon."

Christ and The Woman taken in Adultery
by Rubens.

MY LIFE AND LOVES
Chapter I.

Memory is the Mother of the Muses, the prototype of the Artist. As a rule she selects and relieves out the important, omitting what is accidental or trivial. Now and then, however, she makes mistakes like all other artists. Nevertheless I take Memory in the main as my guide.

I was born on the 14th of February 1855, and named James Thomas, after my father's two brothers: my father was in the Navy, a lieutenant in command of a revenue cutter or gunboat, and we children saw him only at long intervals.

My earliest recollection is being danced on the foot of my father's brother James, the Captain of an Indiaman, who paid us a visit in the south of Kerry when I was about two. I distinctly remember repeating a hymn by heart for him, my mother on the other side of the fireplace, prompting: then I got him to dance me a little more, which was all I wanted. I remember my mother telling him I could read, and his surprise.

The next memory must have been about the same time: I was seated on the floor screaming when my father came in and asked: "What's the matter?"

"It's only Master Jim", replied the nurse crossly, "he's just screaming out of sheer temper, Sir, look, there's not a tear in his eye."

A year or so later, it must have been, I was proud of walking up and down a long room while my mother rested her hand on my head, and called me her walking stick.

Later still I remember coming to her room at night: I whispered to her and then kissed her, but her cheek was cold and she didn't answer, and I woke the house with my shrieking: she was dead. I felt no grief, but something gloomy and terrible in the sudden cessation of the usual household activities.

A couple of days later I saw her coffin carried out, and when the nurse told my sister and me that we would never see our mother again, I was surprised merely and wondered why.

My mother died when I was nearly four, and soon after we moved to Kingstown near Dublin. I used to get up in the night with my sister Annie, four years my senior and go foraging for bread and jam or sugar. One morning about daybreak I stole into the nurse's room, and saw a man beside her in bed, a man with a red moustache. I drew my sister in and she too saw him. We crept out again without waking them. My only emotion was surprise, but next day the nurse denied me sugar on my bread and butter and I said: "I'll tell"—I don't know why: I had then no inkling of modern journalism.

"Tell what?" she asked.

"There was a man in your bed", I replied, "last night."

"Hush, hush!" she said, and gave me the sugar.

After that I found all I had to do was to say "I'll tell!" to get whatever I wanted. My sister even wished to know one day what I had to tell, but I would not say. I distinctly remember my feeling of superiority over her because she had not had sense enough to exploit the sugar mine.

When I was between four and five, I was sent with Annie to a girl's boarding-school in Kingstown kept by a Mrs. Frost. I was put in the class with the oldest girls on account of my proficiency in arithmetic, and I did my best at it because I wanted to be with them, though I had no conscious reason for my preference. I remember how the nearest girl used to lift me up and put me in my high-chair and how I would hurry over the sums set in compound long division and proportion, for as soon as I had finished, I would drop my pencil on the floor, and then turn round and climb down out of my chair, ostensibly to get it, but really to look at the girls' legs. Why? I couldn't have said.

I was at the bottom of the class and the legs got bigger and bigger towards the end of the long table, and I preferred to look at the big ones.

As soon as the girl next to me missed me, she would move her chair back and call me, and I'd pretend to have just found my slate-pencil, which I said had rolled, and she'd lift me back into my high-chair.

One day I noticed a beautiful pair of legs on the other side of the table, near the top. There must have been a window behind the girl; for her legs up to the knees were in full light and they filled me with emotion giving me an indescribable pleasure. They were not the thickest legs, which surprised me. Up to that moment, I had thought it was the thickest legs I liked best; but now I saw that several girls, three anyway, had bigger legs, but none like hers, so shapely, with such slight ankles and tapering lines. I was enthralled and at the same time a little scared.

I crept back into my chair with one idea in my little head: could I get close to those lovely legs and perhaps touch them—breathless expectancy. I knew I could hit my slate-pencil and make it roll up between the files of legs. Next day I did this and crawled right up till I was close to the legs that made my heart beat in my throat and yet gave me a strange delight. I put out my hand to touch them; suddenly the thought came that the girl would simply be frightened by my touch and pull her legs back and I should be discovered and—I was frightened.

I returned to my chair to think, and soon found the solution. Next day I again crouched before the girl's legs, choking with emotion. I put my pencil near her toes, and reached round between her legs with my left hand as if to get it, taking care to touch her calf. She shrieked, and drew back her legs, holding my hand tight between them, and cried: "What are you doing there!"

"Getting my pencil", I said humbly, "it rolled."

"There it is", she said, kicking it with her foot.

"Thanks" I replied, overjoyed, for the feel of her soft legs was still on my hand.

"You're a funny little fellow", she said, but I didn't care; I had had my first taste of Paradise and the forbidden fruit—authentic heaven!

I have no recollection of her face: it seemed pleasant; that's all I remember. None of the girls made any impression on me but I can still recall the thrill of admiration and pleasure her shapely limbs gave me.

I record this incident at length, because it stands alone in my memory, and because it proves that sex-feeling may show itself in early childhood.

One day about 1890 I had Meredith, Walter Pater and Oscar Wilde dining with me in Park Lane and the time of sex-awakening was discussed. Both Pater and Wilde spoke of it as a sign of puberty; Pater thought it began about 13 or 14 and Wilde to my amazement set it as late as 16. Meredith alone was inclined to put it earlier.

"It shows sporadically", he said, "and sometimes before puberty."

I recalled the fact that Napoleon tells how he was in love before he was five years old with a school-mate called Giacominetta, but even Meredith laughed at this and would not believe that any real sex-feeling could show itself so early. To prove the point, I gave my experience as I have told it here, and brought Meredith to pause: "very interesting", he thought, "but peculiar!"

"In her abnormalities", says Goethe, "Nature reveals her secrets"; here is an abnormality, perhaps as such, worth noting.

I hadn't another sensation of sex till nearly six years later when I was eleven, since which time such emotions have been almost incessant.

My exaltation to the oldest class in arithmetic got me into trouble by bringing me into relations with the headmistress, Mrs. Frost, who was very cross and seemed to think that I should spell as correctly as I did sums. When she found I couldn't, she used to pull my ears and got into the habit of digging her long thumb-nail into my ear till it bled. I didn't mind the smart; in fact, I was delighted, for her cruelty brought me the pity of the elder girls who used to wipe my ears with their pocket-handkerchiefs and say that old Frost was a beast and a cat.

One day my father sent for me and I went with a petty officer to his vessel in the harbor: my right ear had bled on to my collar. As soon as my father noticed it and saw the older scars, he got angry and took me back to the school and told Mrs. Frost what he thought of her, and her punishments.

Immediately afterwards, it seems to me I was sent to live with my eldest brother Vernon, ten years older than myself, who was in lodgings with friends in Galway while going to the College.

There I spent the next five years, which passed leaving a blank. I learned nothing in those years except how to play "tig", "hide and seek", "footer" and ball. I was merely a healthy, strong, little animal without an ache or pain or trace of thought.

Then I remember an interlude at Belfast where Vernon and I lodged with an old Methodist who used to force me to go to church with him and drew on a little black skullcap during the Service, which filled me with shame and made me hate him. There is a period in life when every thing peculiar or individual, excites dislike and is in itself an offense.

I learned here to "mitch" and lie simply to avoid school and to play, till my brother found I was coughing and having sent for a doctor, was informed that I had congestion of the lungs; the truth being that I played all day and never came home for dinner, seldom indeed before seven o'clock, when I knew Vernon would be back. I mention this incident because, while confined to the house, I discovered under the old Methodist's bed, a set of doctor's books with colored plates of the insides and the pudenda of men and women. I devoured all the volumes and bits of knowledge from them stuck to me for many a year. But curiously enough the main sex fact was not revealed to me then; but in talks a little later with boys of my own age.

I learned nothing in Belfast but rules of games and athletics. My brother Vernon used to go to a gymnasium every evening and exercise and box. To my astonishment he was not among the best; so while he was boxing I began practicing this and that, drawing myself up till my chin was above the bar, and repeating this till one evening Vernon found I could do it thirty times running: his praise made me proud.

About this time, when I was ten or so, we were all brought together in Carrickfergus; my brothers and sisters then first became living, individual beings to me. Vernon was going to a bank as a clerk, and was away all day. Willie, six years older than I was, Annie four years my senior, and Chrissie two years my junior, went to the same day-school, though the girls went to the girls' entrance and had women teachers. Willie and I were in the same class; though he had grown to be taller than Vernon, I could beat him in most of the lessons. There was, however, one important branch of learning, in which he was easily the best in the school. The first time I heard him recite "The Battle of Ivry" by Macaulay, I was carried off my feet. He made gestures and his voice altered so naturally that I was lost in admiration.

That evening my sisters and I were together and we talked of Willie's talent. My eldest sister was enthusiastic, which I suppose stirred envy and emulation in me, for I got up and imitated him, and to my sisters' surprise I knew the whole poem by heart. "Who taught you?" Annie wanted to know, and when she heard that I had learned it just from hearing Willie recite it once, she was astonished and must have told our teacher, for the next afternoon he asked me to follow Willie and told me I was very good. From this time on, the reciting class was my chief education. I learned every boy's piece and could imitate them all perfectly, except one redheaded rascal who could recite the "African Chief" better than anyone else, better even than the master. It was pure melodrama; but Red-head was a born actor and swept us all away by the realism of his impersonation. Never shall I forget how the boy rendered the words:

"Look, feast thy greedy eyes on gold,

Long kept for sorest need;

Take it, thou askest sums untold

And say that I am freed.

Take it; my wife the long, long day

Weeps by the cocoa-tree,

And my young children leave their play

And ask in vain for me."

I haven't seen or heard the poem these fifty odd years. It seems tawdry stuff to me now; but the boy's accents were of the very soul of tragedy and I realized clearly that I couldn't recite that poem as well as he did. He was inimitable. Every time his accents and manner altered; now he did these verses wonderfully, at another time those, so that I couldn't ape him; always there was a touch of novelty in his intense realization of the tragedy. Strange to say it was the only poem he recited at all well.

An examination came and I was first in the school in arithmetic and first too in elocution; Vernon even praised me, while Willie slapped me and got kicked on the shins for his pains. Vernon separated us and told Willie he should be ashamed of hitting one only half as big as he was. Willie lied promptly, saying I had kicked him first. I disliked Willie; I hardly know why, save that he was a rival in the school life.

After this Annie began to treat me differently and now I seemed to see her as she was and was struck by her funny ways. She wished both Chrissie and myself to call her "Nita"; it was short for "Anita", she said, which was the stylish French way of pronouncing Annie. She hated "Annie"—it was "common and vulgar"; I couldn't make out why.

One evening we were together and she had undressed Chrissie for bed, when she opened her own dress and showed us how her breasts had grown while Chrissie's still remained small, and indeed "Nita's" were ever so much larger and prettier and round like apples. Nita let us touch them gently and was evidently very proud of them. She sent Chrissie to bed in the next room while I went on learning a lesson beside her. Nita left the room to get something, I think, when Chrissie called me and I went into the bedroom wondering what she wanted. She wished me to know that her breasts would grow too, and be just as pretty as Nita's. "Don't you think so!" she asked, and taking my hand put it on them, and I said, "Yes", for indeed I liked her better than Nita who was all airs and graces and full of affectations.

Suddenly Nita called me, and Chrissie kissed me, whispering "don't tell her" and I promised. I always liked Chrissie and Vernon. Chrissie was very clever and pretty, with dark curls and big hazel eyes, and Vernon was a sort of hero and always very kind to me.

I learned nothing from this happening. I had hardly any sex-thrill with either sister, indeed, nothing like so much as I had had, five years before, through the girl's legs in Mrs. Frost's school, and I record the incident here chiefly for another reason. One afternoon about 1890, Aubrey Beardsley and his sister Mabel, a very pretty girl, had been lunching with me in Park Lane. Afterwards we went into the Park. I accompanied them as far as Hyde Park Corner. For some reason or other, I elaborated the theme that men of thirty or forty usually corrupted young girls, and women of thirty or forty in turn corrupted youths.

"I don't agree with you", Aubrey remarked: "It's usually a fellow's sister who gives him his first lessons in sex. I know it was Mabel here, who first taught me."

I was amazed at his outspokenness; Mabel flushed crimson and I hastened to add:

"In childhood girls are far more precocious; but those little lessons are usually too early to matter." He wouldn't have it, but I changed the subject resolutely and Mabel told me some time afterwards that she was very grateful to me for cutting short the discussion: “Aubrey”, she said, “loves all sex things and doesn’t care what he says or does.”

I had seen before that Mabel was pretty: I realised that day when she stooped over a flower that her figure was beautifully slight and round. Aubrey caught my eye at the moment and remarked maliciously:

“Mabel was my first model, weren’t you, Mabs? I was in love with her figure”, he went on judicially, “her breasts were so high and firm and round that I took her as my ideal.” She laughed, blushing a little, and rejoined, “Your figures, Aubrey, are not “exactly ideal”.”

I realised from this little discussion that most men’s sisters were just as precocious as mine and just as likely to act as teachers in the matter of sex.

From about this time on, the individualities of people began to impress me definitely. Vernon suddenly got an appointment in a bank at Armagh and I went to live with him there, in lodgings. The lodging-house keeper I disliked: she was always trying to make me keep hours and rules, and I was as wild as a homeless dog, but Armagh was a wonder city to me. Vernon made me a day-boy at the Royal School: it was my first big school; I learned all the lessons very easily and most of the boys and all the masters were kind to me. The great Mall or park-like place in the centre of the town delighted me; I had soon climbed nearly every tree in it, tree-climbing and reciting being the two sports in which I excelled.

When we were at Carrickfergus, my father had had me on board his vessel and had matched me at climbing the rigging against a cabin-boy and though the sailor was first at the cross-trees, I caught him on the descent by jumping at a rope and letting it slide through my hands, almost at falling speed to the deck. I heard my father tell this afterwards with pleasure to Vernon, which pleased my vanity inordinately and increased, if that were possible, my delight in showing off.

For another reason my vanity had grown beyond measure. At Carrickfergus I had got hold of a book on athletics belonging to Vernon and had there learned that if you went into the water up to your neck and threw yourself boldly forward and tried to swim, you would swim; for the body is lighter than the water and floats.

The next time I went down to bathe with Vernon, instead of going on the beach in the shallow water and wading out, I went with him to the end of the pier and when he dived in, I went down the steps and as soon as he came up to the surface I cried, “Look! I can swim too”, and I boldly threw myself forward and, after a moment’s dreadful sinking and spluttering, did in fact swim. When I wanted to get back I had a moment of appalling fear: “Could

I turn round!" The next moment I found it quite easy to turn and I was soon safely back on the steps again.

"When did you learn to swim?", asked Vernon coming out beside me. "This minute", I replied and as he was surprised, I told him I had read it all in his book and made up my mind to venture the very next time I bathed. A little time afterwards I heard him tell this to some of his men friends in Armagh, and they all agreed that it showed extraordinary courage, for I was small for my age and always appeared even younger than I was.

Looking back, I see that many causes combined to strengthen the vanity in me which had already become inordinate and in the future was destined, to shape my life and direct its purposes. Here in Armagh everything conspired to foster my besetting sin. I was put among boys of my age, I think in the lower Fourth, and the form-master finding that I knew no Latin, showed me a Latin grammar and told me I'd have to learn it as quickly as possible, for the class had already begun to read Caesar: he showed me the first declension *mensa*, as the example, and asked me if I could learn it by the next day. I said I would, and as luck would have it, the Mathematical master passing at the moment, the form-master told him I was backward and should be in a lower form.

"He's very good indeed at figures", the Mathematical master rejoined, "he might be in the Upper Division."

"Really!" exclaimed the Form-master. "See what you can do," he said to me, "you may find it possible to catch up. Here's a Caesar too, you may as well take it with you. We have done only two or three pages."

That evening I sat down to the Latin grammar, and in an hour or so had learned all the declensions and nearly all the adjectives and pronouns. Next day I was trembling with hope of praise and if the form-master had encouraged me or said one word of commendation, I might have distinguished myself in the class work, and so changed perhaps my whole life; but the next day he had evidently forgotten all about my backwardness. By dint of hearing the other boys answer I got a smattering of the lessons, enough to get through them without punishment, and soon a good memory brought me among the foremost boys, though I took no interest in learning Latin.

Another incident fed my self-esteem and opened to me the world of books. Vernon often went to a clergyman's who had a pretty daughter, and I too was asked to their evening parties. The daughter found out I could recite, and soon it became the custom to get me to recite some poem everywhere we went. Vernon bought me the poems of Macaulay and Walter Scott and I had soon learned them all by heart, and used to declaim them with infinite gusto: at first my gestures were imitations of Willie's; but Vernon taught me to be more natural and I bettered his teaching. No doubt my small stature helped the effect and the Irish love of rhetoric did the rest; but every one praised me and the showing off made me very vain and—a more important result—the learning of new poems brought me to the reading of novels and books of adventure. I was soon lost in this new world: though I played at school with the other boys, in the evening I never opened a lesson-book; but devoured Lever and Mayne Reid, Marryat and Fenimore Cooper with unspeakable delight.

I had one or two fights at school with boys of my own age: I hated fighting; but I was conceited and combative and strong and so got to fisticuffs twice or three times. Each time, as soon as an elder boy saw the scrimmage, he would advise us, after looking on for a round or two, to stop and make friends. The Irish are supposed to love fighting better than eating; but my school-days assure me that they are not nearly so combative or perhaps I should say, so brutal, as the English.

In one of my fights a boy took my part and we became friends. His name was Howard and we used to go on long walks together. One day I wanted him to meet Strangways, the Vicar's son, who was fourteen but silly, I thought; Howard shook his head: "he wouldn't want to know me", he said, "I am a Roman Catholic." I still remember the feeling of horror his confession called up in me: "A Roman Catholic! Could anyone as nice as Howard be a Catholic?"

I was thunderstruck and this amazement has always illumined for me the abyss of Protestant bigotry, but I wouldn't break with Howard who was two years older than I and who taught me many things. He taught me to like Fenians, though I hardly knew what the word meant. One day I remember he showed me posted on the Court House a notice offering 5000 Pounds sterling as reward to anyone who would tell the whereabouts of James Stephen, the Fenian Head-Centre. "He's travelling all over Ireland", Howard whispered, "everybody knows him", adding with gusto, "but no one would give the Head-Centre away to the dirty English." I remember thrilling to the mystery and chivalry of the story. From that moment Head-Centre was a sacred symbol to me as to Howard.

One day we met Strangways and somehow or other began talking of sex. Howard knew all about it and took pleasure in enlightening us both. It was Cecil Howard who first initiated Strangways and me too in self-abuse. In spite of my Novel reading, I was still at eleven too young to get much pleasure from the practice; but I was delighted to know how children were made and a lot of new facts about sex. Strangways had hair about his private parts, as indeed Howard had, also, and when he rubbed himself and the orgasm came, a sticky milky fluid spirted from Strangway's cock which Howard told us was the man's seed, which must go right into the woman's womb to make a child.

A week later, Strangways astonished us both by telling how he had made up to the nursemaid of his younger sisters and got into her bed at night. The first time she wouldn't let him do anything, it appeared, but after a night or two he managed to touch her sex and assured us it was all covered with silky hairs. A little later he told us how she had locked her door and how the next day he had taken off the lock and got into bed with her again. At first she was cross, or pretended to be, he said, but he kept on kissing her and begging her, and bit by bit she yielded, and he touched her sex again: "it was a slit", he said. A few nights later, he told us he had put his prick into her and "Oh! by gum, it was wonderful, wonderful!"

"But how did you do it!" we wanted to know and he gave us his whole experience. "Girls love kissing," he said, "and so I kissed and kissed her and put my leg on her, and her hand on my cock and I kept touching her breasts and her cunny (that's what she calls it) and at last I got on her between her legs and she guided my prick into her cunt (God it was wonderful!) and now I go with her every night and often in the day as well. She likes her cunt touched, but very gently", he added, "she showed me how to do it with one finger like this" and he suited the action to the word.

Strangways in a moment became to us not only a hero but a miracle-man; we pretended not to believe him in order to make him tell us more, but in our hearts we knew he was telling us the truth, and we were almost crazy with breathless desire.

I got him to invite me up to the Vicarage and I saw Mary the nurse-girl there, and she seemed to me almost a woman and spoke to him as "Master Will" and he kissed her, though she frowned and said "Leave off" and "Behave yourself", very angrily; but I felt that her anger was put on to prevent my guessing the truth.

I was aflame with desire and when I told Howard, he, too, burned with lust, and took me out for a walk and questioned me all over again and, under a haystack in the country we gave ourselves to a bout of frigging which for the first time thrilled me with pleasure.

All the time we were playing with ourselves I kept thinking of Mary's hot slit, as Strangways had described it, and at length a real orgasm came and shook me; the imagining had intensified my delight.

Nothing in my life up to that moment was comparable in joy to that story of sexual pleasure as described, and acted for us, by Strangways.

MY FATHER.

Father was coming: I was sick with fear: he was so strict and loved to punish. On the ship he had beaten me with a strap because I had gone forward and listened to the sailors talking smut: I feared him and disliked him ever since I saw him once come aboard drunk.

It was the evening of a regatta at Kingston. He had been asked to lunch on one of the big yachts. I heard the officers talking of it. They said he was asked because he knew more about tides and currents along the coast than anyone, more even than the fishermen. The racing skippers wanted to get some information out of him. Another added, "he knows the slants of the wind off Howth Head, ay, and the weather, too, better than anyone living!" All agreed he was a first-rate sailor "one of the best, the very best if he had a decent temper—the little devil."

"D'ye mind when he steered the gig in that race for all? Won? av course he won, he has always won—ah! he's a great little sailor an' he takes care of the men's food too, but he has the divil's own temper—an' that's the truth."

That afternoon of the Regatta, he came up the ladder quickly and stumbled smiling as he stepped down to the deck. I had never seen him like that; he was grinning and walking unsteadily: I gazed at him in amazement. An officer turned aside and as he passed me he said to another: "Drunk as a lord." Another helped my father down to his cabin and came up five minutes afterwards: "he's snoring: he'll soon be all right: it's that champagne they give him, and all that praising him and pressing him to give them tips for this and that."

"No, no!" cried another, "it's not the drink; he only gets drunk when he hasn't to pay for it", and all of them grinned; it was true, I felt, and I despised the meanness inexpressibly.

I hated them for seeing him, and hated him—drunk and talking thick and staggering about; an object of derision and pity!—my "Governor", as Vernon called him; I despised him.

And I recalled other griefs I had against him. A Lord of the Admiralty had come aboard once: father was dressed in his best; I was very young: it was just after I had learned to swim in Carrickfergus. My father used to make me undress and go in and swim round the vessel every morning after my lessons.

That morning I had come up as usual at eleven and a strange gentleman and my father were talking together near the companion. As I appeared my father gave me a frown to go below but the stranger caught sight of me and laughing called me. I came to them and the stranger was surprised on hearing I could swim. "Jump in, Jim!" cried my father, "and swim round."

Nothing loath I ran down the ladder, pulled off my clothes and jumped in. The stranger and my father were above me smiling and talking; my father waved his hand and I swam round the vessel. When I got back, I was about to get on the steps and come aboard when my father said:

"No, no, swim on round till I tell you to stop."

Away I went again quite proud; but when I got round the second time I was tired; I had never swum so far and I had sunk deep in the water and a little spray of wave had gone into my mouth; I was very glad to get near the steps, but as I stretched out my hand to mount them, my father waved his hand.—

"Go on, go on!" he cried, "till you're told to stop."

I went on: but now I was very tired and frightened as well, and as I got to the bow the sailors leant over the bulwarks and one encouraged me: "Go slow, Jim, you'll get round all right." I saw it was big Newton, the stroke-oar of my father's gig, but just because of his sympathy I hated my father the more for making me so tired and so afraid.

When I got round the third time, I swam very slowly and let myself sink very low, and the stranger spoke for me to my father, and then he himself told me to "come up."

I came eagerly, but a little scared at what my father might do; but the stranger came over to me, saying, "he's all blue; that water's very cold, Captain; someone should give him a good towelling."

My father said nothing but "Go down and dress", adding, "get warm."

The memory of my fear made me see that he was always asking me to do too much, and I hated him who could get drunk and shame me and make me run races up the rigging with the cabin boys who were grown men and could beat me. I disliked him.

I was too young then to know that it was probably the habit of command which prevented him from praising me, though I knew in a half-conscious way that he was proud of me, because I was the only one of his children who never got sea-sick.

A little later he arrived in Armagh, and the following week was wretched: I had to come straight home from school every day, and go out for a long walk with the "governor" and he was not a pleasant companion. I couldn't let myself go with him as with a chum; I might in the heat of talk use some word or tell him something and get into an awful row. So I walked beside him silently, taking heed as to what I should say in answer to his simplest question. There was no companionship!

In the evening he used to send me to bed early: even before nine o'clock, though Vernon always let me stay up with him reading till eleven or twelve o'clock. One night I went up to my bedroom on the next floor, but returned almost at once to get a book and have a read in bed, which was a rare treat to me. I was afraid to go into the sitting-room; but crept into the dining-room where there were a few books, though not so interesting as those in the parlour; the door between the two rooms was ajar. Suddenly I heard my father say:

"He's a little Fenian."

"Fenian", repeated Vernon in amazement, "really, Governor, I don't believe he knows the meaning of the word; he's only just eleven, you must remember."

"I tell you" broke in my father, "he talked of James Stephen, the Fenian Head-Centre, today with wild admiration. He's a Fenian alright, but how did he catch it?"

"I'm sure I don't know", replied Vernon, "he reads a great deal and is very quick: I'll find out about it."

"No, no!" said my father, "the thing is to cure him: he must go to some school in England, that'll cure him."

I waited to hear no more but got my book and crept upstairs; so because I loved the Fenian Head-Centre I must be a Fenian.

"How stupid Father is", was my summing up, but England tempted me, England—life was opening out.

It was at the Royal School in the summer after my sex-experiences with Strangways and Howard that I first began to notice dress. A boy in the sixth form named Milman had taken a liking to me and though he was five years older than I was, he often went with Howard and myself for walks. He was a stickler for dress, said that no one but "cads" (a name I learned from him for the first time) and common folk would wear a made-up tie: he gave me one of his scarves and showed me how to make a running lover's knot in it. On another occasion he told me that only "cads" would wear trowsers frayed or repaired.

Was it Milman's talk that made me self-conscious or my sex-awakening through Howard and Strangways? T couldn't say; but at this time I had a curious and prolonged experience. My brother Vernon hearing me once complain of my dress, got me three suits of clothes, one in black with an Eton jacket for best and a tall hat and the others in tweeds: he gave me shirts, too, and ties, and I began to take great care of my appearance. At our evening parties the girls and young women (Vernon's friends) were kinder to me than ever and I found myself wondering whether I really looked "nice" as they said.

I began to wash and bathe carefully and brush my hair to regulation smoothness (only "cads" used pomatum, Milman said) and when I was asked to recite, I would pout and plead prettily that I did not want to, just in order to be pressed.

Sex was awakening in me at this time but was still indeterminate, I imagine; for two motives ruled me for over six months: I was always wondering how I looked and watching to see if people liked me. I used to try to speak with the accent used by the "best people" and on coming into a room I prepared my entrance. Someone, I think it was Vernon's sweetheart, Monica, said that I had an energetic profile, so I always sought to show my profile. In fact, for some six months, I was more a girl than a boy, with all a girl's self-consciousness and manifold affectations and sentimentalities: I often used to think that no one cared for me really and I would weep over my unloved loneliness.

Whenever later, as a writer, I wished to picture a young girl, I had only to go back to this period in my consciousness in order to attain the peculiar view-point of the girl.

LIFE IN AN ENGLISH GRAMMAR SCHOOL.

Chapter II.

If I tried my best, it would take a year to describe the life in that English Grammar School at R.... I had always been perfectly happy in every Irish school and especially in the Royal School at Armagh. Let me give one difference as briefly as possible. When I whispered in the class-room in Ireland, the master would frown at me and shake his head; ten minutes later I was talking again, and he'd hold up an admonitory finger: the third time he'd probably say, "Stop talking, Harris, don't you see you're disturbing your neighbour?" Half an hour later in despair he'd cry, "If you still talk, I'll have to punish you."

Ten minutes afterwards: "You're incorrigible, Harris, come up here" and I'd have to go and stand beside his desk for the rest of the morning, and even this light punishment did not happen more than twice a week, and as I came to be head of my class, it grew rarer.

In England, the procedure was quite different. "That new boy there is talking; take 300 lines to write out and keep quiet."

"Please, Sir", I'd pipe up—"Take 500 lines and keep quiet."

"But, Sir"—in remonstrance.

"Take 1000 lines and if you answer again, I'll send you to the Doctor"—which meant I'd get a caning or a long talking to.

The English masters one and all ruled by punishment; consequently I was indoors writing out lines almost every day, and every half-holiday for the first year. Then my father, prompted by Vernon, complained to the Doctor that writing out lines was ruining my handwriting.

After that I was punished by lines to learn by heart; the lines quickly grew into pages, and before the end of the first half year it was found that I knew the whole school history of England by heart, through these punishments. Another remonstrance from my father, and I was given lines of Vergil to learn. Thank God! that seemed worth learning and the story of Ulysses and Dido on "the wild sea-banks" became a series of living pictures to me, not to be dimmed even, so long as I live.

That English school for a year and a half was to me a brutal prison with stupid daily punishments. At the end of that time I was given a seat by myself, thanks to the Mathematical master; but that's another story.

The two or three best boys of my age in England were far more advanced than I was in Latin and had already waded through half the Greek Grammar, which I had not begun, but I was better in Mathematics than any one in the whole lower school. Because I was behind the English standard in languages, the Form-master took me to be stupid and called me "stupid", and as a result I never learned a Latin or Greek lesson in my two and a half years in the Grammar School. Nevertheless, thanks to the punishment of having to learn Vergil and Livy by heart, I was easily the best of my age in Latin too, before the second year was over.

I had an extraordinary verbal memory. The Doctor, I remember, once mouthed out some lines of the "Paradise Lost" and told us in his pompous way that *Lord* Macaulay knew the "Paradise Lost" by heart from beginning to end. I asked: "Is that hard, Sir!" "When you've learned half of it", he replied, "you'll understand how hard! *Lord* Macaulay was a genius", and he emphasized the "*Lord*" again.

A week later when the Doctor again took the school in literature, I said at the end of the hour: "Please, Sir, I know the 'Paradise Lost' by heart"; he tested me and I remember how he looked at me afterwards from head to foot as if asking himself where I had put all the learning. This "piece of impudence", as the older boys called it, brought me several cuffs and kicks from boys in the Sixth, and much ill-will from many of the others.

All English school life was summed up for me in the "fagging." There was "fagging" in the Royal School in Armagh, but it was kindly. If you wanted to get out of it for a long walk with a chum, you had only to ask one of the Sixth and you got permission to skip it.

But in England the rule was Rhadamanthine; the fags' names on duty were put up on a blackboard, and if you were not on time, ay, and servile to boot, you'd get a dozen from an ash plant on your behind and not laid on perfunctorily and with distaste, as the Doctor did it, but with vim so that I had painful weals on my backside and couldn't sit down for days without a smart.

The fags too, being young and weak, were very often brutally treated just for fun. On Sunday mornings in summer, for instance, we had an hour longer in bed. I was one of the half dozen juniors in the big bedroom; there were two older boys in it, one at each end, presumably to keep order; but in reality to teach lechery and corrupt their younger favorites. If the mothers of England knew what goes on in the dormitories of these boarding-schools throughout England, they would all be closed, from Eton and Harrow upwards or downwards, in a day. If English fathers even had brains enough to understand that the fires of sex need no stoking in boyhood, they too would protect their sons from the foul abuse. But I shall come back to this. Now I wish to speak of the cruelty.

Every form of cruelty was practiced on the younger, weaker and more nervous boys. I remember one Sunday morning, the half dozen older boys pulled one bed along the wall and forced all the seven younger boys underneath it, beating with sticks any hand or foot that showed. One little fellow cried that he couldn't breathe and at once the gang of tormentors began stuffing up all the apertures, saying that they would make a "Black Hole" of it. There were soon cries and strugglings under the bed and at length one of the youngest began shrieking so that the torturers ran away from the prison, fearing lest some master should hear.

One wet Sunday afternoon in midwinter, a little nervous "Mother's darling" from the West Indies who always had a cold and was always sneaking near the fire in the big schoolroom, was caught by two of the Fifth and held near the flames. Two more brutes pulled his trowsers tight over his bottom, and the more he squirmed and begged to be let go, the tighter they held the trowsers and the nearer the flames he was pushed, till suddenly the trowsers split apart scorched through, and as the little fellow tumbled forward screaming, the torturers realized that they had gone too far. The little "Nigger" as he was called, didn't tell how he came to be so scorched but took his fortnight in sick bay as a respite.

We read of a fag at Shrewsbury who was thrown into a bath of boiling water by some older boys because he liked to take his bath very warm; but this experiment turned out badly, for the little fellow died and the affair could not be hushed up, though it was finally dismissed as a regrettable accident.

The English are proud of the fact that they hand over a good deal of the school discipline to the older boys: they attribute this innovation to Arnold of Rugby and, of course, it is possible if the supervision is kept up by a genius, that it may work for good and not for evil; but usually it turns the school into a forcing-house of cruelty and immorality. The older boys establish the legend that only sneaks would tell anything to the masters, and then they are free to give rein to their basest instincts.

The two Monitors in our big bedroom in my time were a strapping big fellow named Dick F..., who tired all the little boys by going into their beds and making them frig him till his semen came. The little fellows all hated to be covered with his filthy slime, but they had to pretend to like doing as he told them, and usually he insisted on frigging them by way of exciting himself. Dick picked me out once or twice but I managed to catch his semen on his own nightshirt, and so after calling me a "dirty little devil" he left me alone.

The other monitor was Jones, a Liverpool boy of about seventeen, very backward in lessons but very strong, the "Cock" of the school at fighting. He used always to go to one young boy's bed whom he favored in many ways. Henry H… used to be able to get off any fagging and he never let out what Jones made him do at night, but in the long run he got to be chums with another little fellow and it all came out. One night when Jones was in Henry's bed, there was a shriek of pain and Jones was heard to be kissing and caressing his victim for nearly an hour afterwards. We all wondered whether Jones had had him, or what had happened. Henry's chum one day let the cat out of the bag. It appeared that Jones used to make the little fellow take his sex in his mouth and frig him and suck him at the same time. But one evening he had brought up some butter and smeared it over his prick and gradually inserted it into Henry's anus and this came to be his ordinary practice. But this night he had forgotten the butter and when he found a certain resistance, he thrust violently forward, causing extreme pain and making his pathic bleed. Henry screamed and so after an interval of some weeks or months the whole procedure came to be known.

If there had been no big boys as Monitors, there would still have been a certain amount of solitary frigging; from twelve or thirteen on, most boys and most girls too, practice self-abuse from time to time on some slight provocation, but the practice doesn't often become habitual unless it is fostered by one's elders and practiced mutually. In Ireland it was sporadic; in England perpetual and in English schools it often led to downright sodomy as in this instance.

In my own case there were two restraining influences, and I wish to dwell on both as a hint to parents. I was a very eager little athlete: thanks to instructions and photographs in a book on athletics belonging to Vernon, I found out how to jump and how to run. To jump high one had to take but a short run from the side and straighten oneself horizontally as one cleared the bar. By constant practice I could at thirteen walk under the bar and then jump it. I soon noticed that if I frigged myself the night before, I could not jump so well, the consequence being that I restrained myself, and never frigged save on Sunday and soon managed to omit the practice on three Sundays out of four.

Since I came to understanding, I have always been grateful to that exercise for this lesson in self-restraint. Besides, one of the boys was always frigging himself: even in school he kept his right hand in his trousers' pocket and continued the practice. All of us knew that he had torn a hole in his pocket so that he could play with his cock; but none of the masters ever noticed anything. The little fellow grew gradually paler and paler until he took to crying in a corner, and unaccountable nervous tremblings shook him for a quarter of an hour at a time. At length, he was taken away by his parents:

what became of him afterwards, I don't know, but I do know that till he was taught self-abuse, he was one of the quickest boys of his age at lessons and given like myself to much reading.

This object-lesson in consequences had little effect on me at the time; but later it was useful as a warning. Such teaching may have affected the Spartans as we read in history that they taught their children temperance by showing them a drunken helot; but I want to lay stress on the fact I was first taught self-control by a keen desire to excel in jumping and in running, and as soon as I found that I couldn't run as fast or jump as high after practicing self-abuse, I began to restrain myself and in return this had a most potent effect on my will-power.

I was over thirteen when a second and still stronger restraining influence made itself felt, and strangely enough this influence grew through my very desire for girls and curiosity about them.

The story marks an epoch in my life. We were taught singing at school and when it was found that I had a good alto voice and a very good ear, I was picked to sing solos, both in school and in the church choir. Before every church festival there was a good deal of practice with the organist, and girls from neighbouring houses joined in our classes. One girl alone sang alto and she and I were separated from the other boys and girls; the upright piano was put across the corner of the room and we two sat or stood behind it almost out of sight of all the other singers; the organist, of course, being seated in front of the piano. The girl E… who sang alto with me was about my own age: she was very pretty or seemed so to me, with golden hair and blue eyes and I always made up to her as well as I could, in my boyish way. One day while the organist was explaining something, E... stood up on the chair and leant over the back of the piano to hear better or see more. Seated in my chair behind her, I caught sight of her legs; for her dress rucked up behind as she leaned over: at once my breath stuck in my throat. Her legs were lovely, I thought, and the temptation came to touch them; for no one could see.

I got up immediately and stood by the chair she was standing on. Casually I let my hand fall against her left leg. She didn't draw her leg away or seem to feel my hand, so I touched her more boldly. She never moved, though now I knew she must have felt my hand, I began to slide my hand up her leg and suddenly my fingers felt the warm flesh on her thigh where the stocking ended above the knee. The feel of her warm flesh made me literally choke with emotion: my hand went on up, warmer and warmer, when suddenly I touched her sex: there was soft down on it. The heart-pulse throbbed in my throat. I have no words to describe the intensity of my sensations.

Thank God, E…. did not move or show any sign of distaste. Curiosity was stronger even than desire in me; I felt her sex all over and at once the idea came into my head that it was like a fig (the Italians, I learned later, call it familiarly "fica"); it opened at my touches and I inserted my finger gently, as Strangways had told me that Mary had taught him to do; still E... did not move. Gently I rubbed the front part of her sex with my finger. I could have kissed her a thousand times out of passionate gratitude.

Suddenly as I went on, I felt her move and then again; plainly she was showing me where my touch gave her most pleasure: I could have died for her in thanks; again she moved and I could feel a little mound or small button of flesh right in the front of her sex, above the junction of the inner lips: of course it was her clitoris. I had forgotten all the old Methodist doctor's books till that moment; this fragment of long forgotten knowledge came back to me: gently I rubbed the clitoris and at once she pressed down on my finger for a moment or two. I tried to insert my finger into the vagina; but she drew away at once and quickly, closing her sex as if it hurt, so I went back to caressing her tickler.

Sudden the miracle ceased. The cursed organist had finished his explanation of the new plain chant, and as he touched the first notes on the piano, E...

drew her legs together; I took away my hand and she stepped down from the chair: "You darling, darling", I whispered; but she frowned, and then just gave me a smile out of the corner of her eye to show me she was not displeased.

Ah, how lovely, how seductive she seemed to me now, a thousand times lovelier and more desirable than ever before. As we stood up to sing again, I whispered to her: "I love you, love you, dear, dear!"

I can never express the passion of gratitude I felt to her for her goodness, her sweetness in letting me touch her sex. E… it was who opened the Gates of Paradise to me and let me first taste the hidden mysteries of sexual delight. Still, after more than fifty years I feel the thrill of the joy she gave me by her response, and the passionate reverence of my gratitude is still alive in me.

This experience with E… had the most important and unlooked for results. The mere fact that girls could feel sex pleasure "just as boys do" increased my liking for them and lifted the whole sexual intercourse to a higher plane in my thought. The excitement and pleasure were so much more intense than anything I had experienced before that I resolved to keep myself for this higher joy. No more self-abuse for me; I knew something infinitely better. One kiss was better, one touch of a girl's sex.

That kissing and caressing a girl could inculcate self-restraint is not taught by our spiritual guides and masters; but is nevertheless true. Another cognate experience came at this time to reinforce the same lesson. I had read all Scott and his heroine Di Vernon made a great impression on me. I resolved now to keep all my passion for some Di Vernon in the future. Thus the first experiences of passion and the reading of a love story completely cured me of the bad habit of self-abuse.

Naturally after this first divine experience, I was on edge for a second and keen as a questing hawk. I could not see E… till the next music-lesson, a week to wait; but even such a week comes to an end, and once more we were imprisoned in our solitude behind the piano; but though I whispered all the sweet and pleading words I could imagine, E… did nothing but frown refusal and shake her pretty head. This killed for the moment all my faith in girls: why did she act so? I puzzled my brain for a reasonable answer and found none. It was part of the damned inscrutability of girls but at the moment it filled me with furious anger. I was savage with disappointment.

"You're mean!" I whispered to her at long last and I would have said more if the organist hadn't called on me for a solo which I sang very badly, so badly indeed that he made me come from behind the piano and thus abolished even the chance of future intimacies. Time and again I cursed organist and girl, but I was always on the alert for a similar experience. As dog fanciers say of hunting dogs, "I had tasted blood and could never afterwards forget the scent of it."

Twenty-five years or more later, I dined with Frederic Chapman, the publisher of "The Fortnightly Review", which I was then editing; he asked me some weeks afterwards had I noticed a lady and described her dress to me, adding, "She was very curious about you. As soon as you came into the room she recognized you and has asked me to tell her if you recognized her; did you?"

I shook my head: "I'm near-sighted, you know", I said, "and therefore to be forgiven, but when did she know me?"

He replied, "As a boy at school; she said you would remember her by her Christian name of E…."

"Of course I do", I cried, "Oh! please tell me her name and where she lives. I'll call on her, I want (and then reflection came to suggest prudence) to ask her some questions", I added lamely.

"I can't give you her name or address", he replied, "I promised her not to, but she's long been happily married I was to tell you."

I pressed him but he remained obstinate, and on second thoughts I came to see that I had no right to push myself on a married woman who did not wish to renew acquaintance with me, but oh! I longed to see her and hear from her own lips the explanation of what to me at the time seemed her inexplicable, cruel change of attitude.

As a man, of course, I know she may have had a very good reason indeed, and her mere name still carries a glamour about it for me, an unforgettable fascination.

My father was always willing to encourage self-reliance in me: indeed, he tried to make me act as a man while I was still a mere child. The Christmas holidays only lasted for four weeks; it was cheaper for me, therefore, to take lodgings in some neighboring town rather than return to Ireland. Accordingly the Headmaster received the request to give me some seven pounds for my expenses and he did so, adding moreover much excellent advice.

My first holiday I spent in the watering-place of Rhyl in North Wales because a chum of mine, Evan Morgan, came from the place and told me he'd make it interesting for me. And in truth he did a good deal to make me like the people and love the place. He introduced me to three or four girls, among whom I took a great fancy to one Gertrude Hanniford. Gertie was over fifteen, tall and very pretty, I thought, with long plaits of chestnut hair; one of the best companions possible. She would kiss me willingly; but whenever

I tried to touch her more intimately, she would wrinkle her little nose with "Don't!" or "Don't be dirty!"

One day I said to her reproachfully: "You'll make me couple 'dirty' with 'Gertie' if you go on using it so often." Bit by bit she grew tamer, though all too slowly for my desires; but luck was eager to help me.

One evening late we were together on some high ground behind the town when suddenly there came a great glare in the sky, which lasted two or three minutes: the next moment we were shaken by a sort of earthquake accompanied by a dull thud.

"An explosion!" I cried, "on the railway: let's go and see!" And away we set off for the railway. For a hundred yards or so Gertie was as fast as I was; but after the first quarter of a mile I had to hold in so as not to leave her. Still for a girl she was very fast and strong. We took a footpath alongside the railway, for we found running over the wooden ties, very slow and dangerous. We had covered a little over a mile when we saw the blaze in front of us and a crowd of figures moving about before the glare.

In a few minutes we were opposite three or four blazing railway carriages and the wreck of an engine.

"How awful!" cried Gertie. "Let's get over the fence", I replied, "and go close!" The next moment I had thrown myself on the wooden paling and half vaulted, half clambered over it. But Gertie's skirts prevented her from imitating me. As she stood in dismay, a great thought came to me: "Step on the low rail, Gertie", I cried, "and then on the upper one and I'll lift you over. Quick!"

At once she did as she was told and while she stood with a foot on each rail hesitating and her hand on my head to steady herself, I put my right hand and arm between her legs and pulling her at the same moment towards me with my left hand, I lifted her over safely but my arm was in her crotch and when I withdrew it, my right hand stopped on her sex and began to touch it:

It was larger than E…'s and had more hairs and was just as soft but she did not give me time to let it excite me so intensely.

"Don't!" she exclaimed angrily: "take your hand away!" And slowly, reluctantly I obeyed, trying to excite her first; as she still scowled: "Come quick!" I cried and taking her hand drew her over to the blazing wreck.

In a little while we learned what had happened: a goods train loaded with barrels of oil had been at the top of the siding; it began to glide down of its own weight and ran into the Irish Express on its way from London to Holyhead. When the two met, the oil barrels were hurled over the engine of the express train, caught fire on the way and poured in flame over the first three carriages, reducing them and their unfortunate inmates to cinders in a very short time. There were a few persons burned and singed in the fourth and fifth carriages; but not many. Open-eyed we watched the gang of workmen lift out charred things like burnt logs rather than men and women, and lay them reverently in rows alongside the rails: about forty bodies, if I remember rightly, were taken out of that holocaust.

Suddenly Gertie realised that it was late and quickly hand in hand we made our way home: "they'll be angry with me", said Gertie, "for being so late, it's after midnight." "When you tell them what you've seen!" I replied, "they won't wonder that we waited." As we parted I said, "Gertie dear, I want to thank you—" "What for" she said shortly. "You know", I said cunningly, "it was so kind of you"—she made a face at me and ran up the steps into her house.

Slowly I returned to my lodgings, only to find myself the hero of the house when I told the story in the morning.

That experience in common made Gertie and myself great friends. She used to kiss me and say I was sweet: once even she let me see her breasts when I told her a girl (I didn't say who it was) had shown hers to me once: her breasts were nearly as large as my sister's and very pretty. Gertie even let me touch her legs right up to the knee; but as soon as I tried to go further, she would pull down her dress with a frown. Still I was always going higher, making progress; persistence brings one closer to any goal; but alas, it was near the end of the Christmas holidays and though I returned to Rhyl at Easter, I never saw Gertie again.

When I was just over thirteen I tried mainly out of pity to get up a revolt of the fags, and at first had a partial success, but some of the little fellows talked and as a ringleader I got a trouncing. The Monitors threw me down on my face on a long desk: one sixth form boy sat on my head and another on my feet, and a third, it was Jones, laid on with an ashplant. I bore it without a groan but I can never describe the storm of rage and hate that boiled in me. Do English fathers really believe that such work is a part of education? It made me murderous. When they let me up, I looked at Jones and if looks could kill, he'd have had short shrift. He tried to hit me but I dodged the blow and went out to plot revenge.

Jones was the head of the cricket First Eleven in which I too was given a place just for my bowling. Vernon of the Sixth was the chief bowler, but I was second, the only boy in the lower school who was in the Eleven at all. Soon afterwards a team from some other school came over to play us: the rival captains met before the tent, all on their best behaviour; for some reason, Vernon not being ready or something, I was given the new ball. A couple of the masters stood near. Jones lost the toss and said to the rival captain very politely, "If you're ready. Sir! we'll go out." The other captain bowed smiling, my chance had come:

"I'm not going to play with you, you brute!" I cried and dashed the ball in Jones's face.

He was very quick and throwing his head aside, escaped the full force of the blow; still the seam of the new ball grazed his cheek-bone and broke the skin: everyone stood amazed: only people who know the strength of English conventions can realise the sensation. Jones himself did not know what to do but took out his handkerchief to mop the blood, the skin being just broken. As for me, I walked away by myself. I had broken the supreme law of our schoolboy honor: never to give away our dissensions to a master, still less to boys and masters from another school; I had sinned in public, too, and before everyone; I'd be universally condemned.

The truth is, I was desperate, dreadfully unhappy, for since the breakdown of the fags' revolt the lower boys had drawn away from me and the older boys never spoke to me if they could help it and then it was always as "Pat."

I felt myself an outcast and was utterly lonely and miserable as only despised outcasts can be. I was sure, too, I should be expelled and knew my father would judge me harshly; he was always on the side of the authorities and masters. However, the future was not to be as gloomy as my imagination pictured it.

The Mathematical Master was a young Cambridge man of perhaps six and twenty, Stackpole by name: I had asked him one day about a problem in algebra and he had been kind to me. On returning to the school this fatal afternoon about six, I happened to meet him on the edge of the playing field and by a little sympathy he soon drew out my whole story.

"I want to be expelled. I hate the beastly school", was my cry. All the charm of the Irish schools was fermenting in me: I missed the kindliness of boy to boy and of the masters to the boys; above all the imaginative fancies of fairies and "the little people" which had been taught us by our nurses and though only half believed in; yet enriched and glorified life,—all this was lost to me. My head in especial, was full of stories of Banshees and fairy queens and heroes, half due to memory, half to my own shaping, which made me a desirable companion to Irish boys and only got me derision from the English.

"I wish I had known that you were being fagged", Stackpole said when he had heard all, "I can easily remedy that", and he went with me to the schoolroom and then and there erased my name from the fags' list and wrote in my name in the First Mathematical Division.

"There", he said with a smile, "you are now in the Upper School where you belong. I think", he added, "I had better go and tell the Doctor what I've done. Don't be down-hearted, Harris", he added, "it'll all come right."

Next day the Sixth did nothing except cut out my name from the list of the First Eleven: I was told that Jones was going to thrash me but I startled my informant by saying: "I'll put a knife into him if he lays a hand on me: you can tell him so."

In fact, however, I was half sent to Coventry and what hurt me most was that it was the boys of the Lower School who were coldest to me, the very boys for whom I had been fighting. That gave me a bitter foretaste of what was to happen to me again and again all through my life.

The partial boycotting of me didn't affect me much; I went for long walks in the beautiful park of Sir W. W— near the school.

I have said many harsh things here of English school life; but for me it had two great redeeming features: the one was the library which was open to every boy, and the other the physical training of the playing fields, the various athletic exercises and the gymnasium. The library to me for some months meant Walter Scott. How right George Eliot was to speak of him as "making the joy of many a young life." Certain scenes of his made ineffaceable impressions on me though unfortunately not always his best work. The wrestling match between the Puritan, Balfour of Burleigh and the soldier was one of my beloved passages. Another favorite page was approved, too, by my maturer judgment, the brave suicide of the little atheist apothecary in the "Fair Maid of Perth." But Scott's finest work, such as the character painting of old Scotch servants, left me cold. Dickens I never could stomach, either as a boy or in later life. His "Tale of Two Cities" and "Nicholas Nickleby" seemed to me then about the best and I've never had any desire since to revise my judgment after reading "David Copperfield" in my student days and finding men painted by a name or phrase or gesture, women by their modesty and souls by some silly catchword; "the mere talent of the caricaturist", I said to myself, "at his best another Hogarth."

Naturally the romances and tales of adventure were all swallowed whole; but few affected me vitally: "The Chase of the White Horse" by Mayne Reid, lives with me still because of the love-scenes with the Spanish heroine, and Marryat's "Peter Simple" which I read a hundred times and could read again tomorrow; for there is better character painting in Chucks, the boatswain, than in all Dickens, in my poor opinion. I remember being astounded ten years later when Carlyle spoke of Marryat with contempt. I knew he was unfair, just as I am probably unfair to Dickens: after all, even Hogarth has one or two good pictures to his credit, and no one survives even three generations without some merit.

In my two years I read every book in the library, and half a dozen are still beloved by me.

I profited, too, from all games and exercises. I was no good at cricket; I was shortsighted and caught some nasty knocks through an unsuspected astigmatism; but I had an extraordinary knack of bowling which, as I have stated, put me in the First Eleven. I liked football and was good at it. I took the keenest delight in every form of exercise: I could jump and run better than almost any boy of my age and in wrestling and a little later in boxing, was among the best in the school. In the gymnasium, too, I practiced assiduously; I was so eager to excel that the teacher was continually advising me to go slow. At fourteen I could pull myself up with my right hand till my chin was above the bar.

In all games the English have a high ideal of fairness and courtesy. No one ever took an unfair advantage of another and courtesy was a law. If another school sent a team to play us at cricket or football, the victors always cheered the vanquished when the game was over, and it was a rule for the Captain to thank the Captain of the visitors for his kindness in coming and for the good game he had given us. This custom obtained too in the Royal Schools in Ireland that were founded for the English garrison, but I couldn't help noting that these courtesies were not practiced in ordinary Irish schools. It was for years the only thing in which I had to admit the superiority of John Bull.

The ideal of a gentleman is not a very high one. Emerson says somewhere that the evolution of the gentleman is the chief spiritual product of the last two or three centuries; but the concept, it seems to me, dwarfs the ideal. A "gentleman" to me is a thing of some parts but no magnitude: one should be a gentleman and much more: a thinker, guide or artist.

English custom in the games taught me the value and need of courtesy, and athletics practiced assiduously did much to steel and strengthen my control of all my bodily desires: they gave my mind and reason the mastery of me. At the same time they taught me the laws of health and the necessity of obeying them.

I found out that by drinking little at meals I could reduce my weight very quickly and was thereby enabled to jump higher than ever; but when I went on reducing I learned that there was a limit beyond which, if I persisted, I began to lose strength: athletics taught me what the French call the juste milieu, the middle path of moderation.

When I was about fourteen I discovered that to think of love before going to sleep was to dream of it during the night. And this experience taught me something else; if I repeated any lesson just before going to sleep, I knew it perfectly next morning; the mind, it seems, works even during unconsciousness. Often since, I have solved problems during sleep in mathematics and in chess that have puzzled me during the day.

SCHOOL DAYS IN ENGLAND.

Chapter III.

In my thirteenth year the most important experience took place of my schoolboy life. Walking out one day with a West Indian boy of sixteen or so, I admitted that I was going to be "confirmed" in the Church of England. I was intensely religious at this time and took the whole rite with appalling seriousness. "Believe and thou shalt be saved" rang in my ears day and night, but I had no happy conviction. Believe what? "Believe in me, Jesus." Of course I believe; then I should be happy, and I was not happy.

"Believe not" and eternal damnation and eternal torture follow. My soul revolted at the iniquity of the awful condemnation. What became of the myriads who had not heard of Jesus? It was all a horrible puzzle to me; but the radiant figure and sweet teaching of Jesus just enabled me to believe and resolve to live as he had lived, unselfishly—purely. I never liked that word "purely" and used to relegate it to the darkest background of my thought. But I would try to be good—I'd try at least!

"Do you believe all the fairy stories in the Bible!" my companion asked.

"Of course I do", I replied, "It's the Word of God, isn't it?" "Who is God?" asked the West Indian.

"He made the world", I added, "all this wonder"—and with a gesture I included earth and sky.

"Who made God!" asked my companion.

I turned away stricken: in a flash I saw I had been building on a word taught to me: "who made God?" I walked away alone, up the long meadow by the little brook, my thoughts in a whirl: story after story that I had accepted were now to me "fairy stories." Jonah hadn't lived three days in a whale's belly. A man couldn't get down a whale's throat. The Gospel of Matthew began with Jesus' pedigree, showing that he had been born of the seed of David through Joseph, his father, and in the very next chapter you are told that Joseph wasn't his father; but the Holy Ghost. In an hour the whole fabric of my spiritual beliefs lay in ruins about me: I believed none of it, not a jot, nor a tittle: I felt as though I had been stripped naked to the cold.

Suddenly a joy came to me: if Christianity was all lies and fairy-tales like Mahometanism, then the prohibitions of it were ridiculous and I could kiss and have any girl who would yield to me. At once I was partially reconciled to my spiritual nakedness: there was compensation.

The loss of my beliefs was for a long time very painful to me. One day I told Stackpole of my infidelity and he recommended me to read "Butler's Analogy" and keep an open mind. Butler finished what the West Indian had begun and in my thirst for some certainty I took up a course of deeper reading. In Stackpole's rooms one day I came across a book of Huxley's Essays; in an hour I had swallowed them and proclaimed myself an "agnostic"; that's what I was; I knew nothing surely, but was willing to learn.

I aged ten years mentally in the next six months: I was always foraging for books to convince me and at length got hold of Hume's argument against miracles. That put an end to all my doubts, satisfied me finally. Twelve years later, when studying philosophy in Goettingen, I saw that Hume's reasoning was not conclusive but for the time I was cured. At midsummer I refused to be confirmed. For weeks before, I had been reading the Bible for the most incredible stories in it and the smut, which I retailed at night to the delight of the boys in the big bedroom.

This year as usual I spent the midsummer holidays in Ireland. My father had made his house with my sister Nita wherever Vernon happened to be sent by his Bank. This summer was passed in Ballybay in County Monaghan, I think. I remember little or nothing about the village save that there was a noble series of reed-fringed lakes near the place which gave good duck and snipe shooting to Vernon in the autumn.

These holidays were memorable to me for several incidents. A conversation began one day at dinner between my sister and my eldest brother about making up to girls and winning them. I noticed with astonishment that my brother Vernon was very deferential to my sister's opinion on the matter, so I immediately got hold of Nita after the lunch and asked her to explain to me what she meant by "flattery." "You said all girls like flattery. What did you mean?"

"I mean", she said, "they all like to be told they are pretty, that they have good eyes or good teeth or good hair, as the case may be, or that they are tall and nicely made. They all like their good points noticed and praised."

"Is that all?" I asked. "Oh no!" she said, "they all like their dress noticed too and especially their hat; if it suits their face, if it's very pretty and so forth.... All girls think that if you notice their clothes you really like them, for most men don't."

"Number two", I said to myself: "is there anything else?"

"Of course", she said, "you must say that the girl you are with, is the prettiest girl in the room or in the town, in fact is quite unlike any other girl, superior to all the rest, the only girl in the world for you. All women like to be the only girl in the world for as many men as possible."

"Number three", I said to myself: "Don't they like to be kissed?" I asked.

"That comes afterwards", said my sister, "lots of men begin with kissing and pawing you about before you even like them. That puts you off. Flattery first of looks and dress, then devotion and afterwards the kissing comes naturally."

"Number four!" I went over these four things again and again to myself and began trying them even on the older girls and women about me and soon found that they all had a better opinion of me almost immediately.

I remember practicing my new knowledge first on the younger Miss Raleigh whom, I thought, Vernon liked. I just praised her as my sister had advised: first her eyes and hair (she had very pretty blue eyes). To my astonishment she smiled on me at once; accordingly I went on to say she was the prettiest girl in the town and suddenly she took my head in her hands and kissed me, saying "You're a dear boy!"

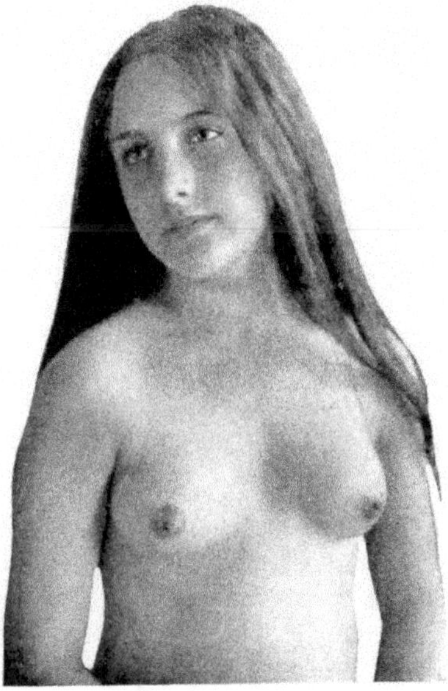

But my great experience was yet to come. There was a very good-looking man whom I met two or three times at parties; I think his name was Tom Connolly: I'm not certain, though I ought not to forget it; for I can see him as plainly as if he were before me now: five feet ten or eleven, very handsome with shaded violet eyes. Everybody was telling a story about him that had taken place on his visit to the Viceroy in Dublin. It appeared that the Vicereine had a very pretty French maid and Tom Connolly made up to the maid. One night the Vicereine was taken ill and sent her husband up stairs to call the maid. When the husband knocked at the maid's door, saying that his wife wanted her, Tom Connolly replied in a strong voice:

"It's unfriendly of you to interrupt a man at such a time."

The Viceroy, of course, apologized immediately and hurried away, but like a fool he told the story to his wife who was very indignant and next day at breakfast she put an aide-de-camp on her right and Tom Connolly's place far down the table. As usual, Connolly came in late and the moment he saw the arrangement of the places, he took it all in and went over to the aide-de-camp.

"Now, young man", he said, "you'll have many opportunities later, so give me my place", and forthwith turned him out of his place and took his seat by the Vicereine, though she would barely speak to him.

At length Tom Connolly said to her: "I wouldn't have thought it of you, for you're so kind. Fancy blaming a poor young girl the first time she yields to a man!"

This response made the whole table roar and established Connolly's fame for impudence throughout Ireland.

Everyone was talking of him and I went about after him all through the gardens and whenever he spoke, my large ears were cocked to hear any word of wisdom that might fall from his lips. At length he noticed me and asked me why I followed him about.

"Everybody says you can win any woman you like, Mr. Connolly"; I said half-ashamed: "I want to know how you do it, what you say to them."

"Faith, I don't know", he said, "but you're a funny little fellow. What age are you to be asking such questions?"

"I'm fourteen", I said boldly.

"I wouldn't have given you fourteen, but even fourteen is too young; you must wait." So I withdrew but still kept within earshot.

I heard him laughing with my eldest brother over my question and so imagined that I was forgiven, and the next day or the day after, finding me as assiduous as ever, he said:

"You know, your question amused me and I thought I would try to find an answer to it and here is one. When you can put a stiff penis in her hand and weep profusely the while, you're getting near any woman's heart. But don't forget the tears." I found the advice a counsel of perfection; I was unable to weep at such a moment; but I never forgot the words.

There was a large barracks of Irish Constabulary in Ballybay and the Sub-Inspector was a handsome fellow of five feet nine or ten named Walter Raleigh. He used to say that he was a descendant of the famous courtier of Queen Elizabeth and he pronounced his name "Rolly" and assured us that his illustrious namesake had often spelt it in this way, which showed that he must have pronounced it as if written with an "o." The reason I mention Raleigh here is that his sisters and mine were great friends and he came in and out of our house almost as if it were his own.

Every evening when Vernon and Raleigh had nothing better to do, they cleared away the chairs in our back parlor, put on boxing gloves and had a set-to. My father used to sit in a corner and watch them: Vernon was lighter and smaller; but quicker; still I used to think that Raleigh did not put out his full strength against him.

One of the first evenings when Vernon was complaining that Raleigh hadn't come in or sent, my father said: "Why not try, Joe?" (my nickname!) In a jiffy I had the gloves on and got my first lesson from Vernon who taught me at least how to hit straight and then how to guard and side-step. I was very quick and strong for my size; but for some time Vernon hit me very lightly. Soon, however, it became difficult for him to hit me at all and then I sometimes got a heavy blow that floored me. But with constant practice I improved rapidly and after a fortnight or so put on the gloves once with Raleigh. His blows were very much heavier and staggered me even to guard them, so I got accustomed to duck or side-step or slip every blow aimed at me while hitting back with all my strength. One evening when Vernon and Raleigh both had been praising me, I told them of Jones and how he bullied me; he had really made my life a misery to me: he never met me outside the school without striking or kicking me and his favorite name for me was "bog-trotter!" His attitude, too, affected the whole school: I had grown to hate him as much as I feared him.

They both thought I could beat him; but I described him as very strong and finally Raleigh decided to send for two pairs of four ounce gloves or fighting gloves and use these with me to give me confidence. In the first half hour with the new gloves Vernon did not hit me once and I had to acknowledge that he was stronger and quicker even than Jones. At the end of the holidays they both made me promise to slap Jones's face the very first time I saw him in the school.

On returning to school we always met in the big schoolroom. When I entered the room there was silence. I was dreadfully excited and frightened, I don't know why; but fully resolved: "he can't kill me", I said to myself a thousand times; still I was in a trembling funk inwardly though composed enough in outward seeming. Jones and two others of the Sixth stood in front of the empty fire-place: I went up to them: Jones nodded, "How d'ye do, Pat!"

"Fairly", I said, "but why do you take all the room?" and I jostled him aside: he immediately pushed me hard and I slapped his face as I had promised. The elder boys held him back or the fight would have taken place then and there: "will you fight?" he barked at me and I replied, "as much as you like, bully!" It was arranged that the fight should take place on the next afternoon, which happened to be a Wednesday and half-holiday. From three to six would give us time enough. That evening Stackpole asked me to his room and told me he would get the Doctor to stop the fight if I wished; I assured him it had to be and I preferred to have it settled.

"I'm afraid he's too old and strong for you", said Stackpole: I only smiled.

Next day the ring was made at the top of the playing field behind the haystack so that we could not be seen from the school. All the Sixth and nearly all the school stood behind Jones; but Stackpole, while ostensibly strolling about, was always close to me. I felt very grateful to him: I don't know why; but his presence took away from my loneliness. At first the fight was almost like a boxing-match. Jones shot out his left hand, my head slipped it and I countered with my right in his face: a moment later he rushed me but I ducked and side-stepped and hit him hard on the chin. I could feel the astonishment of the school in the dead silence:

"Good, good!" cried Stackpole behind me: "that's the way." And indeed it was the "way" of the fight in every round except one. We had been hard at it for some eight or ten minutes when I felt Jones getting weaker or losing his breath: at once I went in attacking with all my might; when suddenly, as luck would have it, I caught a right swing just under the left ear and was knocked clean off my feet: he could hit hard enough, that was clear. As I went into the middle of the ring for the next round Jones jeered at me:

"You got that, didn't ye, Pat!"

"Yes", I replied, "but I'll beat you black and blue for it" and the fight went on. I had made up my mind, lying on the ground, to strike only at his face. He was short and strong and my body-blows didn't seem to make any impression on him; but if I could blacken all his face, the masters and especially the Doctor would understand what had happened.

Again and again Jones swung, first with right hand and then with his left, hoping to knock me down again; but my training had been too varied and complete and the knock-down blow had taught me the necessary caution: I ducked his swings, or side-stepped them and hit him right and left in the face till suddenly his nose began to bleed and Stackpole cried out behind me in huge excitement: "that's the way, that's the way; keep on peppering him!"

As I turned to smile at him, I found that a lot of the fags, former chums of mine, had come round to my corner and now were all smiling encouragement at me and bold exhortations to "give it him hard." I then realized for the first time that I had only to keep on and be careful and the victory would be mine. A cold, hard exultation took the place of nervous excitement in me, and when I struck, I tried to cut with my knuckles as Raleigh had once shown me.

The bleeding of Jones's nose took some time to stop and as soon as he came into the middle of the ring, I started it again with another right-hander. After this round, his seconds and backers kept him so long in his corner that at length, on Stackpole's whispered advice, I went over and said to him: "Either fight or give in: I'm catching cold." He came out at once and rushed at me full of fight, but his face was all one bruise and his left eye nearly closed. Every chance I got, I struck at the right eye till it was in an even worse case.

It is strange to me since that I never once felt pity for him and offered to stop: the truth is, he had bullied me so relentlessly and continually, had wounded my pride so often in public that even at the end I was filled with cold rage against him. I noticed everything: I saw that a couple of the Sixth went away towards the schoolhouse and afterwards returned with Shaddy, the second master. As they came round the haystack, Jones came out into the ring; he struck savagely right and left as I came within striking distance, but I slipped in outside his weaker left and hit him as hard as I could, first right, then left on the chin and down he went on his back.

At once there was a squeal of applause from the little fellows in my corner and I saw that Stackpole had joined Shaddy near Jones's corner. Suddenly Shaddy came right up to the ringside and spoke, to my astonishment, with a certain dignity:

"This fight must stop now", he said loudly, "if another blow is struck or word said, I'll report the disobedience to the Doctor." Without a word I went and put on my coat and waistcoat and collar, while his friends of the Sixth escorted Jones to the schoolhouse.

I had never had so many friends and admirers in my life as came up to me then to congratulate me and testify to their admiration and goodwill. The whole lower school was on my side, it appeared, and had been from the outset, and one or two of the Sixth, Herbert in especial, came over and praised me warmly: "A great fight", said Herbert, "and now perhaps we'll have less bullying: at any rate", he added humorously, "no one will want to bully you: you're a pocket professional: where did you learn to box?"

I had sense enough to smile and keep my own counsel. Jones didn't appear in school that night: indeed, for days after he was kept in sick-bay upstairs. The fags and lower school boys brought me all sorts of stories how the doctor had come and said "he feared erysipelas: the bruises were so large and Jones must stay in bed and in the dark!" and a host of other details.

One thing was quite clear; my position in the school was radically changed: Stackpole spoke to the Doctor and I got a seat by myself in his class-room and only went to the form-master for special lessons: Stackpole became more than ever my teacher and friend.

When Jones first appeared in the school, we met in the Sixth room while waiting for the Doctor to come in. I was talking with Herbert; Jones came in and nodded to me: I went over and held out my hand, "I'm glad you're all right again!" He shook hands but said nothing. Herbert's nod and smile showed me I had done right. "Bygones should be bygones", he said in English fashion. I wrote the whole story to Vernon that night, thanking him, you may be sure, and Raleigh for the training and encouragement they had given me.

My whole outlook on life was permanently altered: I was cock-a-hoop and happy. One night I got thinking of E… and for the first time in months practiced Onanism. But next day I felt heavy and resolved that belief or no belief, self-restraint was a good thing for the health. All the next Christmas holidays spent in Rhyl, I tried to get intimate with some girl; but failed. As soon as I tried to touch even their breasts, they drew away. I liked girls fully formed and they all thought, I suppose, that I was too young and too small: if they had only known!

One more incident belongs in this thirteenth year, and is worthy perhaps of record. Freed of the bullying and senseless cruelty of the older boys who for the most part, still siding with Jones, left me severely alone, the restraints of school life began to irk me. "If I were free", I said to myself, "I'd go after E… or some other girl and have a great time; as it is, I can do nothing, hope for nothing." Life was stale, flat and unprofitable to me. Besides, I had read nearly all the books I thought worth reading in the school library, and time hung heavy on my hands: I began to long for liberty as a caged bird.

What was the quickest way out? I knew that my father as a Captain in the Navy could give me or get me a nomination so that I might become a Midshipman. Of course I'd have to be examined before I was fourteen; but I knew I could win a high place in any test.

The summer vacation after I was thirteen on the 14th of February I spent at home in Ireland as I have told, and from time to time, bothered my father to get me the nomination. He promised he would, and I took his promise seriously. All the autumn I studied carefully the subjects I was to be examined in and from time to time wrote to my father reminding him of his promise. But he seemed unwilling to touch on the matter in his letters which were mostly filled with Biblical exhortations, that sickened me with contempt for his brainless credulity. My unbelief made me feel immeasurably superior to him.

Christmas came and I wrote him a serious letter, insisting that he should keep his promise. For the first time in my life I flattered him, saying that I knew his word was sacred: but the time-limit was at hand and I was getting nervous lest some official delay might make me pass the prescribed limit of age. I got no reply: I wrote to Vernon who said he would do his best with the Governor. The days went on, the 14th of February came and went: I was fourteen. That way of escape into the wide world was closed to me by my father. I raged in hatred of him.

How was I to get free? Where should I go? What should I do? One day in an illustrated paper in '68, I read of the discovery of the diamonds in the Cape, and then of the opening of the Diamond fields. That prospect tempted me and I read all I could about South Africa, but one day I found that the cheapest passage to the Cape cost fifteen pounds and I despaired. Shortly afterwards I read that a steerage passage to New York could be had for five pounds; that amount seemed to me possible to get; for there was a prize of ten pounds for books to be given to the second in the Mathematical scholarship exam that would take place in the summer: I thought I could win that, and I set myself to study Mathematics harder than ever.

The result was—but I shall tell the result in its proper place. Meanwhile I began reading about America and soon learned of the buffalo and Indians on the Great Plains and a myriad entrancing romantic pictures opened to my boyish imagining. I wanted to see the world and I had grown to dislike England; its snobbery, though I had caught the disease, was loathsome and worse still, its spirit of sordid self-interest. The rich boys were favored by all the Masters, even by Stackpole; I was disgusted with English life as I saw it. Yet there were good elements in it which I could not but see, which I shall try to indicate later.

Towards the middle of this winter term it was announced that at Midsummer, besides a scene from a play of Plautus to be given in Latin, the trial scene of "The Merchant of Venice" would also be played—of course, by boys of the Fifth and Sixth form only, and rehearsals immediately began. Naturally I took out "The Merchant of Venice" from the school library and in one day knew it by heart. I could learn good poetry by a single careful reading: bad poetry or prose was much harder.

Nothing in the play appealed to me except Shylock and the first time I heard Fawcett of the Sixth recite the part, I couldn't help grinning: he repeated the most passionate speeches like a lesson in a singsong, monotonous voice. For days I went about spouting Shylock's defiance and one day, as luck would have it, Stackpole heard me. We had become great friends: I had done all Algebra with him and was now devouring trigonometry, resolved to do Conic Sections afterwards, and then the Calculus. Already there was only one boy who was my superior and he was Captain of the Sixth, Gordon, a big fellow of over seventeen, who intended to go to Cambridge with the eighty Pound Mathematical Scholarship that summer.

Stackpole told the Head that I would be a good Shylock: Fawcett to my amazement didn't want to play the Jew: he found it difficult even to learn the part, and finally it was given to me. I was particularly elated for I felt sure I could make a great hit.

One day my sympathy with the bullied got me a friend. The Vicar's son Edwards was a nice boy of fourteen who had grown rapidly and was not strong. A brute of sixteen in the Upper Fifth was twisting his arm and hitting him on the writhen muscle and Edwards was trying hard not to cry. "Leave him alone, Johnson", I said, "why do you bully?" "You ought to have a taste of it", he cried, letting Edwards go, however.

"Don't try it on if you're wise", I retorted.

"Pat would like us to speak to him", he sneered and turned away. I shrugged my shoulders.

Edwards thanked me warmly for rescuing him and I asked him to come for a walk. He accepted and our friendship began, a friendship memorable for bringing me one novel and wonderful experience.

The Vicarage was a large house with a good deal of ground about it. Edwards had some sisters but they were too young to interest me; the French governess, on the other hand, Mlle. Lucille, was very attractive with her black eyes and hair and quick, vivacious manner. She was of medium height and not more than eighteen. I made up to her at once and tried to talk French with her from the beginning. She was very kind to me and we got on together at once. She was lonely, I suppose, and I began well by telling her she was the prettiest girl in the whole place and the nicest. She translated nicest, I remember, as la plus chic.

The next half-holiday Edwards went into the house for something. I told her I wanted a kiss, and she said:

"You're only a boy, mais gentil", and she kissed me. When my lips dwelt on hers, she took my head in her hands, pushed it away and looked at me with surprise.

"You are a strange boy", she said musingly.

The next holiday I spent at the Vicarage. I gave her a little French love-letter I had copied from a book in the school library and I was delighted when she read it and nodded at me, smiling, and tucked it away in her bodice: "near her heart" I said to myself, but I had no chance even of a kiss for Edwards always hung about. But late one afternoon he was called away by his mother for something, and my opportunity came.

We usually sat in a sort of rustic summerhouse in the garden. This afternoon Lucille was seated leaning back in an armchair right in front of the door, for the day was sultry-close, and when Edwards went, I threw myself on the doorstep at her feet: her dress clung to her form, revealing the outlines of her thighs and breasts seductively. I was wild with excitement. Suddenly I noticed her legs were apart; I could see her slim ankles. Pulses awoke throbbing in my forehead and throat: I begged for a kiss and got on my knees to take it: she gave me one; but when I persisted, she repulsed me, saying:

"Non, non! sois sage!"

As I returned to my seat reluctantly, the thought came, "put your hand up her clothes"; I felt sure I could reach her sex. She was seated on the edge of the chair and leaning back. The mere idea shook and scared me: but what can she do, I thought: she can only get angry. I thought again of all possible consequences: the example with E… came to encourage and hearten me. I leaned round and knelt in front of her smiling, begging for a kiss, and as she smiled in return, I put my hand boldly right up her clothes on her sex. I felt the soft hairs and the form of it in breathless ecstasy; but I scarcely held it when she sprang upright: "how dare you!" she cried trying to push my hand away.

My sensations were too overpowering for words or act; my life was in my fingers; I held her cunt. A moment later I tried to touch her gently with my middle finger as I had touched E…: 'twas a mistake: I no longer held her sex and at once Lucille whirled round and was free.

"I have a good mind to strike you", she cried; "I'll tell Mrs. Edwards", she snorted indignantly. "You're a bad, bad boy and I thought you nice. I'll never be kind to you again: I hate you!" she fairly stamped with anger.

I went to her, my whole being one prayer. "Don't please spoil it all", I cried. "You hurt so when you are angry, dear." She turned to me hotly: "I'm really angry, angry", she panted, "and you're a hateful rude boy and I don't like you any more", and she turned away again, shaking her dress straight. "Oh, how could I help it?" I began, "You're so pretty, oh, you are wonderful, Lucille."

"Wonderful", she repeated, sniffing disdainfully, but I saw she was mollified.

"Kiss me", I pleaded, "and don't be cross."

"I'll never kiss you again", she replied quickly, "you can be sure of that." I went on begging, praising, pleading for ever so long, till at length she took my head in her hands, saying:

"If you'll promise never to do that again, never, I'll give you a kiss and try to forgive you."

"I can't promise", I said, "it was too sweet; but kiss me and I'll try to be good."

She kissed me a quick peck and pushed me away.

"Didn't you like it?" I whispered, "I did awfully. I can't tell you how I thrilled: oh, thank you, Lucille, thank you, you are the sweetest girl in all the world, and I shall always be grateful to you, you dear!"

She looked down at me musingly, thoughtfully; I felt I was gaining ground:

"You are lovely there", I ventured in a whisper, "please, dear, what do you call it? I saw 'chat' once: is that right, 'pussy'?"

"Don't talk of it", she cried impatiently, "I hate to think—"

"Be kind, Lucille", I pleaded, "you'll never be the same to me again: you were pretty before, chic and provoking, but now you're sacred. I don't love you, I adore you, reverence you, darling! May I say 'pussy'?"

"You're a strange boy", she said at length, "but you must never do that again; it's nasty and I don't like it. I—"

"Don't say such things!" I cried, pretending indignation, "you don't know what you're saying—nasty! Look, I'll kiss the fingers that have touched your pussy", and I suited the action to the word.

"Oh, don't!" she cried and caught my hand in hers, "don't!" but somehow she leaned against me at the same time and left her lips on mine. Bit by bit my right hand went down to her sex again, this time on the outside of her dress, but at once she tore herself away and would not let me come near her again. My insane desire had again made me blunder! Yet she had half-yielded, I knew, and that consciousness set me thrilling with triumph and hope, but alas! at that moment we heard Edwards shout to us as he left the house to rejoin us.

This experience had two immediate and unlooked for consequences: first of all, I could not sleep that night for thinking of Lucille's sex; it was like a large fig split in the middle, and set in a mesh of soft hairs: I could feel it still on my fingers and my sex stood stiff and throbbed with desire for it.

When I fell asleep I dreamed of Lucille, dreamed that she had yielded to me and I was pushing my sex into hers; but there was some obstacle and while I was pushing, pushing, my seed spirted in an orgasm of pleasure—and at once I awoke and, putting down my hand, found that I was still coming: the sticky, hot, milk-like sperm was all over my hairs and prick.

I got up and washed and returned to bed; the cold water had quieted me; but soon by thinking of Lucille and her soft, hot, hairy "pussy", I grew randy again and in this state fell asleep. Again I dreamed of Lucille and again I was trying, trying in vain to get into her when again the spasm of pleasure overtook me; I felt my seed spirting hot and—awoke.

But lo! when I put my hand down, there was no seed, only a little moisture just at the head of my sex—nothing more. Did it mean that I could only give forth seed once? I tested myself at once: while picturing Lucille's sex, its soft hot roundnesses and hairs, I caressed my sex, moving my hand faster up and down till soon I brought on the orgasm of pleasure and felt distinctly the hot thrills as if my seed were spirting, but nothing came, hardly even the moisture.

Next morning I tested myself at the high jump and found I couldn't clear the bar at an inch lower than usual. I didn't know what to do: why had I indulged so foolishly?

But next night the dream of Lucille came back again, and again I awoke after an acute spasm of pleasure, all wet with my own seed. What was I to do? I got up and washed and put cold water in a sponge on my testicles and sex and all chilled crawled back into bed. But imagination was master. Time and again the dream came and awakened me. In the morning I felt exhausted, washed-out and needed no test to assure me that I was physically below par.

That same afternoon I picked up by chance a little piece of whipcord and at once it occurred to me that if I tied this hard cord round my penis, as soon as the organ began to swell and stiffen in excitement, the cord would grow tight and awake me with the pain.

That night I tied up Tommy and gave myself up to thoughts of Lucille's private parts: as soon as my sex stood and grew stiff, the whipcord hurt dreadfully and I had to apply cold water at once to reduce my unruly member to ordinary proportions. I returned to bed and went to sleep: I had a short sweet dream of Lucille's beauties but then awoke in agony. I got up quickly and sat on the cold marble slab of the washing-stand. That acted more speedily than even the cold water; why? I didn't learn the reason for many a year.

The cord was effective, did all I wanted: after this experience I wore it regularly and within a week was again able to walk under the bar and afterwards jump it, able too to pull myself up with one hand till my chin was above the bar. I had conquered temptation and once more was captain of my body.

The second unsuspected experience was also a direct result, I believe, of my sex-awakening with Lucille and the intense sex-excitement. At all events it came just after the love-passages with her that I have described and post hoc is often propter hoc.

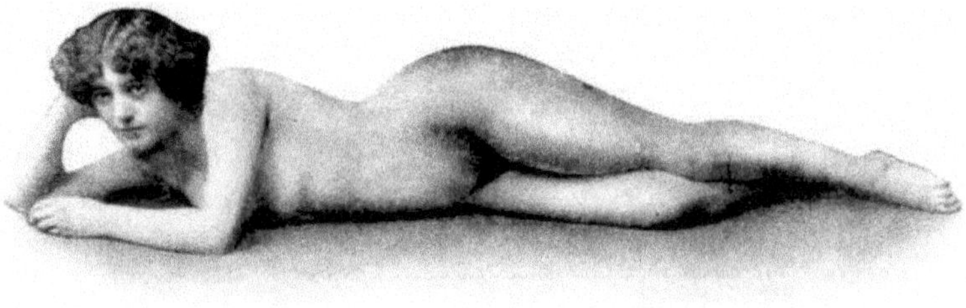

I had never yet noticed the beauties of nature; indeed whenever I came across descriptions of scenery in my reading, I always skipped them as wearisome. Now of a sudden, in a moment, my eyes were unsealed to natural beauties. I remember the scene and my rapt wonder as if it were yesterday. It was a bridge across the Dee near Overton in full sunshine; on my right the river made a long curve, swirling deep under a wooded height, leaving a little tawny sandbank half bare just opposite to me: on my left both banks, thickly wooded, drew together and passed round a curve out of sight. I was entranced and speechless—enchanted by the sheer color-beauty of the scene—sunlit water there and shadowed here, reflecting the gorgeous vesture of the wooded height. And when I left the place and came out again and looked at the adjoining cornfields, golden against the green of the hedgerows and scattered trees, the colors took on a charm I had never noticed before: I could not understand what had happened to me.

It was the awakening of sex-life in me, I believe, that first revealed to me the beauty of inanimate nature.

A night or two later I was ravished by a moon nearly at the full that flooded our playing field with ivory radiance, making the haystack in the corner a thing of supernal beauty.

Why had I never before seen the wonder of the world? the sheer loveliness of nature all about me? From this time on I began to enjoy descriptions of scenery in the books I read and began, too, to love landscapes in painting.

Thank goodness! the miracle was accomplished, at long last, and my life enriched, ennobled, transfigured as by the bounty of a God! From that day on I began to live an enchanted life; for at once I tried to see beauty everywhere, and at all times, of day and night caught glimpses that ravished me with delight and turned my being into a hymn of praise and joy.

Faith had left me and with faith, hope in Heaven or indeed in any future existence: saddened and fearful, I was as one in prison with an undetermined sentence; but now in a moment the prison had become a paradise, the walls of the actual had fallen away into frames of entrancing pictures. Dimly I became conscious that if this life were sordid and mean, petty and unpleasant, the fault was in myself and in my blindness. I began then for the first time to understand that I myself was a magician and could create my own fairyland, ay and my own heaven, transforming this world into the throne-room of a god!

This joy, and this belief I want to impart to others more than almost anything else, for this has been to me a new Gospel of courage and resolve and certain reward, a man's creed teaching that as you grow in wisdom and courage and kindness, all good things are added unto you.

I find that I am outrunning my story and giving here a stage of thought and belief that only became mine much later; but the beginning of my individual soul-life was this experience, that I had been blind to natural beauty and now could see; this was the root and germ, so to speak, of the later faith that guided all my mature life, filling me with courage and spilling over into hope and joy ineffable.

Very soon the first command of it came to my lips almost every hour: "Blame your own blindness! always blame yourself!"

FROM SCHOOL TO AMERICA.

Chapter IV.

Early in January there was a dress rehearsal of the Trial Scene of "The Merchant of Venice." The Grandee of the neighborhood who owned the great park, Sir W. W. W., some M.P.'s, notably a Mr. Whalley who had a pretty daughter and lived in the vicinity, and the Vicar and his family were invited, and others whom I did not know; but with the party from the Vicarage came Lucille.

The big schoolroom had been arranged as a sort of theatre and the estrade at one end where the Head-Master used to throne it on official occasions, was converted into a makeshift stage and draped by a big curtain that could be drawn back or forth at will.

The Portia was a very handsome lad of sixteen named Herbert, gentle and kindly, yet redeemed from effeminacy by the fact that he was the fleetest sprinter in the school and could do the hundred yards in eleven and a half seconds. The "Duke" was, of course, Jones and the merchant "Antonio" a big fellow named Vernon, and I had got Edwards the part of "Bassanio" and a pretty boy in the Fourth Form was taken as "Nerissa." So far as looks went the cast was passable; but the "Duke" recited his lines as if they had been imperfectly learned and so the "Trial Scene" opened badly. But the part of "Shylock" suited me intimately and I had learned how to recite. Now before E… and Lucille, I was set on doing better than my best. When my cue came I bowed low before the "Duke" and then bowed again to left and right of him in silence and formally, as if I, the outcast Jew, were saluting the whole court; then in a voice that at first I simply made slow and clear and hard, I began the famous reply:

"I have possessed your Grace of what I purpose;

And by our Holy Sabbath have I sworn

To have the due and forfeit of my bond."

I don't expect to be believed; but nevertheless I am telling the bare truth when I say that in my impersonation of "Shylock" I brought in the very piece of "business" that made Henry Irving's "Shylock" fifteen years later, "ever memorable", according to the papers.

When at the end, baffled and beaten, Shylock gives in:

"I pray you, give me leave to go from hence,

I am not well: send the deed after me,

And I will sign it,"

the Duke says, "Get thee gone, but do it," and Gratiano insults the Jew—the only occasion, I think, when Shakespeare allows the beaten to be insulted by a gentleman.

On my way to the door as Shylock, I stopped, bent low before the Duke's dismissal; but at Gratiano's insult, I turned slowly round, while drawing myself up to my full height and scanning him from head to foot.

Irving used to return all across the stage and folding his arms on his breast look down on him with measureless contempt.

When fifteen years later Irving, at the Garrick Club one night after supper, asked me what I thought of this new "business"; I replied that if Shylock had done what he did, Gratiano would probably have spat in his face and then kicked him off the stage. Shylock complains that the Christians spat upon his gaberdine.

My boyish, romantic reading of the part, however, was essentially the same as Irving's, and Irving's reading was cheered in London to the echo because it was a rehabilitation of the Jew, and the Jew rules the roost today in all the cities of Europe.

At my first words I could feel the younger members of the audience look about as if to see if such reciting as mine was proper and permitted; then one after the other gave in to the flow and flood of passion. When I had finished everyone cheered, Whalley and Lady W… enthusiastically, and to my delight, Lucille as well.

After the rehearsal, everyone crowded about me: "Where did you learn?" "Who taught you?" At length Lucille came. "I knew you were someone", she said in her pretty way, "quelqu'un", "but it was extraordinary! You'll be a great actor, I'm sure."

"And yet you deny me a kiss", I whispered, taking care no one should hear.

"I deny you nothing", she replied, turning away, leaving me transfixed with hope and assurance of delight. "Nothing", I said to myself, "nothing means everything"; a thousand times I said it over to myself in an ecstasy.

That was my first happy night in England. Mr. Whalley congratulated me and introduced me to his daughter who praised me enthusiastically, and best of all the Doctor said, "We must make you Stage Manager, Harris, and I hope you'll put some of your fire into the other actors."

To my astonishment my triumph did me harm with the boys. Some sneered, while all agreed that I did it to show off. Jones and the Sixth began the boycott again. I didn't mind much, for I had heavier disappointments and dearer hopes.

The worst was I found it difficult to see Lucille in the bad weather; indeed I hardly caught a glimpse of her the whole winter. Edwards asked me frequently to the Vicarage; she might have made half a dozen meetings but she would not, and I was sick at heart with disappointment and the regret of unfulfilled desire. It was March or April before I was alone with her in her schoolroom at the Vicarage. I was too cross with her to be more than polite. Suddenly she said, "Vous me boudez." I shrugged my shoulders.

"You don't like me", I began, "so what's the use of my caring."

"I like you a great deal", she said, "but—"

"No, no", I said, shaking my head, "if you liked me, you wouldn't avoid me and—"

"Perhaps it's because I like you too much—"

"Then you'd make me happy", I broke in.

"Happy", she repeated, "How can I?"

"By letting me kiss you, and—"

"Yes, and—" she repeated significantly.

"What harm does it do you?" I asked.

"What harm", she repeated, "Don't you know it's wrong? One should only do that with one's husband; you know that."

"I don't know anything of the sort", I cried, "That's all silly. We don't believe that today."

"I believe it", she said gravely.

"But if you didn't, you'd let me", I cried, "say that, Lucille, that would be almost as good, for it would show you liked me a little."

"You know I like you a great deal", she replied.

"Kiss me then", I said, "there's no harm in that", and when she kissed me I put my hand over her breasts; they thrilled me they were so elastic-firm, and in a moment my hand slid down her body, but she drew away at once quietly but with resolve.

"No, no", she said, half smiling.

"Please!" I begged.

"I can't", she said, shaking her head, "I mustn't. Let us talk of other things—How is the play getting on?" But I could not talk of the play as she stood there before me. For the first time I divined through her clothes nearly all the beauties of her form. The bold curves of hip and breast tantalized me and her face was expressive and defiant.

How was it I had never noticed all the details before? Had I been blind? or did Lucille dress to show off her figure? Certainly her dresses were arranged to display the form more than English dresses, but I too had become more curious, more observant. Would life go on showing me new beauties I had not even imagined?

My experience with E… and Lucille made the routine of school life almost intolerable to me. I could only force myself to study by reminding myself of the necessity of winning the second prize in the Mathematical Scholarship, which would give me ten pounds, and ten pounds would take me to America.

Soon after the Christmas holidays I had taken the decisive step. The examination in winter was not nearly so important as the one that ended the summer term, but it had been epoch-making to me. My punishments having compelled me to learn two or three books of Vergil by heart and whole chapters of Caesar and Livy, I had come to some knowledge of Latin: in the examination I had beaten not only all my class, but thanks to trigonometry and Latin and history, all the two next classes as well. As soon as the school reassembled I was put in the Upper Fifth. All the boys were from two to three years older than I was, and they all made cutting remarks about me to each other and avoided speaking to "Pat." All this strengthened my resolution to get to America as soon as I could.

Meanwhile I worked as I had never worked: at Latin and Greek as well as Mathematics; but chiefly at Greek, for there I was backward: by Easter I had mastered the grammar—irregular verbs and all—and was about the first in the class. My mind, too, through my religious doubts and gropings and through the reading of the thinkers had grown astonishingly: one morning I construed a piece of Latin that had puzzled the best in the class and the Doctor nodded at me approvingly. Then came the step I spoke of as decisive.

The morning prayers were hardly over one bitter morning when the Doctor rose and gave out the terms of the scholarship Exam at Midsummer; the winner to get eighty pounds a year for three years at Cambridge, and the second ten pounds with which to buy books. "All boys", he added, "who wish to go in for this scholarship will now stand up and give their names." I thought only Gordon would stand up, but when I saw Johnson get up and Fawcett and two or three others I too got up… A sort of derisive growl went through the school; but Stackpole smiled at me and nodded his head as much as to say, "they'll see", and I took heart of grace and gave my name very distinctly. Somehow I felt that the step was decisive.

I liked Stackpole and this term he encouraged me to come to his rooms to talk whenever I felt inclined, and as I had made up my mind to use all the half-holidays for study, this association did me a lot of good and his help was invaluable.

One day when he had just come into his room, I shot a question at him and he stopped, came over to me and put his arm on my shoulder as he answered. I don't know how I knew; but by some instinct I felt a caress in the apparently innocent action. I didn't like to draw away or show him that I objected; but I buried myself feverishly in the Trigonometry and he soon moved away.

When I thought of it afterwards, I recalled the fact that his marked liking for me began after my fight with Jones. I had often been on the point of confessing to him my love-passages; but now I was glad I had kept them strenuously to myself, for day by day I noticed that his liking for me grew or rather his compliments and flatteries increased. I hardly knew what to do: working with him and in his room was a godsend to me; yet at the same time I didn't like him much or admire him really.

In some ways he was curiously dense; he spoke of the school life as the happiest of all and the healthiest; a good moral tone here, he would say, no lying, cheating or scandal, much better than life outside. I used to find it difficult not to laugh in his face. Moral tone indeed! when the Doctor came down out of temper, it was usually accepted among the boys that he had had his wife in the night and was therefore a little below par physically.

Though a really good mathematical scholar and a first-rate teacher, patient and painstaking, with a gift of clear exposition, Stackpole seemed to me stupid and hidebound and I soon found that by laughing at his compliments I could balk his desire to lavish on me his unwelcome caresses.

Once he kissed me, but my amused smile made him blush while he muttered shamefacedly, "You're a queer lad!" At the same time I knew quite well that if I encouraged him, he would take further liberties.

One day he talked of Jones and Henry H… He had evidently heard something of what had taken place in our bedroom; but I pretended not to know what he meant and when he asked me whether none of the big boys had made up to me, I ignored big Fawcett's smutty excursions and said "No" adding that I was interested in girls and not in dirty boys. For some reason or other Stackpole seemed to me younger than I was and not twelve years older, and I had no real difficulty in keeping him within the bounds of propriety till the Math Exam.

I was asked once whether I thought that "Shaddy", as we called the House-master, had ever had a woman. The idea of "Shaddy" as a virgin filled us with laughter; but when one spoke of him as a lover, it was funnier still. He was a man about forty, tall and fairly strong: he had a degree from some college in Manchester, but to us little snobs he was a bounder because he had not been to either Oxford or Cambridge. He was fairly capable, however.

But for some reason or other he had a down on me and I grew to hate him, and was always thinking of how I might hurt him. My new habit of forcing myself to watch and observe everything came to my aid. There were five or six polished oak-steps up to the big bedroom where fourteen of us slept. "Shaddy" used to give us half an hour to get into bed and then would come up, and standing just inside the door under the gas-light would ask us, "Have you all said your prayers?" We all answered: "Yes, sir", then would come his "Goodnight, boys", and our stereotyped reply: "Good night, Sir."

He would then turn out the light and go downstairs to his room. The oak-steps outside were worn in the middle and I had noticed that as one goes downstairs one treads on the very edge of each step.

One day "Shaddy" had maddened me by giving me one hundred lines of Vergil to learn by heart for some trifling peccadillo. That night, having provided myself with a cake of brown Windsor soap, I ran upstairs before the other boys and rubbed the soap freely on the edge of the two top steps, and then went on to undress.

When "Shaddy" put out the light and stepped down to the second step, there was a slip and then a great thud as he half slid, half fell to the bottom. In a moment, for my bed was nearest the door, I had sprung up, opened the door and made incoherent exclamations of sympathy as I helped him to get up.

"I've hurt my hip", he said, putting his hand on it. He couldn't account for his fall.

Grinning to myself as I went back, I rubbed the soap off the top step with my handkerchief and got into bed again, where I chuckled over the success of my stratagem. He had only got what he richly deserved, I said to myself.

At length the long term wore to its end; the Exam was held and after consulting Stackpole I was very sure of the second prize. "I believe", he said one day, "that you'd rather have the second prize than the first." "Indeed I would", I replied without thinking.

"Why?" he asked, "why!" I only just restrained myself in time or I'd have given him the true reason. "You'll come much nearer winning the Scholarship", he said at length, "than any of them guesses."

After the "Exams" came the athletic games, much more interesting than the beastly lessons. I won two first prizes and Jones four, but I gained fifteen "seconds", a record, I believe, for according to my age I was still in the Lower School.

I was fully aware of the secret of my success and strange to say, it did not increase but rather diminished my conceit. I won, not through natural advantages but by will-power and practice. I should have been much prouder had I succeeded through natural gifts. For instance, there was a boy named Reggie Miller, who at sixteen was five feet ten in height, while I was still under five feet: do what I would, he could jump higher than I could, though he only jumped up to his chin while I could jump the bar above my head. I believed that Reggie could easily practice and then outjump me still more. I had yet to learn in life that the resolved will to succeed was more than any natural advantage. But this lesson only came to me later. From the beginning I was taking the highway to success in everything by strengthening my will even more than my body. Thus, every handicap in natural deficiency turns out to be an advantage in life to the brave soul, whereas every natural gift is surely a handicap. Demosthenes had a difficulty in his speech, practising to overcome this, made him the greatest of orators.

The last day came at length and at eleven o'clock all the school and a goodly company of guests and friends gathered in the schoolroom to hear the results of the examinations and especially the award of the scholarships. Though most of the boys were early at the great blackboard where the official figures were displayed, I didn't even go near it till one little boy told me shyly: "You're head of your Form and sure of your remove."

I found this to be true, but wasn't even elated. A Cambridge professor, it appeared, had come down in person to announce the result of the "Math" Scholarship.

He made a rather long talk, telling us that the difficulty of deciding had been unusually great, for there was practical equality between two boys: indeed he might have awarded the scholarship to No. 9 (my number) and not to No. 1, on the sheer merit of the work, but when he found that the one boy was under fifteen while the other was eighteen and ready for the University, he felt it only right to take the view of the Head-Master and give the Scholarship to the older boy, for the younger one was very sure to win it next year and even next year he would still be too young for University life. He therefore gave the Scholarship to Gordon and the second prize of ten pounds to Harris. Gordon stood up and bowed his thanks while the whole school cheered and cheered again: then the Examiner called on me. I had taken in the whole situation. I wanted to get away with all the money I could and as soon as I could. My cue was to make myself unpleasant: accordingly, I got up and thanked the Examiner, saying that I had no doubt of his wish to be fair, "but", I added, "had I known the issue was to be determined by age, I should not have entered. Now I can only say that I will never enter again", and I sat down.

The sensation caused by my little speech was a thousand times greater than I had expected. There was a breathless silence and mute expectancy. The Cambridge Professor turned to the Head of the school and talked with him very earnestly, with visible annoyance, indeed, and then rose again.

"I must say", he began, "I have to say", repeating himself, "that I feel the greatest sympathy with Harris. I was never in so embarrassing a position. I, I must leave the whole responsibility with the Head-Master. I can't do anything else, unfortunately!" and he sat down, evidently annoyed.

The Doctor got up and made a long hypocritical speech: It was one of those difficult decisions one is forced sometimes to make in life: he was sure that everyone would agree that he had tried to act fairly, and so far as he could make it up to the younger boy, he certainly would: he hoped next year to award him the Scholarship with as good a heart as he now gave him his cheque; and he fluttered it in the air.

The Masters all called me and I went up to the platform and accepted the cheque, smiling with delight, and when the Cambridge Professor shook hands with me and would have further excused himself, I whispered shyly, "it's all right, Sir, I'm glad that you decided as you did." He laughed aloud with pleasure, put his arm round my shoulder and said:

"I'm obliged to you, you're certainly a good loser, or winner perhaps I ought to have said, and altogether a remarkable boy. Are you really under sixteen?" I nodded smiling, and the rest of the prize-giving went off without further incident, save that when I appeared on the platform to get the Form prize of books, he smiled pleasantly at me and led the cheering.

I've described the whole incident, for it illustrates to me the English desire to be fair: it is really a guiding impulse in them, on which one may reckon, and so far as my experience goes, it is perhaps stronger in them than in any other race. If it were not for their religious hypocrisies, childish conventions and above all, their incredible snobbishness, their love of fair play alone would make them the worthiest leaders of humanity. All this I felt then as a boy as clearly as I see it today.

I knew that the way of my desire was open to me. Next morning I asked to see the Head; he was very amiable; but I pretended to be injured and disappointed. "My father", I said, "reckons, I think, on my success and I'd like to see him before he hears the bad news from anyone else. Would you please give me the money for my journey and let me go today? It isn't very pleasant for me to be here now."

"I'm sorry", said the Doctor (and I think he was sorry), "of course I'll do anything I can to lighten your disappointment. It's very unfortunate but you must not be down-hearted: Professor S... says that your papers ensure your success next year, and I—well, I'll do anything in my power to help you."

I bowed: "Thank you, Sir. Could I go today? There's a train to Liverpool at noon?"

"Certainly, certainly, if you wish it", he said, "I'll give orders immediately" and he cashed the cheque for ten pounds as well, with only a word that it was nominally to be used to buy books with, but he supposed it did not matter seriously.

By noon I was in the train for Liverpool with fifteen pounds in my pocket, five pounds being for my fare to Ireland. I was trembling with excitement and delight; at length I was going to enter the real world and live as I wished to live. I had no regrets, no sorrows, I was filled with lively hopes and happy presentiments.

As soon as I got to Liverpool, I drove to the Adelphi Hotel and looked out the steamers and soon found one that charged only four pounds for a steerage passage to New York, and to my delight this steamer was starting next day about two o'clock. By four o'clock I had booked my passage and paid for it. The Clerk said something or other about bedding; but I paid no attention. For just on entering his office I had seen an advertisement of "The Two Roses", a "romantic drama" to be played that night, and I was determined to get a seat and see it. Do you know what courage that act required? More than was needed to cut loose from everyone I loved and go to America. For my father was a Puritan of the Puritans and had often spoken of the theatre as the "open door to Hell."

I had lost all belief in Hell or Heaven, but a cold shiver went through me as I bought my ticket and time and again in the next four hours I was on the point of forfeiting it without seeing the play. What if my father was right? I couldn't help the fear that came over me like a vapour.

I was in my seat as the curtain rose and sat for three hours enraptured; it was just a romantic love-story but the heroine was lovely and affectionate and true and I was in love with her at first sight. When the play was over I went into the street, resolved to keep myself pure for some girl like the heroine: no moral lesson I have received before or since can compare with that given me by that first night in a theatre. The effect lasted for many a month and made self-abuse practically impossible to me ever afterwards. The preachers may digest this fact at their leisure.

The next morning I had a good breakfast at the Adelphi Hotel and before ten was on board the steamer, had stowed away my trunk and taken my station by my sleeping place traced in chalk on the deck. About noon the Doctor came round, a young man of good height with a nonchalant manner, reddish hair, roman nose and easy, unconventional ways.

"Whose is this berth?" he asked, pointing to mine.

"Mine, Sir" I replied.

"Tell your father or mother", he said curtly, "that you must have a mattress like this", and he pointed to one, "and two blankets", he added.

"Thank you, Sir", I said and shrugged my shoulders at his interference. In another hour he came round again.

"Why is there no mattress here and no blanket?" he asked.

"Because I don't need 'em", I replied.

"You must have them", he barked, "it's the rule, d'ye understand?" and he hurried on with his inspection. In half an hour he was back again.

"You haven't the mattress yet", he snarled.

"I don't want a mattress", I replied.

"Where's your father or mother", he asked.

"Haven't got any", I retorted.

"Do they let children like you go to America" he cried, "What age are you?"

I was furious with him for exposing my youth there in public before everyone. "How does it matter to you?" I asked disdainfully. "You're not responsible for me, thank God!"

"I am though", he said, "to a certain degree at least. Are you really going to America on your own?"

"I am", I rejoined casually and rudely.

"What to do?" was his next query.

"Anything I can get" I replied.

"Hum", he muttered, "I must see to this."

Ten minutes later he returned again. "Come with me", he said, and I followed him to his cabin—a comfortable stateroom with a good berth on the right of the door as you entered, and a good sofa opposite.

"Are you really alone?" he asked.

I nodded, for I was a little afraid he might have the power to forbid me to go and I resolved to say as little as possible.

"What age are you?" was his next question.

"Sixteen", I lied boldly.

"Sixteen!", he repeated, "you don't look it but you speak as if you had been well educated." I smiled; I had already measured the crass ignorance of the peasants in the steerage.

"Have you any friends in America?" he asked.

"What do you want to question me for?" I demanded, "I've paid for my passage and I'm doing no harm."

"I want to help you", he said, "will you stay here until we draw out and I get a little time?"

"Certainly", I said, "I'd rather be here than with those louts and if I might read your books—"

I had noticed that there were two little oak bookcases, one on each side of the washing-stand, and smaller books and pictures scattered about.

"Of course you may", he rejoined and threw open the door of the bookcase. There was a Macaulay staring at me.

"I know his poetry", I said, seeing that the book contained his "Essays" and was written in prose. "I'd like to read this."

"Go ahead", he said smiling, "in a couple of hours I'll be back." When he returned he found me curled upon his sofa, lost in fairyland. I had just come to the end of the essay on Clive and was breathless. "You like it?" he asked. "I should just think I did", I replied, "it's better even than his poetry", and suddenly I closed the book and began to recite:

"With all his faults, and they were neither few nor small, only one cemetery was worthy to contain his remains. In the Great Abbey—"

The Doctor took the book from me where I held it.

"Are you reciting from Clive?" he asked.

"Yes", I said, "but the essay on Warren Hastings is just as good", and I began again:

"He looked like a great man, and not like a bad one. A person small and emaciated, yet deriving dignity from a carriage which, while it indicated deference to the Court, indicated also habitual self-possession and self-respect. A high and intellectual forehead; a brow pensive but not gloomy, a mouth of inflexible decision, a face on which was written as legibly as under the great picture in the Council Chamber of Calcutta, *Mens aequa in arduis*: such was the aspect with which the great proconsul presented himself to his judges."

"Have you learned all this by heart?" cried the Doctor laughing.

"I don't have to learn stuff like that", I replied, "one reading is enough."

He stared at me.

"I was surely right in bringing you down here", he began, "I wanted to get you a berth in the Intermediate; but there's no room: if you could put up with that sofa, I'd have the steward make up a bed for you on it."

"Oh, would you!" I cried, "how kind of you, and you'll let me read your books?" "Everyone of 'em", he replied, adding, "I only wish I could make as good use of them."

The upshot of it was that in an hour he had drawn some of my story from me and we were great friends. His name was Keogh. "Of course he's Irish", I said to myself, as I went to sleep that night: "no one else would have been so kind."

The ordinary man will think I am bragging here about my memory. He's mistaken. Swinburne's memory especially for poetry was far, far better than mine, and I have always regretted the fact that a good memory often prevents one thinking for oneself. I shall come back to this belief of mine when I later explain how want of books gave me whatever originality I possess. A good memory and books at command are two of the greatest dangers of youth and form by themselves a terrible handicap, but like all gifts a good memory is apt to make you friends among the unthinking, especially when you are very young.

As a matter of fact, Doctor Keogh went about bragging of my memory and power of reciting, until some of the Cabin passengers became interested in the extraordinary schoolboy. The outcome was that I was asked to recite one evening in the First Cabin and afterwards a collection was taken up for me and a first-class passage paid and about twenty dollars over and above was given to me. Besides, an old gentleman offered to adopt me and play second father to me, but I had not got rid of one father to take on another, so I kept as far away from him as I decently could.

I am again, however, running ahead of my story. The second evening of the voyage, the sea got up a little and there was a great deal of sickness. Doctor Keogh was called out of his cabin and while he was away, someone knocked at the door. I opened it and found a pretty girl.

"Where's the Doctor?" she asked. I told her he had been called to a cabin passenger.

"Please tell him", she said, "when he returns, that Jessie Kerr, the chief Engineer's daughter, would like to see him."

"I'll go after him now if you wish, Miss Jessie", I said. "I know where he is."

"It isn't important", she rejoined, "but I feel giddy and he told me he could cure it."

"Coming up on deck is the best cure", I declared: "the fresh air will soon blow the sick feeling away. You'll sleep like a top and tomorrow morning you'll he alright. Will you come?" She consented readily and in ten minutes admitted that the slight nausea had disappeared in the sharp breeze. As we walked up and down the dimly lighted deck I had now and then to support her, for the ship was rolling a little under a sou-wester. Jessie told me something about herself; how she was going to New York to spend some months with an elder married sister and how strict her father was. In return she had my whole story and could hardly believe I was only sixteen. Why she was over sixteen, and she could never have stood up and recited piece after piece as I did in the Cabin: she thought it "wonderful."

Before she went down, I told her she was the prettiest girl on board and she kissed me and promised to come up the next evening and have another walk. "If you've nothing better to do" she said at parting, "you might come forward to the little Promenade Deck of the Second Cabin and I'll get one of the men to arrange a seat in one of the boats for us." "Of course", I promised gladly and spent the next afternoon with Jessie in the stern-sheets of the great launch where we were out of sight of everyone, and out of hearing as well.

There we were, tucked in with two rugs and cradled, so to speak, between sea and sky, while the keen air whistling past increased our sense of solitude. Jessie, though rather short, was a very pretty girl with large hazel eyes and fair complexion.

I soon got my arm round her and kept kissing her till she told me she had never known a man so greedy of kisses as I was. It was delicious flattery to me to speak of me as a man and in return I raved about her eyes and mouth and form; caressing her left breast I told her I could divine the rest and knew she had a lovely body. But when I put my hand up her clothes, she stopped me when I got just above her knee and said:

"We'd have to be engaged before I could let you do that. Do you really love me?"

Of course I swore I did, but when she said she'd have to tell her father that we were engaged to be married, cold shivers went down my back.

"I can't marry for a long time yet", I said, "I'll have to make a living first and I'm not very sure where I'll begin." But she had heard that an old man wished to adopt me and everyone said that he was very rich, and even her father admitted that I'd be "well fixed."

Meanwhile my right hand was busy: I had got my fingers to her warm flesh between the stockings and the drawers and was wild with desire; soon mouth on mouth I touched her sex.

What a gorgeous afternoon we had! I had learned enough now to go slow and obey what seemed to be her moods. Gently, gently I caressed her sex with my finger till it opened and she leaned against me and kissed me of her own will, while her eyes turned up and her whole being was lost in thrills of ecstasy. When she asked me to stop and take my hand away, I did her bidding at once and was rewarded by being told that I was a "dear boy" and "a sweet" and soon the embracing and caressing began again. She moved now in response to my lascivious touchings and when the ecstasy came on her, she clasped me close and kissed me passionately with hot lips and afterwards in my arms wept a little and then pouted that she was cross with me for being so naughty. But her eyes gave themselves to me even while she tried to scold.

The dinner bell rang and she said she'd have to go, and we made a meeting for afterwards on the top deck; but as she was getting up, she yielded again to my hand with a little sigh and I found her sex all wet, wet!

She got down out of the boat by the main rigging and I waited a few moments before following her. At first our caution seemed likely to be rewarded, chiefly, I have thought since, because everyone believed me to be too young and too small to be taken seriously. But everything is quickly known on seaboard at least by the sailors.

I went down to Dr. Keogh's cabin, once more joyful and grateful as I had been with E… My fingers were like eyes gratifying my curiosity, and the curiosity was insatiable. Jessie's thighs were smooth and firm and round: I took delight in recalling the touch of them, and her bottom was firm like warm marble. I wanted to see her naked and study her beauties one after the other. Her sex too was wonderful, fuller even than Lucille's and her eyes were finer. Oh, Life was a thousand times better than school. I thrilled with joy and passionate wild hopes—perhaps Jessie would let me, perhaps—I was breathless.

Our walk on deck that evening was not so satisfactory: the wind had gone down and there were many other couples and the men all seemed to know Jessie, and it was Miss Kerr here, and Miss Kerr there, till I was cross and disappointed; I couldn't get her to myself, save at moments, but then I had to admit she was as sweet as ever and her Aberdeen accent even was quaint and charming to me.

I got some long kisses at odd moments and just before we went down I drew her behind a boat in the davits and was able to caress her little breasts and when she turned her back to me to go, I threw my arms round her hips and drew them against me and felt her sex and she leant her head back over her shoulder and gave me her mouth with dying eyes. The darling! Jessie was apt at all Love's lessons.

The next day was cloudy and rain threatened, but we were safely ensconced in the boat by two o'clock, as soon as lunch was over, and we hoped no one had seen us. An hour passed in caressings and fondlings, in love's words and love's promises: I had won Jessie to touch my sex and her eyes seemed to deepen as she caressed it.

"I love you, Jessie, won't you let it touch yours?"

She shook her head. "Not here, not in the open", she whispered and then, "wait a little till we get to New York, dear", and our mouths sealed the compact.

Then I asked her about New York and her sister's house, and we were discussing where we should meet, when a big head and beard showed above the gunwale of the boat and a deep Scotch voice said: "I want ye, Jessie, I've been luiking everywhere for ye."

"Awright, father", she said, "I'll be down in a minute."

"Come quick", said the voice as the head disappeared.

"I'll tell him we love each other and he won't be angry for long", whispered Jessie; but I was doubtful. As she got up to go my naughty hand went up her dress behind and felt her warm, smooth buttocks. Ah, the poignancy of the ineffable sensations; her eyes smiled over her shoulder at me and she was gone—and the sunlight with her.

I still remember the sick disappointment as I sat in the boat alone. Life then like school had its chagrins, and as the pleasures were keener, the balks and blights were bitterer. For the first time in my life vague misgivings came over me, a heart-shaking suspicion that everything delightful and joyous in life had to be paid for—I wouldn't harbor the fear. If I had to pay, I'd pay; after all, the memory of the ecstasy could never be taken away while the sorrow was fleeting. And that faith I still hold.

Next day the Chief Steward allotted me a berth in a cabin with an English midshipman of seventeen going out to join his ship in the West Indies. William Ponsonby was not a bad sort, but he talked of nothing but girls from morning till night and insisted that negresses were better than white girls: they were far more passionate, he said.

He showed me his sex; excited himself before me, while assuring me he meant to have a Miss LeBreton, a governess who was going out to take up a position in Pittsburg.

"But suppose you put her in the family way?" I asked.

"That's not my funeral", was his answer, and seeing that the cynicism shocked me, he went on to say there was no danger if you withdrew in time. Ponsonby never opened a book and was astoundingly ignorant: he didn't seem to care to learn anything that hadn't to do with sex. He introduced me to Miss LeBreton the same evening. She was rather tall, with fair hair and blue eyes, and she praised my reciting. To my wonder she was a woman and pretty, and I could see by the way she looked at Ponsonby that she was more than a little in love with him. He was above middle height, strong and good-tempered, and that was all I could see in him.

Miss Jessie kept away the whole evening and when I saw her father on the "upper deck", he glowered at me and went past without a word. That night I told Ponsonby my story, or part of it, and he declared he would find a sailor to carry a note to Jessie next morning if I'd write it.

Besides, he proposed we should occupy the cabin alternate afternoons; for example, he'd take it next day and I mustn't come near it, and if at any time one of us found the door locked, he was to respect his chum's privacy. I agreed to it all with enthusiasm and went to sleep in a fever of hope. Would Jessie risk her father's anger and come to me? Perhaps she would: at any rate I'd write and ask her and I did. In one hour the same sailor came back with her reply. It ran like this: "Dear love, father is mad, we shall have to take great care for two or three days: as soon as it's safe, I'll come—your loving Jess", with a dozen crosses for kisses.

That afternoon, without thinking of my compact with Ponsonby, I went to our cabin and found the door locked: at once our compact came into my head and I went quietly away. Had he succeeded so quickly? and was she with him in bed? The half certainty made my heart beat.

That evening Ponsonby could not conceal his success but as he used it partly to praise his mistress. I forgave him.

"She has the prettiest figure you ever saw", he declared, "and is really a dear. We had just finished when you came to the door. I said it was some mistake and she believed me. She wants me to marry her but I can't marry. If I were rich I'd marry quick enough. It's better than risking some foul disease", and he went on to tell about one of his colleagues, John Lawrence, who got Black Pox, as he called syphilis, caught from a negress.

"He didn't notice it for three months", Ponsonby went on, "and it got into his system; his nose got bad and he was invalided home, poor devil. Those black girls are foul", he continued, "they give everyone the clap and that's bad enough, I can tell you; they're dirty devils." His ruttish sorrows didn't interest me much, for I had made up my mind never at any time to go with any prostitute.

I came to several such uncommon resolutions on board that ship, and I may set down the chief of them here very briefly. First of all, I resolved that I would do every piece of work given to me as well as I could, so that no one coming after me could do it better. I had found out at school in the last term that if you gave your whole mind and heart to anything, you learned it very quickly and thoroughly. I was sure even before the trial that my first job would lead me straight to fortune. I had seen men at work and knew it would be easy to beat any of them. I was only eager for the trial.

I remember one evening I had waited for Jessie and she never came and just before going to bed, I went up into the bow of the ship where one was alone with the sea and sky, and swore to myself this great oath, as I called it in my romantic fancy: whatever I undertook to do, I would do it to the uttermost in me.

If I have had any success in life or done any good work, it is due in great part to that resolution.

I could not keep my thoughts from Jessie; if I tried to put her out of my head, I'd either get a little note from her, or Ponsonby would come begging me to leave him the cabin the whole day: at length in despair I begged her for her address in New York, for I feared to lose her forever in that maelstrom. I added that I would always be in my cabin and alone from one to half past if she could ever come.

That day she didn't come, and the old gentleman who said he would adopt me, got hold of me, told me he was a banker and would send me to Harvard, the University near Boston; from what the Doctor had said of me, he hoped I would do great things. He was really kind and tried to be sympathetic, but he had no idea that what I wanted chiefly was to prove myself, to justify my own high opinion of my powers in the open fight of life. I didn't want help and I absolutely resented his protective airs.

Next day in the cabin came a touch on the door and Jessie all flustered was in my arms. "I can only stay a minute", she cried, "Father is dreadful, says you are only a child and won't have me engage myself and he watches me from morning to night, I could only get away now because he had to go down to the machine-room."

Before she had finished, I had locked the cabin door.

"Oh, I must go", she cried, "I must really; I only came to give you my address in New York, here it is", and she handed me the paper that I put at once in my pocket. And then I put both my arms under her clothes and my hands were on her warm hips, and I was speechless with delight; in a moment my right hand came round in front and as I touched her sex our lips clung together and her sex opened at once, and my finger began to caress her and we kissed and kissed again. Suddenly her lips got hot and while I was still wondering why, her sex got wet and her eyes began to flutter and turn up. A moment or two later she tried to get out of my embrace.

"Really, dear, I'm frightened: he might come and make a noise and I'd die; please let me go now: we'll have lots of time in New York"—but I could not bear to let her go. "He'd never come here where there are two men", I said, "never, he might find the wrong one", and I drew her to me, but seeing she was only half reassured, I said while lifting her dress, "Let mine just touch yours, and I'll let you go" and the next moment my sex was against hers and almost in spite of herself she yielded to the throbbing warmth of it; but when I pushed in, she drew away and down on it a little and I saw anxiety in her eyes that had grown very dear to me.

At once I stopped and put away my sex and let her clothes drop. "You're such a sweet, Jess", I said, "who could deny you anything; in New York then, but now one long kiss."

She gave me her mouth at once and her lips were hot. I learned that morning that when a girl's lips grow hot, her sex is hot first and she is ready to give herself and ripe for the embrace.

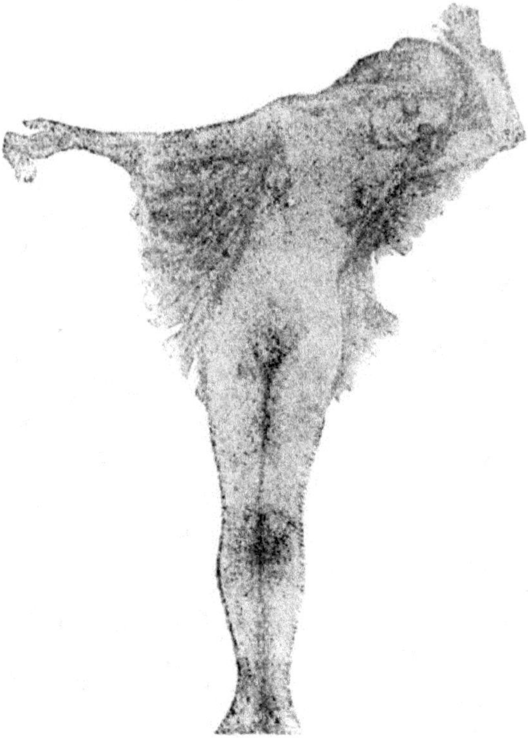

THE GREAT NEW WORLD!

Chapter V.

A stolen kiss and fleeting caress as we met on the deck at night were all I had of Jessie for the rest of the voyage. One evening landlights flickering in the distance drew crowds to the deck; the ship began to slow down. The cabin passengers went below as usual, but hundreds of immigrants sat up as I did and watched the stars slide down the sky till at length dawn came with silver lights and startling revelations.

I can still recall the thrills that overcame me when I realized the great waterways of that land-locked harbor and saw Long Island Sound stretching away on one hand like a sea and the magnificent Hudson River with its palisades on the other, while before me was the East River, nearly a mile in width. What an entrance to a new world! A magnificent and safe ocean port which is also the meeting place of great water paths into the continent.

No finer site could be imagined for a world capital; I was entranced with the spacious grandeur, the manifest destiny of this Queen City of the Waters.

The Old Battery was pointed out to me and Governor's Island and the prison and where the bridge was being built to Brooklyn: suddenly Jessie passed on her father's arm and shot me one radiant, lingering glance of love and promise.

I remember nothing more till we landed and the old banker came up to tell me he had had my little box taken from the "H's" where it belonged and put with his luggage among the "S's."

"We are going", he added, "to the Fifth Avenue Hotel away up town in Madison Square: we'll be comfortable there", and he smiled self-complacently. I smiled too, and thanked him; but I had no intention of going in his company. I went back to the ship and thanked Dr. Keogh with all my heart for his great goodness to me; he gave me his address in New York and incidentally I learned from him that if I kept the key of my trunk, no one could open it or take it away; it would be left in charge of the Customs till I called for it.

In a minute I was back in the long shed on the dock and had wandered nearly to the end when I perceived the stairs: "Is that the way into the town?" I asked and a man replied, "Sure." One quick glance around to see that I was not noticed and in a moment I was down the stairs and out in the street: I raced straight ahead of me for two or three blocks and then asked and was told that Fifth Avenue was right in front. As I turned up Fifth Avenue, I began to breathe freely; "no more fathers for me." The old Greybeard who had bothered me was consigned to oblivion without regret. Of course, I know now that he deserved better treatment. Perhaps indeed I should have done better had I accepted his kindly, generous help, but I'm trying to set down the plain, unvarnished truth, and here at once I must say that children's affections are much slighter than most parents imagine. I never wasted a thought on my father; even my brother Vernon who had always been kind to me and fed my inordinate vanity, was not regretted: the new life called me: I was in a flutter of expectancy and hope.

Some way up Fifth Avenue I came into the great Square and saw the Fifth Avenue Hotel, but I only grinned and kept right on till at length I reached Central Park. Near it, I can't remember exactly where, but I believe it was near where the Plaza Hotel stands today, there was a small wooden house with an outhouse at the other end of the lot. While I stared a woman came out with a bucket and went across to the outhouse. In a few moments she came back again and noticed me looking over the fence.

"Would you please give me a drink?" I asked. "Sure I will", she replied with a strong Irish brogue. "Come right in" and I followed her into her kitchen.

"You're Irish", I said, smiling at her. "I am", she replied, "how did ye guess?" "Because I was born in Ireland too", I retorted. "You were not!" she cried emphatically, more for pleasure than to contradict. "I was born in Galway", I went on and at once she became very friendly and poured me out some milk warm from the cow, and when she heard I had had no breakfast and saw I was hungry, she pressed me to eat and sat down with me and soon heard my whole story or enough of it to break out in wonder again and again.

In turn she told me how she had married Mike Mulligan, a longshoreman who earned good wages and was a good husband but took a drop too much now and again, as a man will when tempted by one of "thim saloons." It was the saloons, I learned, that were the ruination of all the best Irishmen and "they were the best men anyway, an'—an'—" and the kindly, homely talk flowed on, charming me.

When the breakfast was over and the things cleared away I rose to go with many thanks but Mrs. Mulligan wouldn't hear of it. "Ye're a child", she said, "an' don't know New York: it's a terrible place and you must wait till Mike comes home an'—"

"But I must find some place to sleep", I said, "I have money."

"You'll sleep here", she broke in decisively, "and Mike will put ye on yer feet; sure he knows New York like his pocket, an' yer as welcome as the flowers in May, an'—"

What could I do but stay and talk and listen to all sorts of stories about New York, and "toughs" that were "hard cases" and "gunmen" an' "wimmin that were worse—bad scran to them."

In due time Mrs. Mulligan and I had dinner together, and after dinner I got her permission to go into the Park for a walk, but "mind now and be home by six or I'll send Mike after ye", she added laughing.

I walked a little way in the Park and then started down-town again to the address Jessie had given me near the Brooklyn Bridge. It was a mean street, I thought, but I soon found Jessie's sister's house and went to a nearby restaurant and wrote a little note to my love, that she could show if need be, saying that I proposed to call on the 18th, or two days after the ship we had come in was due to return to Liverpool. After that duty which made it possible for me to hope all sorts of things on the 18th, 19th or 20th, I sauntered over to Fifth Avenue and made my way up town again. At any rate I was spending nothing in my present lodging.

When I returned that night I was presented to Mike: I found him a big, good-looking Irishman who thought his wife a wonder and all she did perfect. "Mary", he said, winking at me, "is one of the best cooks in the wurrld and if it weren't that she's down on a man when he has a drop in him, she'd be the best gurrl on God's earth. As it is, I married her and I've never been sorry: have I Mary?" "Ye've had no cause, Mike Mulligan."

Mike had nothing particular to do next morning and so he promised he would go and get my little trunk from the Custom House. I gave him the key. He insisted as warmly as his wife that I should stay with them till I got work: I told them how eager I was to begin and Mike promised to speak to his chief and some friends and see what could be done.

Next morning I got up about five-thirty as soon as I heard Mike stirring, and went down Seventh Avenue with him till he got on the horse-car for down-town and left me. About seven-thirty to eight o'clock a stream of people began walking down-town to their offices. On several corners were bootblack shanties. One of them happened to have three customers in it and only one bootblack.

"Won't you let me help you shine a pair or two?", I asked. The bootblack looked at me: "I don't mind", he said and I seized the brushes and went to work. I had done the two just as he finished the first: he whispered to me "halves" as the next man came in and he showed me how to use the polishing rag or cloth. I took off my coat and waistcoat and went to work with a will; for the next hour and a half we both had our hands full. Then the rush began to slack off but not before I had taken just over a dollar and a half. Afterwards we had a talk and Allison, the bootblack, told me he'd be glad to give me work any morning on the same terms. I assured him I'd be there and do my best till I got other work. I had earned three shillings and had found out I could get good board for three dollars a week, so in a couple of hours I had earned my living. The last anxiety left me.

Mike had a day off, so he came home for dinner at noon and he had great news. They wanted men to work under water in the iron caissons of Brooklyn Bridge and they were giving from five to ten dollars a day.

"Five dollars", cried Mrs. Mulligan, "it must be dangerous or unhealthy or somethin'—sure, you'd never put the child to work like that."

Mike excused himself, but the danger, if danger there was, appealed to me almost as much as the big pay: my only fear was that they'd think me too small or too young. I had told Mrs. Mulligan I was sixteen, for I didn't want to be treated as a child and now I showed her the eighty cents I had earned that morning boot-blacking, and she advised me to keep on at it and not go to work under the water; but the promised five dollars a day won me.

Next morning Mike took me to Brooklyn Bridge soon after five o'clock to see the Contractor: he wanted to engage Mike at once but shook his head over me. "Give me a trial", I pleaded, "You'll see, I'll make good." After a pause, "O.K.", he said, "four shifts have gone down already underhanded; you may try."

I've told about the work and its dangers at some length in my novel "The Bomb", but here I may add some details just to show what labor has to suffer.

In the bare shed where we got ready the men told me no one could do the work for long without getting the "bends"; the "bends", it appeared, were a sort of convulsive fit that twisted one's body like a knot and often made you an invalid for life. They soon explained the whole procedure to me. We worked, it appeared, in a huge bell-shaped caisson of iron that went to the bottom of the river and was pumped full of compressed air to keep the water from entering it from below: the top of the caisson is a room called the "material chamber" into which the stuff dug out of the river passes up and is carted away. On the side of the caisson is another room, called the "airlock", into which we were to go to be "compressed." As the compressed air is admitted, the blood keeps absorbing the gasses of the air till the tension of the gasses in the blood becomes equal to that in the air: when this equilibrium has been reached, men can work in the caisson for hours without serious discomfort if sufficient pure air is constantly pumped in. It was the foul air that did the harm, it appeared; "if they'd pump in good air, it would be O.K.: but that would cost a little time and trouble and men's lives are cheaper." I saw that the men wanted to warn me, thinking I was too young, and accordingly I pretended to take little heed.

When we went into the "airlock" and they turned on one aircock after another of compressed air, the men put their hands to their ears and I soon imitated them for the pain was very acute. Indeed, the drums of the ears are often driven in and burst if the compressed air is brought in too quickly. I found that the best way of meeting the pressure was to keep swallowing air and forcing it up into the middle ear where it acted as an air-pad on the inner side of the drum and so lessened the pressure from the outside.

It took about half an hour or so to "compress" us and that half an hour gave me lots to think about. When the air was fully compressed, the door of the airlock opened at a touch and we all went down to work with pick and shovel on the gravelly bottom. My headache soon became acute. The six of us were working naked to the waist in a small iron chamber with a temperature of about 180 Fahrenheit: in five minutes the sweat was pouring from us and all the while we were standing in icy water that was only kept from rising by the terrific air pressure. No wonder the headaches were blinding. The men didn't work for more than ten minutes at a time, but I plugged on steadily, resolved to prove myself and get constant employment; only one man, a Swede named Anderson, worked at all as hard. I was overjoyed to find that together we did more than the four others. The amount done each week was estimated, he told me, by an inspector. Anderson was known to the Contractor and received half a wage extra as head of our gang. He assured me I could stay as long as I liked, but he advised me to leave at the end of a month: it was too unhealthy: above all, I mustn't drink and should spend all my spare time in the open. He was kindness itself to me as indeed were all the others. After two hours' work down below we went up into the airlock room to get gradually "decompressed", the pressure of air in our veins having to be brought down gradually to the usual air pressure. The men began to put on their clothes and passed round a bottle of Schnapps; but though I was soon as cold as a wet rat and felt depressed and weak to boot, I would not touch the liquor. In the shed above I took a cupful of hot cocoa with Anderson which stopped the shivering and I was soon able to face the afternoon's ordeal.

I had no idea one could feel so badly when being "decompressed" in the airlock, but I took Anderson's advice and got into the open as soon as I could, and by the time I had walked home in the evening and changed, I felt strong again, but the headache didn't leave me entirely and the earache came back every now and then and to this day a slight deafness reminds me of that spell of work under water.

I went into Central Park for half an hour; the first pretty girl I met reminded me of Jessie: in one week I'd be free to see her and tell her I was making good and she'd keep her promise, I felt sure; the mere hope led me to fairyland. Meanwhile nothing could take away the proud consciousness that with my five dollars I had earned two weeks' living in a day: a month's work would make me safe for a year.

When I returned I told the Mulligans I must pay for my board, said "I'd feel better, if you'll let me" and finally they consented, though Mrs. Mulligan thought three dollars a week too much. I was glad when it was settled and went to bed early to have a good sleep. For three or four days things went fairly well with me but on the fifth or sixth day we came on a spring of water or "gusher" and were wet to the waist before the air pressure could be increased to cope with it. As a consequence a dreadful pain shot through both my ears: I put my hands to them tight and sat still a little while. Fortunately the shift was almost over and Anderson came with me to the horse-car. "You'd better knock off", he said, "I've known 'em go deaf from it."

The pain had been appalling but it was slowly diminishing and I was resolved not to give in. "Could I get a day off?" I asked Anderson: he nodded, "of course: you're the best in the shift, the best I've ever seen, a great little pony."

Mrs. Mulligan saw at once something was wrong and made me try her household remedy—a roasted onion cut in two and clapped tight on each ear with a flannel bandage. It acted like magic: in ten minutes I was free of pain: then she poured in a little warm sweet oil and in an hour I was walking in the Park as usual. Still the fear of deafness was on me and I was very glad when Anderson told me he had complained to the Boss and we were to get an extra thousand feet of pure air. It would make a great difference, Anderson said, and he was right, but the improvement was not sufficient.[1]

> 1. In Germany I have since learned the State requires that ten times as much pure air must be supplied as we had and in consequence the serious illnesses which with us amounted to eighty per cent in three months have been reduced to eight. Paternal Government, it appears, has certain good points.

One day just as the "decompression" of an hour and a half was ending, an Italian named Manfredi fell down and writhed about, knocking his face on the floor till the blood spurted from his nose and mouth. When we got him into the shed, his legs were twisted like plaited hair. The surgeon had him taken to the hospital. I made up my mind that a month would be enough for me.

At the end of the first week I got a note from Jessie saying that her father was going on board that afternoon and she could see me the next evening. I went and was introduced to Jessie's sister who, to my surprise, was tall and large but without a trace of Jessie's good looks.

"He's younger than you, Jess", she burst out laughing. A week earlier I'd have been hurt to the soul, but I had proved myself, so I said simply, "I'm earning five dollars a day, Mrs. Plummer, and money talks." Her mouth fell open in amazement. "Five dollars", she repeated, "I'm sorry, I—I—"

"There, Maggie", Jessie broke in, "I told you, you had never seen anyone like him; you'll be great friends yet. Now come and we'll have a walk", she added and out we went.

To be with her even in the street was delightful and I had a lot to say, but making love in a New York street on a summer evening is difficult and I was hungry to kiss and caress her freely. Jessie, however, had thought of a way: if her sister and husband had theatre tickets, they'd go out and we'd be alone in the apartment; it would cost two dollars, however, and she thought that a lot. I was delighted: I gave her the bills and arranged to be with her next night before eight o'clock. Did Jessie know what was going to happen? Even now I'm uncertain, though I think she guessed.

Next night I waited till the coast was clear and then hurried to the door. As soon as we were alone in the little parlor and I had kissed her, I said, "Jessie, I want you to undress. I'm sure your figure is lovely, but I want to know it."

"Not at once, eh?" she pouted, "talk to me first. I want to know how you are?" and I drew her to the big armchair and sat down with her in my arms. "What am I to tell you?" I asked, while my hand went up her dress to her warm thighs and sex. She frowned but I kissed her lips and with a movement or two stretched her out on me so that I could use my finger easily. At once her lips grew hot and I went on kissing and caressing till her eyes closed and she gave herself to the pleasure. Suddenly she wound herself upon me and gave me a big kiss. "You don't talk", she said.

"I can't", I exclaimed, making up my mind. "Come", and I lifted her to her feet and took her into the bedroom. "I'm crazy for you", I said, "take off your clothes, please." She resisted a little but when I began loosening her dress, she helped me and took it off. Her knickers, I noticed, were new. They soon fell off and she stood in her chemise and black stockings. "That's enough, isn't it?" she said, "Mr. Curious", and she drew the chemise tight about her. "No", I cried, "beauty must unveil, please!" The next moment the chemise slipping down caught for a moment on her hips and then slid circling round her feet.

Her nakedness stopped my heart; desire blinded me: my arms went round her, straining her soft form to me: in a moment I had lifted her on to the bed, pulling the bed clothes back at the same time. The foolish phrase of being in bed together deluded me: I had no idea that she was more in my power just lying on the edge of the bed; in a moment I had torn off my clothes and boots and got in beside her. Our warm bodies lay together: a thousand hot pulses beating in us: soon I separated her legs and lying on her tried to put my sex into hers, but she drew away almost at once. "O—O, it hurts" she murmured and each time I tried to push my sex in, her "O's" of pain stopped me.

My wild excitement made me shiver; I could have struck her for drawing away; but soon I noticed that she let my sex touch her clitoris with pleasure and I began to use my cock as a finger, caressing her with it. In a moment or two I began to move it more quickly and as my excitement grew to the height, I again tried to slip it into her pussy, and now as her love-dew came, I got my sex in a little way which gave me inexpressible pleasure; but when I pushed to go further, she drew away again with a sharp cry of pain. At the same moment my orgasm came on for the first time and seed like milk spurted from my sex. The pleasure thrill was almost unbearably keen: I could have screamed with the pang of it; but Jessie cried out, "Oh, you're wetting me" and drew away with a frightened "Look, look!" And there, sure enough, on her round white thighs were patches of crimson blood. "Oh! I'm bleeding", she cried, "what have you done?"

"Nothing", I answered, a little sulky, I'm afraid, at having my indescribable pleasure cut short, "nothing" and in a moment I had got out of bed, and taking my handkerchief soon wiped away the telltale traces.

But when I wanted to begin again, Jessie wouldn't hear of it at first:

"No, no", she said. "You've hurt me really, Jim, (my Christian name, I had told her, was James) and I'm scared, please be good." I could only do her will, till a new thought struck me. At any rate I could see her now and study her beauties one by one, and so still lying by her I began kissing her left breast and soon the nipple grew a little stiff in my mouth. Why, I didn't know and Jessie said she didn't, but she liked it when I said her breasts were lovely and indeed they were, small and firm while the nipples pointed straight out. Suddenly the thought came, surprising me: it would have been much prettier if the circle surrounding the nipples had been rose-red instead of merely umber brown. I was thrilled by the bare idea. But her flanks and belly were lovely; the navel like a curled sea-shell, I thought, and the triangle of silky brown hairs on the Mount of Venus seemed to me enchanting, but Jessie kept covering her beauty-place. "It's ugly", she said, "please, boy", but I went on caressing it and soon I was trying to slip my sex in again; though Jessie's "O's" of pain began at once and she begged me to stop.

"We must get up and dress", she said, "they'll soon be back", so I had to content myself with just lying in her arms with my sex touching hers. Soon she began to move against my sex, and to kiss me, and then she bit my lips just as my sex slipped into hers again; she left it in for a long moment and then as her lips grew hot: "it's so big", she said, "but you're a dear." The moment after she cried: "We must get up, boy! if they caught us, I'd die of shame." When I tried to divert her attention by kissing her breasts, she pouted, "That hurts too. Please, boy, stop and don't look", she added as she tried to rise, covering her sex the while with her hand, and pulling a frowning face. Though I told her she was mistaken and her sex was lovely, she persisted in hiding it, and in truth her breasts and thighs excited me more, perhaps because they were in themselves more beautiful.

I put my hand on her hips; she smiled, "Please, boy" and as I moved away to give her room, she got up and stood by the bed, a perfect little figure in rosy, warm outline. I was entranced, but the cursed critical faculty was awake. As she turned, I saw she was too broad for her height; her legs were too short, her hips too stout. It all chilled me a little. Should I ever find perfection?

Ten minutes later she had arranged the bed and we were seated in the sitting-room but to my wonder Jessie didn't want to talk over our experience. "What gave you most pleasure?" I asked. "All of it", she said, "you naughty dear; but don't let's talk of it."

I told her I was going to work for a month, but I couldn't talk to her: my hand was soon up her clothes again playing with her sex and caressing it, and we had to move apart hurriedly when we heard her sister at the door.

I didn't get another evening alone with Jessie for some time. I asked for it often enough, but Jessie made excuses and her sister was very cold to me. I soon found out it was by her advice that Jessie guarded herself. Jessie confessed that her sister accused her of letting me "act like a husband: she must have seen a stain on my chemise", Jessie added, "when you made me bleed, you naughty boy; any way something gave her the idea and now you must be good."

That was the conclusion of the whole matter. If I had known as much then as I knew ten years later, neither the pain nor her sister's warnings could have dissuaded Jessie from giving herself to me. Even at the time I felt that a little more knowledge would have made me the arbiter.

The desire to have Jessie completely to myself again, was one reason why I gave up the job at the Bridge as soon as the month was up. I had over a hundred and fifty dollars clear in my pocket and I had noticed that though the pains in my ears soon ceased, I had become a little hard of hearing. The first morning I wanted to lie in bed and have one great lazy day, but I awoke at five as usual, and it suddenly occurred to me that I should go down and see Allison, the bootblack, again. I found him busier than ever and I had soon stripped off and set to work. About ten o'clock we had nothing to do, so I told him of my work under water; he boasted that his "stand" brought him in about four dollars a day: there wasn't much to do in the afternoons, but from six to seven again he usually earned something more.

I was welcome to come and work with him any morning on halves and I thought it well to accept his offer.

That very afternoon I took Jessie for a walk in the Park, but when we had found a seat in the shade she confessed that her sister thought we ought to be engaged, and as soon as I got steady work we could be married: "A woman wants a home of her own", she said, "and oh, Boy! I'd make it so pretty! and we'd go out to the theatres and have a gay old time."

I was horrified; married at my age, no, Sir! It seemed absurd to me and with Jessie. I saw she was pretty and bright, but she knew nothing, never had read anything: I couldn't marry her. The idea made me snort. But she was dead in earnest, so I agreed to all she said, only insisting that first I must got regular work; I'd buy the engagement ring too: but first we must have another great evening. Jessie didn't know whether her sister would go out, but she'd see. Meanwhile we kissed and kissed and her lips grew hot and my hand got busy, and then we walked again, on and on, and finally went into the great Museum.

Here I got one of the shocks of my life. Suddenly Jessie stopped before a picture representing, I think, Paris choosing the Goddess of Beauty, Paris being an ideal figure of youthful manhood.

"Oh, isn't he splendid!" cried Jessie, "just like you", she added with feminine wit, pouting out her lips as if to kiss me. If she hadn't made the personal application, I might not have realized the absurdity of the comparison. But Paris had long, slim legs while mine were short and stout, and his face was oval and his nose straight, while my nose jutted out with broad, scenting nostrils.

The conviction came to me in a flash: I was ugly with irregular features, sharp eyes and short squat figure: the certainty overpowered me: I had learned before that I was too small to be a great athlete, now I saw that I was ugly to boot: my heart sank: I can not describe my disappointment and disgust.

Jessie asked; what was the matter and at length I told her. She wouldn't have it: "You've a lovely white skin", she cried, "and you're quick and strong: no one would call you ugly!—the idea!" But the knowledge was in me indisputable, never to leave me again for long. It even led me to some erroneous inferences then and there: for example, it seemed clear to me that if I had been tall and handsome like Paris, Jessie would have given herself to me in spite of her sister; but further knowledge of women makes me inclined to doubt this: they have a luscious eye for good looks in the male, naturally; but other qualities, such as strength and dominant self-confidence have an even greater attraction for the majority, especially for those who are richly endowed sexually and I am inclined to think that it was her sister's warnings and her own matter-of-fact hesitation before the irrevocable that induced Jessie to withhold her sex from complete abandonment. But the pleasure I had experienced with her, made me keener than ever, and more enterprising. The conviction of my ugliness, too, made me resolve to develop my mind and all other faculties as much as I could.

Finally, I saw Jessie home and had a great hug and long kiss and was told she had had a bully afternoon and we made another appointment.

I worked at boot-blacking every morning and soon got some regular customers, notably a young, well-dressed man who seemed to like me. Either Allison, or he himself, told me his name was Kendrick and he came from Chicago. One morning he was very silent and absorbed. At length I said, "Finished" and "Finished", he repeated after me: "I was thinking of something else", he explained. "Intent", I said smiling. "A business deal", he explained, "but why do you say intent?" "The Latin phrase came into my head", I replied without thinking, "'Intentique ore tenebant', Vergil says."

"Good God!" he cried, "fancy a bootblack quoting Vergil. You're a strange lad, what age are you?" "Sixteen", I replied. "You don't look it", he said, "but now I must hurry; one of these days we'll have a talk." I smiled, "Thank you, Sir", and away he hastened.

The very next day he was in still greater haste: "I must get down-town", he said, "I'm late already; just give me a rub or two", he cried impatiently, "I must catch that train" and he fumbled with some bills in his hand. "It's all right", I said, and smiling added; "Hurry! I'll be here tomorrow." He smiled and went off without paying, taking me at my word.

The next day I strolled down-town early; for Allison had found that a stand and lean-to were to be sold on the corner of 13th Street and Seventh Avenue, and as he was known, he wanted me to go and have a look at the business done from seven to nine. The Dago who wished to sell out and go back to Dalmatia, wanted three hundred dollars for the outfit, asserting that the business brought in four dollars a day. He had not exaggerated unduly, I found, and Allison was hot that we should buy it together and go fifty-fifty. "You'll make five or six dollars a day at it", he said, "if the Dago makes four. It's one of the good pitches and with three dollars a day coming in, you'll soon have a stand of your own."

While we were discussing it, Kendrick came up and took his accustomed seat. "What were you so hot about?" he asked, and as Allison smiled, I told him. "Three dollars a day seems good", he said, "but boot-blacking's not your game. How would you like to come to Chicago and have a place as night-clerk in my hotel? I've got one with my uncle", he added, "and I think you'd make good."

"I'd do my best", I replied, the very thought of Chicago and the Great West drawing me, "Will you let me think it over?"

"Sure, sure!", he replied, "I don't go back till Friday; that gives you three days to decide."

Allison stuck to his opinion, that a good stand would make more money; but when I talked it over with the Mulligans, they were both in favor of the hotel. I saw Jessie that same evening and told her of the "stand" and begged for another evening, but she stuck to it that her sister was suspicious and cross with me and would not leave us alone again. Accordingly, I said nothing to her of Chicago.

I had already noticed that sexual pleasure is in its nature profoundly selfish. So long as Jessie yielded to me and gave me delight, I was attracted by her; but as soon as she denied me, I became annoyed and dreamed of more pliant beauties. I was rather pleased to leave her without even a word; "that'll teach her!" my wounded vanity whispered, "she deserves to suffer a little for disappointing me."

But parting with the Mulligans was really painful: Mrs. Mulligan was a dear, kind woman who would have mothered the whole race if she could; one of those sweet Irish women whose unselfish deeds and thoughts are the flowers of our sordid human life. Her husband too was not unworthy of her; very simple and straight and hard-working, without a mean thought in him, a natural prey to good fellowship and songs and poteen.

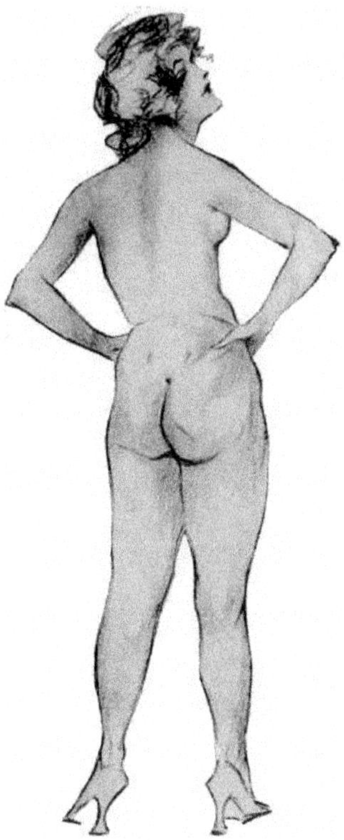

On Friday afternoon I left New York for Chicago with Mr. Kendrick. The country seemed to me very bare, harsh and unfinished, but the great distances enthralled me; it was indeed a land to be proud of, every broad acre of it spoke of the future and suggested hope.

My first round, so to speak, with American life was over. What I had learned in it remains with me still. No people is so kind to children and no life so easy for the handworkers; the hewers of wood and drawers of water are better off in the United States than anywhere else on earth. To this one class and it is by far the most numerous class, the American democracy more than fulfills its promises. It levels up the lowest in a most surprising way. I believed then with all my heart what so many believe today, that all deductions made, it was on the whole, the best civilization yet known among men.

In time, deeper knowledge made me modify this opinion more and more radically. Five years later I was to see Walt Whitman, the noblest of all Americans, living in utter poverty at Camden, dependent upon English admirers for a change of clothes or a sufficiency of food, and Poe had suffered in the same way.

Bit by bit the conviction was forced in upon me that if the American democracy does much to level up the lowest class, it is still more successful in leveling down the highest and best. No land on earth is so friendly to the poor illiterate toilers, no land so contemptuous-cold to the thinkers and artists, the guides of humanity. What help is there here for men of letters and artists, for the seers and prophets? Such guides are not wanted by the idle rich and are ignored by the masses, and after all the welfare of the head is more important even than that of the body and feet.

What will become of those who stone the prophet? and persecute the teachers? The doom is written in flaming letters on every page of history.

LIFE IN CHICAGO!

Chapter VI.

The Fremont House, Kendrick's hotel was near the Michigan Street Depot. In those days when Chicago had barely 300,000 inhabitants, it was an hotel of the second class. Mr. Kendrick had told me that his uncle, a Mr. Cotton really owned the House, but left him the chief share in the management, adding "What uncle says, goes always." In the course of time, I understood the nephew's loyalty; for Mr. Cotton was really kindly and an able man of business. My duties as night-clerk were simple; from eight at night till six in the morning, I was master in the office and had to apportion bedrooms to the incoming guests and give bills and collect the monies due from the outgoing public. I set myself at once to learn the good and bad points of the hundred odd bedrooms in the house and the arrival and departure times of all the night trains. When guests came in, I met them at the entrance, found out what they wanted and told this or that porter or bellboy to take them to their rooms. However curt or irritable they were, I always tried to smooth them down and soon found I was succeeding. In a week Mr. Kendrick told me that he had heard golden opinions of me from a dozen visitors. "You have a dandy night-clerk," he was told; "Spares no pains … pleasant manners … knows everything ... "*some*" clerk; yes, sir!"

My experience in Chicago assured me that if one does his very best, he comes to success in business in a comparatively short time; so few do all they can. Going to bed at six, I was up every day at 1 o'clock for dinner as it was called and after dinner I got into the habit of going into the billiard-room at one end of which was a large bar. By five o'clock or so, the billiard-room was crowded and there was no one to superintend things, so I spoke to Mr. Kendrick about it and took the job on my own shoulders. I had little to do but induce newcomers to await their turn patiently and to mollify old customers who expected to find tables waiting for them. The result of a little courtesy and smiling promises was so marked that at the end of the very first month the bookkeeper, a man named Curtis, told me with a grin that I was to get sixty dollars a month and not forty dollars as I had supposed. Needless to say the extra pay simply quickened my desire to make myself useful. But now I found the way up barred by two superiors, the bookkeeper was one and the steward, a dry taciturn Westerner named Payne was the other. Payne bought everything and had control of the dining-room and waiters while Curtis ruled the office and the bell-boys. I was really under Curtis; but my control of the billiard-room gave me a sort of independent position.

I soon made friends with Curtis; got into the habit of dining with him and when he found that my handwriting was very good, he gave me the day-book to keep and in a couple of months had taught me bookkeeping while entrusting me with a good deal of it. He was not lazy; but most men of forty like to have a capable assistant. By Christmas that year I was keeping all the books except the ledger and I knew, as I thought, the whole business of the hotel.

The dining-room, it seemed to me was very badly managed; but as luck would have it, I was first to get control of the office. As soon as Curtis found out that I could safely be trusted to do his work, he began going out at dinner time and often stayed away the whole day. About New Year he was away for five days and confided in me when he returned, that he had been on a "bust." He wasn't happy with his wife, it appeared, and he used to drink to drown her temper. In February he was away for ten days; but as he had given me the key of the safe I kept everything going. One day Kendrick found me in the office working and wanted to know about Curtis: "how long had he been away!" "A day or two," I replied. Kendrick looked at me and asked for the ledger: "it's written right up!" he exclaimed, "did you do it?" I had to say I did; but at once I sent a bellboy for Curtis. The boy didn't find him at his house and next day I was brought up before Mr. Cotton. I couldn't deny that I had kept the books and Cotton soon saw that I was shielding Curtis out of loyalty. When Curtis came in next day, he gave the whole show away; he was half-drunk still and rude to boot. He had been unwell, he said; but his work was in order. He was 'fired' there and then by Mr. Cotton and that evening Kendrick asked me to keep things going properly till he could persuade his uncle that I was trustworthy and older than I looked.

In a couple of days I saw Mr. Cotton and Mr. Kendrick together. "Can you keep the books and be night-clerk and take care of the billiard-room?" Mr. Cotton asked me sharply. "I think so" I replied, "I'll do my best." "Hm!" he grunted: "what pay do you think you ought to have?" "I'll leave that to you sir," I said, "I shall be satisfied whatever you give me." "The devil you will," he said grumpily, "suppose I said, keep on at your present rate?" I smiled; "O.K. Sir."

"Why do you smile?" he asked. "Because, sir, pay like water tends to find its level!" "What the devil d'ye mean by its level?" "The level," I went on, "is surely the market price; sooner or later it'll rise towards that and I can wait." His keen grey eyes suddenly bored into me. "I begin to think you're much older, than you look, as my nephew here tells me," he said. "Put yourself down at a hundred a month for the present and in a little while we'll perhaps find the 'level,'" and he smiled. I thanked him and went out to my work.

It seemed as if incidents were destined to crowd my life.... A day or so after this the taciturn steward, Payne, came and asked me if I'd go out with him to dinner and some theatre or other? I had not had a day off in five or six months so I said "Yes." He gave me a great dinner at a famous French restaurant (I forget the name now) and wanted me to drink champagne. But I had already made up my mind not to touch any intoxicating liquor till I was twenty one and so I told him simply that I had taken the pledge. He beat about the bush a great deal, but at length said that as I was bookkeeper in place of Curtis, he hoped we should get along as he and Curtis had done. I asked him just what he meant but he wouldn't speak plainly which excited my suspicions. A day or two afterwards I got into talk with a butcher in another quarter of the town and asked him what he would supply seventy pounds of beef and fifty pounds of mutton for, daily for a hotel; he gave me a price so much below the price Payne was paying that my suspicions were confirmed. I was tremendously excited. In my turn I invited Payne to dinner and led up to the subject. At once he said "of course there's a 'rake-off' and if you'll hold in with me, I'll give you a third as I gave Curtis. The 'rake-off' don't hurt anyone," he went on, "for I buy below market-price." Of course I was all ears and eager interest when he admitted that the 'rake-off' was on everything he bought and amounted to about 20 per cent. of the cost. By this he changed his wages from two hundred dollars a month into something like two hundred dollars a week.

As soon as I had all the facts clear, I asked the nephew to dine with me and laid the situation before him. I had only one loyalty—to my employers and the good of the ship. To my astonishment he seemed displeased at first; "more trouble," he began, "why can't you stick to your own job and leave the others alone? What's in a commission after all?" When he came to understand what the commission amounted to and that he himself could do the buying in half an hour a day, he altered his tone. "What will my uncle say now?" he cried and went off to tell the owner his story. There was a tremendous row two days later for Mr. Cotton was a business man and went to the butcher we dealt with and ascertained for himself how important the 'rake-off' really was. When I was called into the uncle's room Payne tried to hit me; but he found it was easier to receive than to give punches and that "the damned kid" was not a bit afraid of him.

Curiously enough, I soon noticed that the "rake-off" had had the secondary result of giving us an inferior quality of meat; whenever the butcher was left with a roast he could not sell, he used to send it to us confident that Payne wouldn't quarrel about it. The negro cook declared that the meat now was far better; all that could be desired in fact, and our customers too were not slow to show their appreciation.

One other change the discharge of Payne brought about; it made me master of the dining-room. I soon picked a smart waiter and put him as chief over the rest and together we soon improved the waiting and discipline among the waiters out of all comparison. For over a year I worked eighteen hours out of the twenty four and after the first six months or so, I got one hundred and fifty dollars a month and saved practically all of it.

Some experience in this long, icy-cold winter in Chicago enlarged my knowledge of American life and particularly of life on the lowest level. I had been about three months in the hotel when I went out one evening for a sharp walk, as I usually did, about seven o'clock. It was bitterly cold, a western gale raked the streets with icy teeth, the thermometer was about ten below zero. I had never imagined anything like the cold. Suddenly I was accosted by a stranger, a small man with red moustache and stubbly unshaven beard:

"Say, mate, can you help a man to a meal?" The fellow was evidently a tramp: his clothes shabby and dirty: his manner servile with a backing of truculence. I was kindly and not critical. Without a thought, I took my roll of bills out of my pocket. I meant to take off a dollar bill. As the money came to view the tramp with a pounce grabbed at it, but caught my hand as well. Instinctively I held on to my roll like grim Death, but while I was still under the shock of surprise the hobo hit me viciously in the face and plucked at the bills again. I hung on all the tighter, and angry now, struck the man in the face with my left fist. The next moment we had clenched and fallen. As luck and youth would have it, I fell on top. At once I put out all my strength, struck the fellow hard in the face and at the same time tore my bills away. The next moment I was on my feet with my roll deep in my pocket and both fists ready for the next assault. To my astonishment the hobo picked himself up and said confidingly:

"I'm hungry, weak, or you wouldn't have downed me so easy." And then he went on with what to me seemed incredible impudence:

"You should peel me off a dollar at least for hittin' me like that," and he stroked his jaw as if to ease the pain.

"I've a good mind to give you in charge," said I, suddenly realizing that I had the law on my side.

"If you don't cash up," barked the hobo, "I'll call the cops and say you've grabbed my wad."

"Call away," I cried: "we'll see who'll be believed."

But the hobo knew a better trick. In a familiar wheedling voice he began again:

"Come, young fellow, you'll never miss one dollar and I'll put you wise to a good many things here in Chicago. You had no business to pull out a wad like that, in a lonely place to tempt a hungry man...."

"I was going to help you," I said hesitatingly. "I know," replied my weird acquaintance, "but I prefer to help myself," and he grinned. "Take me to a hash-house: I'm hungry and I'll put you wise to many things; you're a tenderfoot and show it."

Clearly the hobo was the master of the situation and somehow or other his whole attitude stirred my curiosity.

"Where are we to go!" I asked. "I don't know any restaurant near here except the Fremont House."

"Hell," cried the hobo, "only millionaires and fools go to hotels. I follow my nose for grub," and he turned on his heel and led the way without another word down a side street and into a German dive set out with bare wooden tables and sanded floor.

Here he ordered hash and I, hot coffee and when I came to pay I was agreeably surprised to find that the bill was only forty cents and we could talk in our corner undisturbed as long as we liked.

In ten minutes' chat the hobo had upset all my preconceived ideas and given me a host of new and interesting thoughts. He was a man of some reading if not of education and the violence of his language attracted me almost as much as the novelty of his point of view.

All rich men were thieves, all workmen, sheep and fools, was his creed. The workmen did the work, created the wealth, and the employers robbed them of nine-tenths of the product of their labor and so got rich. It all seemed simple. The tramp never meant to work; he lived by begging and went wherever he wanted to go.

"But how do you get about?" I cried.

"Here in the middle west," he replied, "I steal rides in freight cars and box-cars and on top of coal wagons, but in the real west and south I get inside the cars and ride, and when the conductor turns me off I wait for the next train. Life is full of happenings—some of 'em painful," he added, thoughtfully rubbing his jaw again.

He appeared to be a tough little man whose one object in life it was to avoid work and in spite of himself, he worked hard in order to do nothing.

The experience had a warning, quickening effect on me. I resolved to save all I could.

When I stood up to go the hobo grinned amicably:

"I guess I've earned that dollar?" I could not help laughing. "I guess you have," I replied, but took care to turn aside as I stripped off the bill.

"So long," said the tramp as we parted at the door and that was all the thanks I ever got.

Another experience of this time told a sadder story. One evening a girl spoke to me; she was fairly well-dressed and as we came under a gas-lamp I saw she was good-looking with a tinge of nervous anxiety in her face.

"I don't buy love," I warned her: "but how much do you generally get?" "From one dollar to five," she replied; "but tonight I want as much as I can get."

"I'll give you five," I replied; "but you must tell me all I want to know."

"All right," she said eagerly, "I'll tell all I know: it's not much," she added bitterly; "I'm not twenty yet; but you'd have taken me for more, now wouldn't you?" "No," I replied, "you look about eighteen: in a few minutes we were climbing the stairs of a tenement house. The girl's room was poorly furnished and narrow, a hall bedroom just the width of the corridor, perhaps six feet by eight. As soon as she had taken off her thick cloak and hat, she hastened out of the room saying she'd be back in a minute. In the silence, I thought I heard her running up the stairs; a baby somewhere near cried; and then silence again, till she opened the door, drew my head to her and kissed me:

"I like you," she said, "though you're funny."

"Why funny?" I asked.

"It's a scream," she said, "to give five dollars to a girl and never touch her: but I'm glad for I was tired tonight and anxious."

"Why anxious?" I queried, "and why did you go out if you were tired?" "Got to," she replied through tightly closed lips. "You don't mind if I leave you again for a moment?" she added and before I could answer she was out of the room again. When she returned in five minutes I had grown impatient and put on my overcoat and hat.

"Goin?" she asked in surprise:

"Yes", I replied, "I don't like this empty cage while you go off to someone else."

"Someone else" she repeated and then as if desperate: "it's my baby if you must know: a friend takes care of her when I'm out or working."

"Oh, you poor thing," I cried, "fancy you with a baby at this life!"

"I wanted a baby", she cried defiantly. "I wouldn't be without her for anything! I always wanted a baby: there's lots of girls like that."

"Really?" I cried astounded.

"Do you know her father?" I went on.

"Of course I do," she retorted. "He's working in the stock yards; but he's tough and won't keep sober."

"I suppose you'd marry him if he would go straight?" I asked.

"Any girl would marry a decent feller!" she replied.

"You're pretty," I said.

"D'ye think so?" she asked eagerly pushing her hair back from the sides of her head. "I used to be but now—this life—" and she shrugged her shoulders expressively.

"You don't like it?" I asked.

"No," she cried; "though when you get a nice feller, it's not so bad; but they're scarce," she went on bitterly, "and generally when they're nice, they've no bucks. The nice fellers are all poor or old," she added reflectively.

I had had the best part of her wisdom, so I stripped off a five dollar bill and gave it to her. "Thanks," she said, "you're a dear and if you want to come an' see me any time, just come an' I'll try to give you a good time."—Away I went. I had had my first talk with a prostitute and in her room! The idea that a girl could want a baby was altogether new to me: her temptations very different from a boy's, very!

For the greater part of my first year in Chicago I had no taste of love: I was often tempted by this chambermaid or that; but I knew I should lose prestige if I yielded and I simply put it all out of my head resolvedly as I had abjured drink. But towards the beginning of the summer temptation came to me in a new guise. A Spanish family, named Vidal, stopped at the Fremont House.

Señor Vidal was like a French officer, middle height, trim figure, very dark with grey moustache waving up at the ends. His wife, motherly but stout, with large dark eyes and small features; a cousin, a man of about thirty, rather tall with a small black moustache, like a tooth brush, I thought, and sharp imperious ways. At first I did not notice the girl who was talking to her Indian maid. I understood at once that the Vidals were rich and gave them the best rooms: "all communicating—except yours," I added, turning to the young man: "it is on the other side of the corridor, but large and quiet." A shrug and contemptuous nod was all I got for my pains from Señor Arriga. As I handed the keys to the bellboy, the girl threw back her black mantilla.

"Any letters for us?" she asked quietly. For a minute I stood dumbfounded, enthralled, then "I'll see," I muttered and went to the rack, but only to give myself a countenance—I knew there were none.

"None, I'm sorry to say," I smiled watching the girl as she moved away.

"What's the matter with me?" I said to myself angrily. "She's nothing wonderful, this Miss Vidal; pretty, yes, and dark with fine dark eyes, but nothing extraordinary." But it would not do; I was shaken in a new way and would not admit it even to myself. In fact the shock was so great that my head took sides against heart and temperament at once as if alarmed. "All Spaniards are dank," I said to myself, trying to depreciate the girl and so regain self-control; "besides her nose is beaked a little." But there was no conviction in my criticism. As soon as I recalled the proud grace of carriage and the magic of her glance, the fever-fit shook me again: for the first time my heart had been touched.

Next day I found out that the Vidals had come from Spain and were on their way to their hacienda near Chihuahua in Northern Mexico. They meant to rest in Chicago for three or four days because Señora Vidal had heart trouble and couldn't stand much fatigue. I discovered besides that Señor Arriga was either courting his cousin or betrothed to her and at once I sought to make myself agreeable to the man. Señor Arriga was a fine billiard player and I took the nearest way to his heart by reserving for him the best table, getting him a fair opponent and complimenting him upon his skill. The next day Arriga opened his heart to me: "What is there to do in this dull hole? Did I know of any amusement? Any pretty women?"

I could do nothing but pretend to sympathize and draw him out and this I easily accomplished, for Señor Arriga loved to boast of his name and position in Mexico and his conquests. "Ah, you should have seen her as I led her in the baile (dance)—an angel!" and he kissed his fingers gallantly.

"As pretty as your cousin?" I ventured. Señor Arriga flashed a sharp suspicious glance at me, but apparently reassured by my frankness, went on:

"In Mexico we never talk of members of our family," he warned: "The Senorita is pretty, of course, but very young; she has not the charm of experience, the caress of—I know so little American, I find it difficult to explain."

But I was satisfied. "He doesn't love her", I said to myself; "loves no one except himself."

In a thousand little ways I took occasion to commend myself to the Vidals. Every afternoon they drove out and I took care they should have the best buggy and the best driver and was at pains to find out new and pretty drives, though goodness knows the choice was limited. The beauty of the girl grew on me in an extraordinary way: yet it was the pride and reserve in her face that fascinated me more even than her great dark eyes or fine features or splendid coloring. Her figure and walk were wonderful; I thought: I never dared to seek epithets for her eyes, or mouth or neck. Her first appearance in evening dress was a revelation to me: she was my idol, enskied and sacred.

It is to be presumed that the girl saw how it was with me and was gratified. She made no sign, betrayed herself in no way, but her mother noticed that she was always eager to go downstairs to the lounge and missed no opportunity of making some inquiry at the desk.

"I want to practice my English," the girl said once and the mother smiled: "Los ojos, you mean your eyes, my dear," and added to herself: "But why not? Youth—" and sighed for her own youth now foregone, and the petals already fallen.

One little talk I got with my goddess: she came to the office to ask about reserving a Pullman drawing-room for El Paso. I undertook at once to see to everything, and when the dainty little lady added in her funny accent: "We have so many baggage, twenty-six bits"; I said as earnestly as if my life depended on it:

"Please trust me. I shall see to everything. I only wish," I added, "I could do more for you."

"That's kind," said the coquette: "very kind," looking full at me. Emboldened by despair at her approaching departure I added: "I'm so sorry you're going. I shall never forget you, never."

Taken aback by my directness, the girl laughed saucily, "*Never* means a week, I suppose."

"You will see," I went on hurriedly as if driven, as indeed I was. "If I thought I should not see you again and soon, I should not wish to live."

"A declaration", she laughed merrily, still looking me brightly in the face.

"Not of independence," I cried, "but of—" as I hesitated between "affection" and "love" the girl put her finger to her lips.

"Hush, hush," she said gravely, "you are too young to take vows and I must not listen", but seeing my face fall, she added: "You have been very kind. I shall remember my stay in Chicago with pleasure," and she stretched out her hand. I took it and held it treasuring every touch.

Her look and the warmth of her fingers I garnered up in my heart as purest treasure.

As soon as she had gone and the radiance with her, I cudgeled my brains to find some pretext for another talk. "She goes tomorrow," hammered in my brain and my heartache choked me, almost prevented my thinking. Suddenly the idea of flowers came to me. I'd buy a lot. No; everyone would notice them and talk. A few would be better. How many? I thought and thought.

When they came into lounge next day ready to start I was watching my opportunity, but the girl gave me a better one than I could have picked. She waited till her father and Arriga had left the hall and then came over to the desk.

"You have ze checks?" she asked.

"Everything will be given you at the train," I said, "but I have these for you. Please accept them!" and I handed her three splendid red rosebuds, prettily tied up with maiden hair fern.

"How kind!" she exclaimed, coloring, "and how pretty," she added, looking at the roses. "Just three?"

"One for your hair," I said with love's cunning, "one for your eyes and one for your heart—will you remember?" I added in a low voice intensely.

She nodded and then looked up sparkling: "As long—as ze flowers last," she laughed, and was back with her mother.

I saw them into the omnibus and got kind words from all the party, even from Señor Arriga, but cherished most her look and word as she went out of the door.

Holding it open for her, I murmured as she passed, for the others were within hearing: "I shall come soon."

The girl stopped, at once, pretending to look at the tag on a trunk the porter was carrying. "El Paso is far away," she sighed, "and the hacienda ten leagues further on. When shall we arrive—when?" she added glancing up at me.

"When?" was the significant word to me for many a month; her eyes had filled it with meaning.

I've told of this meeting with Miss Vidal at length, because it marked an epoch in my life; it was the first time that love had cast her glamor over me making beauty superlative, intoxicating. The passion rendered it easier for me to resist ordinary temptation, for it taught me there was a whole gorgeous world in Love's Kingdom that I had never imagined, much less explored. I had scarcely a lewd thought of Gloria. It was not till I saw her bared shoulders in evening dress that I stripped her in imagination and went almost wild in uncontrollable desire. Would she ever kiss me? What was she like undressed? My imagination was still untutored: I could picture her breasts better than her sex and I made up my mind to examine the next girl I was lucky enough to see naked, much more precisely.

At the back of my mind was the fixed resolve to get to Chihuahua somehow or other in the near future and meet my charmer again and that resolve in due course shaped my life anew.

In early June, that year, three strangers came to the Hotel, all cattlemen I was told, but of a new sort: Reece and Dell and Ford, the "Boss", as he was called. Reece was a tall dark Englishman or rather Welshman, always dressed in brown leather riding boots, Bedford Cord breeches and dark tweed cutaway coat: he looked a prosperous gentleman farmer; Dell was almost a copy of him in clothes, about middle height and sturdier—in fact an ordinary Englishman. The Boss was fully six feet, taller even than Reece with a hatchet-thin, bronzed face and eagle profile—evidently a Western cattle-man from head to foot. The headwaiter told me about them and as soon as I saw them I had them transferred to a shady-cool table and saw that they were well waited on.

A day or two afterwards we had made friends and a little later, Reece got me measured for two pairs of cord-breeches and had promised to teach me how to ride. They were cowpunchers, he said, with his strong English accent and were going down to the Rio Grande to buy cattle and drive 'em back to market here or in Kansas City. Cattle, it appeared, could be bought in South Texas for a dollar a head or less and fetched from fifteen to twenty dollars each in Chicago.

"Of course we don't always get through unscathed" Reece remarked, "The Plain Indians—Cherokees, Blackfeet and Sioux—take care of that; but one herd in two gets through and that pays big."

I found they had brought up a thousand head of cattle from their ranch near Eureka, Kansas and a couple of hundred head of horses.

To cut a long story short, Reece fascinated me: he told me that Chihuahua was the Mexican province just across the Rio Grande from Texas and at once, I resolved to go on the Trail with these cowpunchers if they'd take me. In two or three days Reece told me I shaped better at riding than anyone he had ever seen, though, he added "when I saw your thick short legs I thought you'd never make much of a hand at it." But I was strong and had grown nearly six inches in my year in the States and I turned in my toes as Reece directed and hung on to the English saddle by the grip of my knees till I was both tired and sore. In a fortnight Reece made me put five cent pieces between my knees and the saddle and keep them there when galloping or trotting.

This practice soon made a rider of me so far as the seat was concerned and I had already learned that Reece was a past-master in the deeper mysteries of the art for he told me he used to ride colts in the hunting field in England and "that's how you learn to know horses" he added significantly.

One day I found out that Dell knew some poetry, literature too, and economics and that won me completely; when I asked them would they take me with them as a cowboy, they told me I'd have to ask the Boss, but there was no doubt he'd consent, and he consented, after one sharp glance.

Then came my hardest task: I had to tell Kendrick and Mr. Cotton that I must leave. They were more than astonished: at first they took it to be a little trick to extort a rise in salary: when they saw it was sheer boyish adventure-lust they argued with me but finally gave in. I promised to return to them as soon as I got back to Chicago or got tired of cowpunching. I had nearly eighteen hundred dollars saved, which, by Mr. Cotton's advice, I transferred to a Kansas City bank he knew well.

LIFE ON THE TRAIL.

On the tenth of June, we took train to Kansas City, the Gate at that time of the "Wild West." In Kansas City I became aware of three more men belonging to the outfit: Bent, Charlie and Bob, the Mexican. Charlie, to begin with the least important, was a handsome American youth, blue-eyed and fair-haired, over six feet in height, very strong, careless, light-hearted: I always thought of him as a big, kind, Newfoundland dog, rather awkward but always well-meaning. Bent was ten years older, a war-veteran, dark, saturnine, purposeful; five feet nine or ten in height with muscles of whipcord and a mentality that was curiously difficult to fathom. Bob, the most peculiar and original man I had ever met up to that time, was a little dried up Mexican, hardly five feet three in height, half Spaniard, half Indian, I believe, who might be thirty or fifty and who seldom opened his mouth except to curse all Americans in Spanish. Even Reece admitted that Bob could ride "above a bit" and knew more about cattle than anyone else in his world. Reece's admiration directed my curiosity to the little man and I took every opportunity of talking to him and of giving him cigars—a courtesy so unusual that at first he was half inclined to resent it.

It appeared that these three men had been left in Kansas City to dispose of another herd of cattle and to purchase stores needed at the ranch. They were all ready, so the next day we rode out of Kansas City, about four o'clock in the morning; our course roughly south by west. Everything was new and wonderful to me. In three days we had finished with roads and farmsteads and were on the open prairie; in two or three days more, the prairie became the great plains which stretched four or five thousand miles from north to south with a breadth of some seven hundred. The plains wore buffalo grass and sage-brush for a garment, and little else save in the river-bottoms, trees like the cottonwood; everywhere rabbits, prairie chicken, deer and buffalo abounded.

We covered about thirty miles a day: Bob sat in the wagon and drove the four mules, while Bent and Charlie made us coffee and biscuits in the morning and cooked us sow-belly and any game we might bring in for dinner and supper. There was a small keg of rye whisky on the wagon; but we kept it for snake-bite or some emergency.

I became the hunter to the outfit, for it was soon discovered that by some sixth sense I could always find my way back to the wagon on a bee-line, and only Bob of the whole party possessed the same instinct. Bob explained it by muttering "No Americano!" The instinct itself which has stood me in good stead more times than I can count, is in essence inexplicable: I feel the direction; but the vague feeling is strengthened by observing the path of the sun and the way the halms of grass lean, and the bushes grow. But it made me a valuable member of the outfit instead of a mere parasite midway between master and man, and it was the first step to Bob's liking which taught me more than all the other haps of my early life. I had bought a shotgun and and a Winchester rifle and revolver in Kansas City and Reece had taught me how to get weapons that would fit me and this fact helped to make me a fair shot almost at once. But soon to my grief I found that I would never be a great shot; for Bob and Charlie and even Dell could see things far beyond my range of vision. I was shortsighted in fact through astigmatism and even glasses I discovered later, could not clear my blurred sight.

It was the second or third disappointment of my life the others being the conviction of my personal ugliness and the fact that I should always be too short and small to be a great fighter or athlete.

As I went on in life I discovered more serious disabilities but they only strengthened my deep-seated resolve to make the most of any qualities I might possess and meanwhile the life was divinely new and strange and pleasureful.

After breakfast, about five o'clock in the morning, I would ride away from the wagon till it was out of sight and then abandon myself to the joy of solitude, with no boundary between plain and sky. The air was brisk and dry, as exhilarating as champagne and even when the sun reached the zenith and became blazing hot, the air remained lightsome and invigorating. Mid Kansas is 2000 odd feet above sea-level and the air is so dry that an animal when killed, dries up without stinking and in a few months the hide's filled with mere dust. Game was plentiful, hardly an hour would elapse before I had got half a dozen ruffed grouse or a deer and then I would walk my pony back to the midday camp with perhaps a new wildflower in hand whose name I wished to learn.

After the midday meal I used to join Bob in the wagon and learn some Spanish words or phrases from him or question him about his knowledge of cattle. In the first week we became great friends: I found to my amusement that Bob was just as voluble in Spanish as he was tongue-tied in English, and his command of Spanish oaths, objurgations and indecencies was astounding. Bob despised all things American with an unimaginable ferocity and this interested me by its apparent unreason.

Once or twice on the way down we had a race; but Reece on a big Kentucky thoroughbred called 'Shiloh' won easily. He told me however, that there was a young mare called 'Blue Devil' at the ranch which was as fast as Shiloh and of rare stay and stamina: "You can have her, if you can ride her," he threw out carelessly and I determined to win the 'Devil' if I could.

In about ten days we reached the ranch near Eureka; it was set in five thousand acres of prairie, a big frame dwelling, that would hold twenty men; but it wasn't nearly so well-built as the great, brick stable, the pride of Reece's eye, which would house forty horses and provide half a dozen with good loose boxes besides, in the best English style.

The house and stable were situated on a long billowy rise perhaps three hundred yards away from a good-sized creek which I soon christened Snake-Creek for snakes of all sorts and sizes simply swarmed in the brush and woodland of the banks. The big sitting-room of the ranch was decorated with revolvers and rifles of a dozen different kinds and pictures, strange to say, cut out of the illustrated papers: the floor was covered with buffalo and bear rugs and rarer skins of mink and beaver hung here and there on the wooden walls. We got to the ranch late one night and I slept in a room with Dell, he taking the bed while I rolled myself in a rug on the couch. But I slept like a top and next morning was out before sunrise to take stock so to speak. An Indian lad showed me the stable and as luck would have it Blue Devil in a loose box, all to herself and very uneasy.

"What's the matter with her?" I asked, and the Indian told me she had rubbed her ear raw where it joins the head and the flies had got on it and plagued her: I went to the house and got Peggy, the mulatto cook to fill a bucket with warm water and with this bucket and a sponge I entered the loose box: Blue Devil came for me and nipped my shoulder but as soon as I clapped the sponge with warm water on her ear, she stopped biting and we soon became friends. That same afternoon, I led her out in front of the ranch saddled and bridled, got on her and walked her off as quiet as a lamb. "She's yours!" said

Reece; "but if she ever gets your foot in her mouth, you'll know what pain is!"

It appeared that that was a little trick she had, to tug and tug at the reins till the rider let them go loose and then at once she would twist her head round, get the rider's toes in her mouth and bite like a fiend. No one she disliked could mount her; for she fought like a man with her fore-feet; but I never had any difficulty with her and she saved my life more than once. Like most feminine creatures she responded immediately to kindness and was faithful to affection.

I'm compelled to notice that if I tell the other happenings in this eventful year at as great length as I've told the incidents of the fortnight that brought me from Chicago to the ranch at Eureka, I'd have to devote at least a volume to them, so I prefer to assure my readers that one of these days if I live, I'll publish my novel "On the Trail" which gives the whole story in great detail. Now I shall content myself with saying that two days after reaching the ranch we set out, ten men strong and two wagons filled with our clothes and provender and dragged by four mules each, to cover the twelve hundred miles to Southern Texas or New Mexico where we hoped to buy 5000 or 6000 head of cattle at a dollar a head and drive them to Kansas City, the nearest train point.

When we got on the Great Trail a hundred miles from Fort Dodge, the days passed in absolute monotony. After sunset a light breeze usually sprang up to make the night pleasantly cool and we would sit and chat about the camp-fire for an hour or two. Strange to say the talk usually turned to bawd or religion or the relations of capital and labor. It was curious how eagerly these rough cattle-men would often discuss the mysteries of this unintelligible world, and as a militant sceptic I soon got a reputation among them; for Dell usually backed me up and his knowledge of books and thinkers seemed to us extraordinary.

These constant evening discussions, this perpetual arguing, had an unimaginable effect on me. I had no books with me and I was often called on to deal with two or three different theories in a night: I had to think out the problems for myself and usually I thought them out when hunting by myself in the daytime. It was as a cowpuncher that I taught myself how to think:—a rare art among men and seldom practised. Whatever originality I possess comes from the fact that in youth, while my mind was in process of growth, I was confronted with important modern problems and forced to think them out for myself and find some reasonable answer to the questionings of half a dozen different minds.

For example, Bent asked one night what the proper wage should be of the ordinary workman? I could only answer that the workman's wage should increase at least in measure as the productivity of labor increased; but I could not then see how to approach this ideal settlement. When I read Herbert Spencer ten years later in Germany, I was delighted to find that I had divined the best of his sociology and added to it materially. His idea that the amount of individual liberty in a country depends on "the pressure from the outside", I knew to be only half-true. Pressure from the outside is one factor but not even the most important: the centripetal force in the society itself is often much more powerful: how else can one explain the fact that during the world-war, liberty almost disappeared in these States in spite of the First Amendment to the Constitution. At all times indeed there is much less regard for liberty here than in England or even in Germany or in France: one has only to think of prohibition to admit this. The pull towards the centre in every country is in direct proportion to the mass and accordingly the herd-feeling in America is unreasonably strong.

If we were not arguing or telling smutty stories, Bent would be sure to get out cards and the gambling instinct would keep the boys busy till the stars paled in the eastern sky.

One incident I must relate here, for it broke the monotony of the routine in a curious way.

Our fire at night was made up of buffalo "chips" as the dried excrement was called, and Peggy had asked me, as I got up the earliest, always to replenish the fire before riding away. One morning I picked up a chip with my left hand and as luck would have it, disturbed a little prairie rattlesnake that had been attracted probably by the heat of the camp-fire. As I lifted the chip, the snake struck me on the back of my thumb, then coiled up in a flash and began to rattle. Angered I put my right foot on him and killed him, and at the same moment bit out the place on my thumb where I had been stung, and then, still unsatisfied, rubbed my thumb in the red embers, especially above the wound. I paid little further attention to the matter; it seemed to me that the snake was too small to be very poisonous; but on returning to the wagon to wake Peggy, he cried out and called the Boss and Reece and Dell and was manifestly greatly perturbed and even anxious. Reece too agreed with him that the bite of the little prairie rattlesnake was just as venomous as that of his big brother of the woods.

The Boss produced a glass of whisky and told me to drink it: I didn't want to take it; but he insisted and I drank it off. "Did it burn?" he asked: "No, 'twas just like water!" I replied and noticed that the Boss and Reece exchanged a meaning look.

At once the Boss declared I must walk up and down and each taking an arm they walked me solemnly round and round for half an hour. At the end of that time I was half asleep; the Boss stopped and gave me another jorum of whisky: for a moment it awakened me, then I began to get numb again and deaf. Again they gave me whisky: I revived but in five minutes I sagged down and begged them to let me sleep.

"Sleep be d—d!" cried the Boss, "you'd never wake. Pull yourself together," and again I was given whisky. Then, dimly I began to realise that I must use my will-power and so I started to jump about and shake off the overpowering drowsiness. Another two or three drinks of whisky and much frisking about occupied the next couple of hours, when suddenly I became aware of a sharp, intense pang of pain in my left thumb.

"Now you can sleep," said the Boss, "if you're minded to; I guess whisky has wiped out the rattler!"

The pain in my burnt thumb was acute: I found too I had a headache for the first time in my life. But Peggy gave me hot water to drink and the headache soon disappeared. In a day or two I was as well as ever, thanks, to the vigorous regimen of the Boss; in the course of a single year we lost two young men just through the little prairie snakes that seemed so insignificant.

The days passed quickly till we came near the first towns in southern Texas: then every man wanted his arrears of salary from the Boss and proceeded to shave and doll up in wildest excitement. Charlie was like a madman. Half an hour after reaching the chief saloon in the town, everyone of them save Bent was crazy drunk and intent on finding some girl with whom to spend the night. I didn't even go to the saloon with them and begged Charlie in vain not to play the fool. "That's what I live for", he shouted, and raced off.

I had got accustomed to spend all my spare time with Reece, Dell, Bob or the Boss, and from all of them I learned a good deal. In a short time I had exhausted the Boss and Reece; but Dell and Bob each in his own way was richly equipped, and while Dell introduced me to literature and economics, Bob taught me some of the mysteries of cowpunching and the peculiar morals of Texan cattle. Every little herd of those half-wild animals had its own leader, it appeared and followed him fanatically. When we brought together a few different bunches in our corral, there was confusion worse confounded till after much hooking and some fighting a new leader would be chosen whom all would obey. But sometimes we lost five or six animals in the mellay. I found that Bob could ride his pony in among the half-savage brutes and pick out the future leader for them. Indeed, at the great sports held near Taos, he went in on foot where many herds had been corralled and led out the leader amid the triumphant cheers of his compatriots who challenged los Americanos to emulate that feat. Bob's knowledge of cattle was uncanny and all I know I learned from him.

For the first week or so, Reece and the Boss were out all day buying cattle; Reece would generally take Charlie and Jack Freeman, young Americans, to drive his purchases home to the big corral; while the Boss called indifferently first on one and then on another to help him. Charlie was the first to lay off: he had caught a venereal disease, the very first night and had to lie up for more than a month. One after the other, all the younger men fell to the same plague. I went into the nearest town and consulted doctors and did what I could for them; but the cure was often slow for they would drink now and again to drown care and several in this way, made the disease chronic. I could never understand the temptation; to get drunk was bad enough; but in that state to go with some dirty Greaser woman, or half-breed prostitute was incomprehensible to me.

Naturally I enquired about the Vidals; but no one seemed to have heard of them and though I did my best, the weeks passed without my finding a trace of them. I wrote, however, to the address Gloria had given me before leaving Chicago so that I might be able to forward any letters; but I had left Texas before I heard from her: indeed her letter reached me in the Fremont House when I got back to Chicago. She simply told me that they had crossed the Rio Grande and had settled in their hacienda on the other side, where perhaps, she added coyly, I would pay them a visit some day. I wrote thanking her and assuring her that her memory transfigured the world for me—which was the bare truth: I took infinite pains to put this letter into good Spanish though I fear that in spite of Bob's assistance it had a dozen faults. But I'm outrunning my story.

Rapidly the herd was got together. Early in July we started northwards driving before us some 6000 head of cattle which certainly hadn't cost five thousand dollars. That first year everything went well with us; we only saw small bands of Plain Indians and we were too strong for them. The Boss had allowed me to bring 500 head of cattle on my own account: he wished to reward me, he said, for my incessant hard work; but I was sure it was Reece and Dell who put the idea into his head.

The fact that some of the cattle were mine made me a most watchful and indefatigable herdsman. More than once my vigilances sharpened by Bob's instinct, made a difference to our fortunes. When we began to skirt the Indian Territory, Bob warned me that a small band or even a single Indian might try some night to stampede the herd. About a week later, I noticed that the cattle were uneasy: "Indians!" said Bob when I told him the signs, "cunning beasts!" That night I was off duty, but was on horseback circling round as usual, when about midnight, I saw a white figure leap from the ground with an unearthly yell. The cattle began to run together so I threw my rifle up and fired at the Indian and though I didn't hit him, he thought it better to drop the sheet and decamp. In five minutes we had pacified the cattle again and nothing unfortunate happened that night or indeed till we reached Wichita which was then the outpost of civilization. In ten days more we were in Kansas City entraining, though we sold a fourth of our cattle there at about fifteen dollars a head. We reached Chicago about the first of October and put the cattle in the yards about the Michigan St. Depot. Next day we sold more than half the herd and I was lucky enough to get a purchaser at fifteen dollars a head for three hundred of my beasts. If it hadn't been for the Boss who held out for three cents a pound, I should have sold all I had. As it was I came out with more than five thousand dollars in the Bank and felt myself another Croesus. My joy, however, was short-lived.

Of course I stayed in the Fremont, and was excellently received. The management had slipped back a good deal, I thought, but I was glad that I was no longer responsible and could take my ease in my inn. But my six months on the Trail had marked my very being. It made a workman of me and above all, it taught me that tense resolution, will-power was the most important factor of success in life. I made up my mind to train my will by exercise as I would train a muscle and each day I proposed to myself a new test. For example I liked potatoes so I resolved not to eat one for a week, or again I foreswore coffee that I loved, for a month, and I was careful to keep to my determination. I had noticed a French saying that intensified my decision, celui qui veut, celui-là peut:—'he who wills, can.' My mind should govern me, not my appetites, I decided.

THE GREAT FIRE OF CHICAGO.

Chapter VII.

I wish I could persuade myself that I was capable of picturing the events of the week after we reached Chicago.

We arrived, if I remember rightly, on a Wednesday and put our cattle and horses in the stockyards near the Michigan Street depot. As I have related, we sold on Thursday and Friday about three-fifths of the cattle. I wanted to sell all, but followed the judgment of the Boss and sold three hundred head and put a little over five thousand dollars in my banking account.

On Saturday night the alarm bells began to ring and awoke me. I slipped into my breeches, shirt and boots and a youthful curiosity exciting me, I raced downstairs, got Blue Devil from the stable and rode out to the fire. I was infinitely impressed by the rapidity with which the firemen acted and the marvelous efficiency of the service. Where in England there would have been perhaps half a dozen fire-engines, the Americans sent fifty, but they all found work and did it magnificently. At one o'clock the fire was out and I returned to the hotel through two or three miles of uninjured streets. Of course, I told Reece and Ford all about it the next day. To my astonishment, no one seemed to pay much attention; a fire was so common a thing in the wooden shanties on the outskirts of American towns that nobody cared to listen to my epic.

Next night, Sunday, the alarm bell began ringing about eleven o'clock: I was still dressed in my best. I changed into my working clothes, I do not know why, put my belt about me with a revolver in it and again took out the mare and rode to the fire. When still a quarter of a mile away, I realized that this fire was much more serious than that of the previous night: first of all, a gale of wind was blowing right down on the town. Then, when I wondered why there were so few fire-engines, I was told that there were two other fires and the man with whom I talked did not scruple to ascribe them to a plot and determination to burn down the town! "Them damned foreign anarchists are at the bottom of it," he said, "three fires do not start on the very outskirts of the town with a gale of wind blowing, without some reason."

And indeed, it looked as if he were right. In spite of all the firemen could do, the fire spread with incredible rapidity. In half an hour I saw they were not going to master it soon or easily and I rode back to get Reece, who had told me that he would have come with me the previous night if he had known where the fire was. When I got back to the hotel, Reece had gone out on his own and so had Dell and the Boss. I went back to the fire. It had caught on in the most extraordinary way. The wooden streets now were all blazing; the fire was swallowing block after block and the heat was so tremendous that the fire-engines could not get within two hundred yards of the blaze. The roar of the fire was unearthly.

Another thing I noticed almost immediately: the heat was so terrific that the water decomposed into its elements and the oxygen gas in the water burned vehemently on its own account. The water, in fact, added fuel to the flames. As soon as I made sure of this, I saw that the town was doomed and walked my pony back a block or two to avoid flying sparks.

This must have been about three or four o'clock in the morning. I had gone back about three blocks when I came across a man talking to a group of men at the corner of a street. He was the one man of insight and sense I met that night. He seemed to me a typical, down-east Yankee: he certainly talked like one. The gist of his speech was as follows:

"I want you men to come with me right now to the Mayor and tell him to give orders to blow up at least two blocks deep all along this side of the town; then, if we drench the houses on the other side, the flames will be stopped: there's no other way."

"That's sense", I cried, "that's what ought to be done at once. There's no other way of salvation; for the heat is disintegrating the water and the oxygen in the water is blazing fiercely, adding fuel to the flames."

"Gee! that's what I have been preaching for the last hour", he cried.

A little later fifty or sixty citizens went to the Mayor, but he protested that he had no power to blow up houses and evidently, too, shirked the responsibility. He decided, however, to call in some of the councilmen and see what could be done. Meanwhile I went off and wandered towards the Randolph Street bridge and there saw a scene that appalled me.

Some men had caught a thief, they said, plundering one of the houses and they proceeded to string the poor wretch up to a lamp-post.

In vain I pleaded for his life, declared that he ought to be tried, that it was better to let off ten guilty men than hang one innocent one, but my foreign accent robbed my appeal, I think, of any weight and before my eyes the man was strung up. It filled me with rage; it seemed to me a dreadful thing to have done: the cruelty of the executioners, the hard purpose of them, shut me away from my kin. Later I was to see these men from a better angle.

By the early morning the fire had destroyed over a mile deep of the town and was raging with unimaginable fury. I went down on the lakeshore just before daybreak. The scene was one of indescribable magnificence: there were probably a hundred and fifty thousand homeless men, women and children grouped along the lake shore. Behind us roared the fire; it spread like a red sheet right up to the zenith above our heads, and from there was borne over the sky in front of us by long streamers of fire like rockets: vessels four hundred yards out in the bay were burning fiercely, and we were, so to speak, roofed and walled by flame. The danger and uproar were indeed terrifying and the heat, even in this October night, almost unbearable.

I wandered along the lake shore, noting the kind way in which the men took care of the women and children. Nearly every man was able to erect some sort of shelter for his wife and babies, and everyone was willing to help his neighbor. While working at one shelter for a little while, I said to the man I wished I could get a drink.

"You can get one", he said, "right there", and he pointed to a sort of makeshift shanty on the beach. I went over and found that a publican had managed to get four barrels down on the beach and had rigged up a sort of low tent above them; on one of the barrels he had nailed his shingle, and painted on it were the words, "What do you think of our hell? No drinks less than a dollar!" The wild humor of the thing amused me infinitely and the man certainly did a roaring trade.

A little later it occurred to me that our cattle might possibly burn, so I went out and hurried back to the Michigan Street stockyards. An old Irishman was in charge of the yard, but though he knew me perfectly well, he refused to let me take out a steer. The cattle were moving about wildly, evidently in a state of intense excitement. I pleaded with the man and begged him, and at length tied my mare up to the lamp-post at the corner and went back and got into the stockyard when he wasn't looking. I let down two or three of the bars and the next moment started the cattle through the opening. They went crazy wild and choked the gateway. In five minutes there were ten or twelve dead cattle in the entrance and the rest had to go over them. Suddenly, just as I got through the gap, the mad beasts made a rush and carried away the rails on both sides of the gateway. The next moment I was knocked down and I had just time to drag myself through the fence and so avoid their myriad trampling heels.

A few minutes later, I was on Blue Devil, trying to get the cattle out of the town and on to the prairie. The herd broke up at almost every corner but I managed to get about six hundred head right out into the country.

I drove them on the dead run for some miles. By this time it was daybreak and at the second or third farmhouse I came to, I found a farmer willing to take in the cattle. I bargained with him a little and at length told him I would give him a dollar a head if he kept them for the week or so we might want to leave them with him. In two minutes he brought out his son and an Irish helper and turned the cattle back and into his pasture. There were six hundred and seventy-six of them, as near as I could count, out of practically two thousand head.

By the time I had finished the business and returned to the hotel, it was almost noon and as I could get nothing to eat, I wandered out again to see the progress of the fire. Already I found that relief trains were being sent in with food from all neighboring towns and this was the feature of the next week in starving Chicago.

Strangely enough, at that time the idea was generally accepted that a man or woman could only live three days without food. It was years before Dr. Tanner showed the world that a man could fast for forty days or more. Everyone I met acted as if he believed that if he were fully three days without food, he must die incontinently. I laughed at the idea which seemed to me absurd, but so strong was the universal opinion and the influence of the herd-sentiment, that on the third day I too felt particularly empty and thought I had better take my place in the bread line. There were perhaps five thousand in front of me and there were soon fifty or sixty thousand behind me. We were five deep moving to the depot where the bread trains were discharging, one after the other. When I got pretty close to the food wagons, I noticed that the food supply was coming to an end, and next moment I noticed something else.

Again and again women and girls came into our bread line and walked through the lines of waiting men, who, mark you, really believed they were going to die that night if they could not get food, but instead of objecting they one and all made way for the women and girls and encouraged them: "Go right on, Madam, take all you want:" "This way, Missee, you won't be able to carry much, I'm afraid";—proof on proof, it seemed to me, of courage, good humor and high self-abnegation. I went into that bread line an Irish boy and came out of it a proud American, but I did not get any bread that night or the next. In fact, my first meal was made when I ran across Reece on the Friday or Saturday after: Reece, as usual, had fallen on his feet and found a hotel where they had provisions—though at famine prices.

He insisted that I should come with him and soon got me my first meal. In return, I told him and Ford of the cattle I had saved. They were, of course, delighted and determined next day to come out and retrieve them. "One thing is certain," said Ford, "six hundred head of cattle are worth as much today in Chicago as fifteen hundred head were worth before the fire, so we hain't lost much."

Next day I led Reece and the Boss straight to the farmer's place, but to my surprise he told me that I had agreed to give him two dollars a head, whereas I had bargained with him for only one dollar. His son backed up the farmer's statement and the Irish helper declared that he was sorry to disagree with me, but I was mistaken; it was two dollars I had said. They little knew the sort of men they had to deal with. "Where are the cattle?" Ford asked, and we went down to the pasture where they were penned. "Count them, Harris," said Ford, and I counted six hundred and twenty head. Fifty odd had disappeared, but the farmer wanted to persuade me that I had counted wrongly.

Ford went about and soon found a rough lean-to stable where there were thirty more head of Texan cattle. These were driven up and soon disappeared in the herd; Reece and I began to move the herd towards the entrance. The farmer declared he would not let us go, but Ford looked at him a little while and then said very quietly, "You have stolen enough cattle to pay you. If you bother with us, I will make meat of you—see!—cold meat", and the farmer moved aside and kept quiet.

That night we had a great feast and the day after Ford announced that he had sold the whole of the cattle to two hotel proprietors and got nearly as much money as if we had not lost a hoof.

My five thousand dollars became six thousand, five hundred.

The courage shown by the common people in the fire, the wild humor coupled with the consideration for the women, had won my heart. This is the greatest people in the world, I said to myself, and was proud to feel at one with them.

ON THE TRAIL!

Chapter VIII.

Prompted by Dell, before leaving Chicago I bought some books for the winter evenings, notably Mill's "Political Economy"; Carlyle's "Heroes and Hero Worship" and "Latter Day Pamphlets"; Col. Hay's "Dialect Poems", too and three medical books, and took them down with me to the ranch. We had six weeks of fine weather, during which I broke in horses under Reece's supervision, and found out that gentleness and especially carrots and pieces of sugar were the direct way to the heart of the horse; discovered, too, that a horse's bad temper and obstinacy were nearly always due to fear. A remark of Dell that a horse's eye had a magnifying power and that the poor, timid creatures saw men as trees walking, gave me the clue and soon I was gratified by Reece saying that I could "gentle" horses as well as anyone on the ranch, excepting Bob.

As winter drew down and the bitter frost came, outdoor work almost ceased. I read from morning till night and not only devoured Mill, but saw through the fallacy of his Wage-Fund theory. I knew from my own experience that the wages of labor depended primarily on the productivity of labor. I liked Mill for his humanitarian sympathies with the poor; but I realized clearly that he was a second-rate intelligence, just as I felt pretty sure that Carlyle was one of the Immortals. I took Carlyle in small doses, for I wanted to think for myself. After the first chapters I tried to put down first, chapter by chapter, what I thought or knew about the subject treated, and am still inclined to believe that that is a good way to read in order to estimate what the author has taught you.

Carlyle was the first dominant influence in my life and one of the most important: I got more from him than from any other writer. His two or three books learned almost by heart, taught me that Dell's knowledge was skimpy and superficial and I was soon Sir Oracle among the men on all deep subjects. For the medical books, too, turned out to be excellent and gave me almost the latest knowledge on all sex-matters. I was delighted to put all my knowledge at the disposal of the boys, or rather to show off to them how much I knew.

That fall brought me to grief: early in October I was taken by ague; "chills and fever" as it was called. I suffered miseries and though Reece induced me to ride all the same and spend most of the daytime in the open, I lost weight till I learned that arsenic was a better specific even than quinine. Then I began to mend, but, off and on, every fall and spring afterwards, so long as I stayed in America, I had to take quinine and arsenic to ward off the debilitating attacks.

I was very low indeed when we started down on the Trail; the Boss being determined, as he said, to bring up two herds that summer. Early in May he started north from near St. Anton' with some five thousand head, leaving Reece, Dell, Bob, Peggy the cook, Bent, Charlie and myself to collect another herd. I never saw the Boss again; understood, however, from Reece's cursing that he had got through safely, sold the cattle at a good price and made off with all the proceeds, though he owed Reece and Dell more than one-half.

Charlie's love-adventure that ended so badly didn't quiet him for long. In our search for cheap cattle we had gone down nearly to the Rio Grande and there, in a little half-Mexican town, Charlie met his fate.

As it so happened, I had gone to the saloon with him on his promise that he would only drink one glass, and though the glass would be full of forty-rod whisky, I knew it would have only a passing effect on Charlie's superb strength. But it excited him enough to make him call up all the girls for a drink: they all streamed laughing to the bar, all save one. Naturally Charlie went after her and found a very pretty blond girl, who had a strain of Indian blood in her, it was said. At first she didn't yield to Charlie's invitation, so he turned away angrily, saying:

"You don't want to drink probably because you want to cure yourself or because you're ugly where women are usually beautiful." Answering the challenge the girl sprang to her feet, tore off her jacket and in a moment was naked to her boots and stockings.

"Am I ugly?" she cried, pushing out her breasts, "or do I look ill, you fool!" and whirled around to give us the back view!

She certainly had a lovely figure with fair youthful breasts and peculiarly full bottom and looked the picture of health. The full cheeks of her behind excited me intensely, I didn't know why: therefore, it didn't surprise me when Charlie, with a half-articulate shout of admiration, picked her up bodily in his arms and carried her out of the room.

When I remonstrated with him afterwards, he told me he had a sure way of knowing whether the girl, Sue, was diseased or not.

I contradicted him and found that this was his infallible test: as soon as he was alone with a girl, he pulled out ten or twenty dollars, as the case might be, and told her to keep the money. "I'll not give you more in any case", he would add: "now tell me, dear, if you are ill and we'll have a last drink and then I'll go. If she's ill, she's sure to tell you—see!" and he laughed triumphantly.

"Suppose she doesn't know she's ill?" I asked: but he replied: "they always know and they'll tell the truth when their greed is not against you."

For some time it looked as if Charlie had enjoyed his Beauty without any evil consequences, but a month or so later he noticed a lump in his right groin and soon afterwards a syphilitic sore showed itself just under the head of his penis. We had already started northwards, but I had to tell Charlie the plain truth.

"Then it's serious", he cried in astonishment, and I replied.

"I'm afraid so, but not if you take it in time and go under a rigorous regimen."

Charlie did everything he was told to do and always bragged that gonorrhea was much worse, as it is certainly more painful, than syphilis; but the disease in time had its revenge.

As he began to get better on the Trail, thanks to the good air, regular exercise and absence of drink, he became obstreperous from time to time and I at any rate forgot about his ailment.

The defection of the Boss made a serious difference to us; Reece and Dell with three or four Mexicans and Peggy went on slowly buying cattle; but Bob and Bent put a new scheme into my head. Bent was always preaching that the Boss's defection had ruined Reece and that if I would put in, say five thousand dollars, I could be Reece's partner and make a fortune with him. Bob, too, was keen on this and told me incidentally that he could get cattle from the Mexicans for nothing. I had a talk with Reece who said he'd have to be content with buying 3000 head for cattle had gone up in price twofold and the Boss's swindle had crippled him. If I would pay Bent's, Charlie's and Bob's wages, he'd be delighted, he said, to join forces with me: on Bob's advice, I consented and with his help, I managed to secure three thousand head for little more than three thousand dollars. And this is how we managed it.

For some reason or other, perhaps, because I had learnt a few words of Spanish, Bob had taken a fancy to me and was always willing to help me except when he was mad with drink. He now assured me that if I would go with him down the Rio Grande a hundred miles or so, he'd get me a thousand head of cattle for nothing. I consented, for Bent, too, and Charlie, were on Bob's side.

The next morning before sunrise we started out and rode steadily to the southeast. We carried enough food for two or three days. Bob saw to that without any question, but generally he brought us about eight o'clock near some house or other where we could get food and shelter. His knowledge of the whole frontier was as uncanny as his knowledge of cattle.

On the fourth or fifth day about nine in the morning he stopped us by a little wooded height looking over a gorge of the river. To the left the river spread out almost to a shallow lake, and one did not need to be told that a little lower down there must be one or more fords where cattle could cross almost without wetting themselves.

Bob got off his horse in a clump of cottonwood trees which he said was a good place to camp without being seen. I asked him where the cattle were and he told me "across the river." Within two or three miles, it appeared, there was a famous hacienda with great herds. As soon as it got dark he proposed to go across and find out all about it and bring us the news. We were to be careful not to be seen and he hoped that we would not even make a fire but lie close till he returned.

We were more than willing, and when we got tired of talking Bent produced an old deck of cards and we would play draw poker or euchre or casino for two or three hours. The first night passed quickly enough. We had been in the saddle for ten hours a day for four or five days and slept a dreamless sleep. Bob did not return that day or the next and on the third day Bent began to curse him, but I felt sure he had good reason for the delay and so waited with what patience I could muster. On the third night he was suddenly with us just as if he had come out of the earth.

"Welcome back", I cried. "Everything right?"

"Everything", he said: "It was no good coming sooner; they have brought some cattle within four miles of the river; the orders are to keep 'em away seven or eight miles, so that they could not be driven across without rousing the whole country; but Don José is very rich and carefree and there is a herd of fifteen hundred that will suit us not three miles from the river in a fold of the prairie guarded only by two men whom I'll make so very drunk that they'll hear nothing till next morning. A couple of bottles of aguardiente will do the bizness, and I'll come back for you tomorrow night by eight or nine o'clock."

It all turned out as Bob had arranged. The next night he came to us as soon as it was dark. We rode some two miles down the river to a ford, splashed through the rivulets of water and came out on the Mexican side. In single file and complete silence we followed Bob at a lope for perhaps twenty minutes when he put up his hand and we drew down to a walk. There below us between two waves of prairie were the cattle.

In a few words Bob told Bent and Charlie what they were to do. Bent was to stay behind and shoot in case we were followed—unlikely but always possible. Charlie and I were to move the cattle towards the ford, quietly all the way if we could, but if we were pursued, then as hard as we could drive them.

For the first half hour all went according to program. Charlie and I moved the cattle together and drove them over the waves of prairie towards the river; it all seemed as easy as eating and we had begun to push the cattle into a fast walk when suddenly there was a shot in front and a sort of stampede!

At once Charlie shot out on the left as I shot out on the right and using our whips, we quickly got the herd into motion again, the rear ranks forcing the front ones on; the cattle were soon pressed into a shuffling trot and the difficulty seemed overcome. Just at that moment I saw two or three bright flames half a mile away on the other side of Charlie and suddenly I heard the zip of a bullet pass my own head and turning, saw pretty plainly a man riding fifty yards away from me. I took very careful aim at his horse and fired and was delighted to see horse and man come down and disappear. I paid no further attention to him and kept on forcing the pace of the cattle. But Charlie was very busily engaged for two or three minutes because the fusillade was kept up from behind till he was joined by Bent and shortly afterwards by Bob. We were all now driving the cattle as hard as they could go, straight towards the ford. The shots behind us continued and even grew more frequent, but we were not further molested till three quarters of an hour later we reached the Rio Grande and began urging the cattle across the ford. There progress was necessarily slow. We could scarcely have got across had it not been that about the middle Bob came up and made his whip and voice a perfect terror to the beasts in the rear.

When we got them out on the other side I began to turn them westwards towards our wooded knoll, but the next moment Bob was beside me shouting—"Straight ahead, straight ahead; they are following us and we shall have to fight. You get on with the herd always straight north and I'll bring Charlie back to the bank so as to hold 'em off."

Boylike, I said I would rather go and fight, but he said: "You go on. If Charlie killed, no matter. I want you." And I had perforce to do what the little devil ordered.

When Texan cattle have been brought up together the largest herd can be driven like a small bunch. They have their leader and they follow him religiously and so one man can drive a thousand head with very little trouble.

For two or three miles I kept them on the trot and then I let them gradually get down to a walk. I did not want to lose any more of them; some fat cows had already died in their tracks through being driven so fast.

About two o'clock in the morning I passed a log-house and soon an American rode up beside me and wanted to know who I was, where I had brought the cattle from and where I was going! I told him the owner was behind me, and the boys and I were driving them straight ahead because some greasers had been interfering with us.

"That's the shooting I heard", he said. "You have driven them across the river: haven't you?"

"I've driven them from the river," I replied; "some of them were getting a drink."

I could feel him grin though I was not looking at him.

"I guess I'll see your friends pretty soon," he said, "but this raiding is bad business. Them greasers'll come across and give me trouble. We border-folk don't want a fuss, hatched up by you foreigners!"

I placated him as well as I could; but at first was unsuccessful. He didn't say much but he evidently intended to come with me to the end because wherever I rode, I found him right behind the herd when I returned.

Day had broken when I let the cattle halt for the first time. I reckoned I had gone twelve miles from the ford and the beasts were foot-sore and very tired; more and more of them requiring the whip in order to keep up even a walk. I bunched them together and came back to my saturnine acquaintance.

"You are young to be at this game", he said. "Who is your Boss?"

"I don't keep a boss", I answered, taking him in with hostile scrutiny. He was a man of about forty, tall and lean with an enormous quid of tobacco in his left cheek—a typical Texan.

His bronco interested me; instead of being an Indian pony of thirteen hands or so it was perhaps fifteen and a half and looked to be three-quarters bred.

"A good horse you have there", I said.

"The best in the hull country," he replied, "easy."

"That's only your conceit", I retorted. "The mare I am on right now can give him a hundred yards in a mile."

"You don't want to risk any money on that, do you?" he remarked.

"Oh, yes", I smiled.

"Well, we can try it out one of these days, but here comes your crowd", and indeed, although I had not expected them, in five minutes Bent and Bob and Charlie rode up.

"Get the cattle going", cried Bob, as he came within earshot. "We must go on. The Mexicans have gone back but they will come right after us again. Who is this?" he added, ranging up beside the Texan.

"My name is Locker", said my acquaintance; "and I guess your raiding will set the whole border boiling. Can't you buy cattle decently, like we all have to?"

"How do you know how decently we paid for them?" cried Bent, thrusting forward his brown face like a weasel's, his dog teeth showing.

"I guess Mr. Locker is all right", I cried laughing; "I propose he should help us and take two or three hundred head as payment, or the value of them—"

"Now you're talking", said Locker. "I call that sense. There is a herd of mine about a mile further on; if two or three hundred of your José steers join it, I can't hinder 'em; but I'd rather have dollars; cash is scarce!"

"Are they herded?" asked Bob.

"Sure", replied Locker. "I am too near the river to let any cattle run round loose though nobody has interfered with me in the last ten years."

Bob and I began moving the cattle on leaving Bent with Locker to conclude the negotiations. In an hour we had found Locker's herd that must have numbered at least six thousand head and were guarded by three herdsmen.

Locker and Bent had soon come to a working agreement. Locker it turned out had another herd some distance to the east from which he could draw three or four herdsmen. He had also a couple of boys, sons of his, whom he could send to rouse some of the neighboring farmers if the need was urgent. It turned out that we had done well to be generous to him for he knew the whole of the countryside like a book and was a good friend in our need.

Late in the afternoon, Locker was informed by one of his sons, a youth of about sixteen, that twenty Mexicans had crossed the river and would be up to us in a short time. Locker sent him after the younger boy to round up as many Texans as possible but before they could be collected, a bunch of greasers, twenty or so, in number, rode up and demanded the return of the cattle. Bent and Locker put them off and as luck would have it, while they were arguing, three or four Texans came up, and one of them, a man of about forty years of age named Rossiter, took control of the whole dispute. He told the Mexican leader, who said he was Don Luis, a son of Don José, that if he stayed any longer he would probably be arrested and put in prison for raiding American territory and threatening people.

The Mexican seemed to have a good deal of pluck, and declared that he would not only threaten but carry out his threat. Rossiter told him to wade right in. The loud talk began again, and a couple more Texans came up and the Mexican leader realizing that unless he did something at once he would be too late, started to circle round the cattle, no doubt thinking that if he did some thing his superior numbers would scare us.

In five minutes the fight had begun. In ten more it was all over. Nothing could stand against the deadly shooting of the Westerners. In five minutes one or two of the Mexicans had been killed and several wounded; half a dozen horses had gone down; it was perfectly evident that the eight or ten of us were more than a match for the twenty Mexicans, for except Don Luis, none of them seemed to have any stomach for the work, and Luis got a bullet through his arm in the first five minutes. Finally they drew off threatening and yelling and we saw no more of them.

After the battle we all adjourned to Locker's and had a big drink. Nobody took the fight seriously: whipping Greasers was nothing to brag about; but Rossiter thought that a claim should be made against the Mexican Government for raiding United States territory: said he was going to draw up the papers and send them to the State District Attorney at Austin. The proposal was received with whoops and cheers. The idea of punishing the Mexicans for getting shot trying to recapture their own cattle appealed to us Americans as something intensely humorous. All the Texans gave their names solemnly as witnesses, and Rossiter swore he would draw up the document. Years afterwards Bent whom I met by chance, told me that Rossiter had got forty thousand dollars on that claim.

Three days later we began to move our cattle eastward to rejoin Reece and Dell. I gave one hundred dollars as a reward to Locker's two boys who had helped us from start to finish most eagerly.

A week or so later we got back to the main camp. Reece and Dell had their herd ready and fat, and after a talk we resolved to go each on his own and join afterwards for the fall and winter on the ranch, if it pleased us. We took three weeks to get our bunch of cattle into condition and so began driving North in July. I spent every night in the saddle and most of the day, even though the accursed fever was shaking me.

All went well with us at first: I promised my three lieutenants a third share in the profits and a small wage besides: they were as keen as mustard and did all men could do. As soon as we reached the latitude of the Indian territory our troubles began. One wild night Indians, who wore sheets and had smeared their hands with phosphorus, stampeded the cattle and though the boys did wonders we lost nearly a thousand head and some hundred horses all of them broken in carefully.

It was a serious loss but not irreparable. The Plain Indians, however, were as persistent that summer as mosquitoes. I never went out after game but they tried to cut me off and once at least nothing but the speed and stamina of Blue Devil saved me. I had to give up serious shooting and depend on luck bringing us near game. Gradually the Indians following us grew more numerous and bolder. We were attacked at nightfall and daybreak three or four days running and the half wild cattle began to get very scary.

Bob did not conceal his anxiety. "Bad Injuns! very mean Injuns—!" One afternoon they followed us openly; there were at one time over a hundred in view; evidently they were getting ready for a serious attack. Bob's genius got us a respite. While Charlie was advising a pitched battle, Bob suddenly remembered that there was a scrub-oak forest some five miles further on to our right that would give us a refuge. Charlie and Bent, the best shots, lay down and began to shoot and soon made the Indians keep out of sight. In three hours we reached the scrub-oak wood and the bay or bight in it where Bob said the cattle would be safe; for nothing could get through scrub-oak and as soon as we had driven the cattle deep into the bay and brought our wagon to the centre, on the arc of the bight, so to speak, no Indians could stampede the cattle without blotting us out first. For the moment we were safe and as luck would have it, the water in a little creek near by was drinkable. Still we were besieged by over a hundred Indians and those odds were heavy as even Bob admitted.

Days passed and the siege continued: the Indians evidently meant to tire us out and get the herd, and our tempers didn't improve under the enforced idleness and vigilance. One evening Charlie was sprawling at the fire taking up more than his share of it, when Bent who had been looking after the cattle, came in. "Take up your legs, Charlie," he said roughly, "you don't want the whole fire." Charlie didn't hear or paid no attention: the next moment Bent had thrown himself down on Charlie's long limbs. With a curse Charlie pushed him off: the next moment Bent had hurled himself on Charlie and had shoved his head down in the fire. After a short struggle Charlie got free and in spite of all I could do, struck Bent.

Bent groped for his gun at once; but Charlie was at him striking and swinging like a wild man and Bent had to meet the attack.

Till the trial came, everyone would have said that Charlie was far and away the better man, younger too and astonishingly powerful. But Bent evidently was no novice at the game. He side-stepped Charlie's rush and hit out straight and hard and Charlie went down; but was up again like a flash, and went for his man in a wild rush: soon he was down again and everyone realized that sooner or later Bent must win. Fighting, however, has a large element of chance in it and as luck would have it just when Bent seemed most certain of winning, one of Charlie's wild swings caught him on the point of the jaw and to our amazement he went, down like a log and could not be brought to for some ten minutes. It was the first time I had seen this blow and naturally we all exaggerated the force of it not knowing that a light blow up against the chin jars the spinal cord and knocks any man insensible, in fact, in many cases, such a blow results in partial paralysis and life-long weakness.

Charlie was inclined to brag of his victory but Bob told him the truth and on reflection Bent's purpose and fighting power made the deeper impression on all of us and he himself took pains next day to warn Charlie:

"Don't get in my way again", he said to him drily, "or I'll make meat of you."

The dire menace in his hard, face was convincing. "Oh, Hell", replied Charlie, "who wants to get in your way!"

Reflection teaches me that all the worst toughs on the border in my time were ex-soldiers: it was the Civil war that had bred those men to violence and the use of the revolver; it was the civil war that produced the "Wild Bills" and Bents who forced the good-humored Westerners to hold life cheaply and to use their guns instead of fists.

One evening we noticed a large increase in the force of Indians besieging us: one chief too on a piebald mustang appeared to be urging an immediate attack and soon we found some of the "braves" stealing down the creek to outflank us, while a hundred others streamed past us at four hundred yards' distance firing wildly. Bob and I went under the creek banks to stop the flankers while Bent and Charlie and Jo brought down more than one horse and man and taught the band of Indians that a direct attack would surely cost them many lives.

Still there were only five of us and a chance bullet or two might make the odds against us desperate.

Talking it over we came to the conclusion that one man should ride to Fort Dodge for help and I was selected as the lightest save Bob and altogether the worst shot besides being the only man who would certainly find his way. Accordingly I brought up Blue Devil at once, took some pounds of jerked beef with me and a goat-water skin I had bought in Taos; a girth and stirrups quickly turned a blanket into a makeshift, light saddle and I was ready.

It was Bob's uncanny knowledge both of the Trail and of Indian ways that gave me my chance. All the rest advised me to go North out of our bay and then ride for it. He advised me to go south where the large body of Indians had stationed themselves. "They'll not look for you there", he said and "you may get through unseen; half an hour's riding more will take you round them; then you have one hundred and fifty miles north on the Trail—you may pick up a herd—and then one hundred and twenty miles straight west. You ought to be in Dodge in five days and back here in five more; you'll find us", he added significantly. The little man padded Blue Devil's hooves with some old garments he cut up and insisted on leading her away round the bight and far to the south, and I verily believe beyond the Indian camp.

There he took off the mare's pads, while I tightened the girths and started to walk keeping the mare between me and the Indians and my ears cocked for the slightest sound. But I heard nothing and saw nothing and in an hour more had made the round and was on the Trail for the north determined in my own mind to do the two or three hundred miles in four days at most.... On the fourth day I got twenty troopers from the Fort with Lieutenant Winder and was leading them in a bee-line to our Refuge. We got there in six days; but in the mean time the Indians had been busy.

They cut a way through the scrub-oak brush that we regarded as impassable and stampeded the cattle one morning just at dawn and our men were only able to herd off about six or seven hundred head and protect them in the extreme north corner of the bend. The Indians had all drawn off the day before I arrived with the U. S. Cavalry troopers.... Next morning we began the march northwards and I had no difficulty in persuading Lieutenant Winder to give us his escort for the next four or five days....

A week later we reached Wichita where we decided to rest for a couple of days and there we encountered another piece of bad luck. Ever since he had caught syphilis, Charlie seemed to have lost his gay temper: he became gloomy and morose and we could do nothing to cheer him up. The very first night he had to be put to bed at the gambling saloon in Wichita where he had become speechlessly drunk. And next day he was convinced that he had been robbed of his money by the man who kept the bank and went about swearing that he would get even with him at all costs. By the evening he had infected Bent and Jo with his insane determination and finally I went along hoping to save him, if I could, from some disaster.

Already I had asked Bob to get another herdsman and drive the cattle steadily towards Kansas City: he consented and for hours before we went to the saloon, Bob had been trekking north. I intended to rejoin him some five or six miles further on and drive slowly for the rest of the night. Somehow or other, I felt that the neighborhood was unhealthy for us.

The gambling saloon was lighted by three powerful oil lamps: two over the faro-table and one over the bar. Jo stationed himself at the bar while Bent and Charlie went to the table: I walked about the room trying to play the indifferent among the twenty or thirty men scattered about. Suddenly about 10 o'clock Charlie began disputing with the banker: they both rose, the banker drawing a big revolver from the table drawer in front of him. At the same moment Charlie struck the lamp above him and I saw him draw his gun just as all the lights went out leaving us in pitch darkness.

I ran to the door and was carried through it in a sort of mad stampede. A minute afterwards Bent joined me and then Charlie came rushing out at top speed with Jo hard after him. In a moment we were at the corner of the street where we had left our ponies and were off: one or two shots followed; I thought we had got off scot free; but I was mistaken.

We had ridden hell for leather, for about an hour when Charlie without apparent reason pulled up and swaying fell out of his saddle: his pony stopped dead and we all gathered round the wounded man:

"I'm finished", said Charlie in a weak voice, "but I've got my money back and I want you to send it to my mother in Pleasant Hill, Missouri. It's about a thousand dollars, I guess."

"Are you badly hurt?" I asked.

"He drilled me through the stomach first go off" Charlie said pointing, "and I guess I've got it at least twice more through the lungs: I'm done."

"What a pity, Charlie!" I cried, "you'll get more than a thousand dollars from your share of the cattle: I've told Bob, that I intend to share equally with all of you: this money must go back; but the thousand shall be sent to your mother I promise you:"—

"Not on your life!", cried the dying man, lifting himself up on one elbow: "This is my money: it shan't go back to that oily sneak thief": the effort had exhausted him; even in the dim light we could see that his face was drawn and gray: he must have understood this himself for I could just hear his last words: "Good-bye, boys!" his head fell back, his mouth opened: the brave boyish spirit was gone.

I couldn't control my tears: the phrase came to me: "I better could have lost a better man," for Charlie was at heart a good fellow!

I left Bent to carry back the money and arrange for Charlie's burial, leaving Jo to guard the body: in an hour I was again with Bob and had told him everything. Ten days later we were in Kansas City where I was surprised by unexpected news.

My second brother Willie, six years older than I was, had come out to America and hearing of me in Kansas had located himself in Lawrence as a real-estate agent; he wrote asking me to join him. This quickened my determination to have nothing more to do with cowpunching. Cattle too, we found, had fallen in price and we were lucky to get ten dollars or so a head for our bunch which made a poor showing from the fact that the Indians had netted all the best. There was about six thousand dollars to divide: Jo got five hundred dollars and Bent, Bob, Charlie's mother and myself divided the rest. Bob told me I was a fool: I should keep it all and go down south again:

but what had I gained by my two years of cowpunching? I had lost money and caught malarial fever; I had won a certain knowledge of ordinary men and their way of living and had got more than a smattering of economics and of medicine, but I was filled with an infinite disgust for a merely physical life. What was I to do now? I'd see Willie and make up my mind.

STUDENT LIFE AND LOVE.

Chapter IX.

That railway journey to Lawrence, Kansas, is as vivid to me now as if it had taken place yesterday yet it all happened more than fifty years ago. It was a blazing hot day and in the seat opposite to me was an old grey-haired man who appeared to be much troubled by the heat: he moved about restlessly, mopped his forehead, took off his vest and finally went out probably to the open observation platform, leaving a couple of books on his seat. I took one of them up heedlessly—it was "The Life and Death of Jason", by William Morris. I read a page or two, was surprised by the easy flow of the verse; but not gripped, so I picked up the other volume:—"Laus Veneris: Poems and Ballads" by Algernon Charles Swinburne. It opened at the Anactoria and in a moment, I was carried away entranced as no poetry before or since has ever entranced me. Venus, herself, spoke in the lines:

"Alas! that neither rain nor snow nor dew

Nor all cold things can purge me wholly through,

Assuage me nor allay me, nor appease,

Till supreme sleep shall bring me bloodless ease,

Till Time wax faint in all her periods,

Till Fate undo the bondage of the Gods

To lay and slake and satiate me all through,

Lotus and Lethe on my lips like dew,

And shed around and over and under me

Thick darkness and the insuperable sea."

I haven't seen the poem since and there may be verbal inaccuracies in my version; but the music and passion of the verses enthralled me and when I came to "The Leper", the last stanzas brought hot tears to my eyes and in the "Garden of Proserpine", I heard my own soul speaking with divine if hopeless assurance. Was there ever such poetry? Even the lighter verses were charming:

"Remembrance may recover

And time bring back to time

The name of your first lover,

The ring of my first rhyme:

But rose-leaves of December,

The storms of June shall fret;

The day that you remember,

The day that I forget.

And then the gay defiance:

In the teeth of the glad salt weather,

In the blown wet face of the sea;

While three men hold together,

Their Kingdoms are less by three.

And the divine songs to Hugo and to Whitman and the superb "Dedication": the last verse of it a miracle:

Though the many lights dwindle to one light,

There is help if the Heavens have one;

Though the stars be discrowned of the sunlight;

And the earth dispossessed of the Sun:

They have moonlight and sleep for repayment;

When refreshed as a bride and set free;

With stars and sea-winds in her raiment

Night sinks on the sea."

My very soul was taken: I had no need to read them twice: I've never seen them since: I shall not forget them so long as this machine lasts. They flooded my eyes with tears, my heart with passionate admiration. In this state the old gentlemen came back and found me, a cowboy to all appearance, lost, tear-drowned in Swinburne.

"I think that's my book", he said calling me back to dull reality. "Surely", I replied bowing; "but what magnificent poetry and I never heard of Swinburne before." "This is his first book I believe", said the old gentleman, "but I'm glad you like his verses." "Like", I cried, "who could help adoring them!" and I let myself go to recite the Proserpine:

"From too much love of living,
From hope and fear set free,
We thank with brief thanksgiving
Whatever Gods may be
That no life lives forever,
That dead men rise up never,
That even the weariest river
Winds somewhere safe to sea."

"Why you've learned it by heart!", cried the old man in wonder; "learned", I repeated, "I know half the book by heart: if you had stayed away another half hour, I'd have known it all" and I went on reciting for the next ten minutes.

"I never heard of such a thing in my life", he cried: "fancy a cowboy who learns Swinburne by merely reading him. It's astounding! Where are you going?" "To Lawrence," I replied. "We're almost there," he added and then, "I wish you would let me give you the book. I can easily get another copy and I think it ought to be yours."

I thanked him with all my heart and in a few minutes more got down at Lawrence station then as now far outside the little town clasping my Swinburne in my hand.

I record this story not to brag of my memory for all gifts are handicaps in life; but to show how kind Western Americans were to young folk and because the irresistible, unique appeal of Swinburne to youth has never been set forth before, so far as I know.

In a comfortable room at the Eldridge House, in the chief street of Lawrence, I met my brother: Willie seemed woefully surprised by my appearance: "You're as yellow as a guinea; but how you've grown", he cried. "You may be tall yet but you look ill, very ill!"

He was the picture of health and even better-looking than I had remembered him: a man of five feet ten or so with good figure and very handsome dark face: hair, small moustache and goatee beard jet black, straight thin nose and superb long hazel eyes with black lashes: he might have stood for the model of a Greek god were it not that his forehead was narrow and his eyes set close.

In three months he had become enthusiastically American, "America is the greatest country in the world", he assured me from an abysmal ignorance; "any young man who works can make money here; if I had a little capital I'd be a rich man in a very few years; it's some capital I need, nothing more." Having drawn my story out of me especially the last phase when I divided up with the boys, he declared I must be mad. "With five thousand dollars", he cried, "I could be rich in three years, a millionaire in ten. You must be mad; don't you know that everyone is for himself in this world: good gracious! I never heard of such insanity: if I had only known!"

For some days I watched him closely and came to believe that he was perfectly suited to his surroundings, eminently fitted to succeed in them. He was an earnest Christian, I found, who had been converted and baptised in the Baptist Church; he had a fair tenor voice and led the choir; he swallowed all the idiocies of the incredible creed; but drew some valuable moral sanctions from it; he was a teetotaler and didn't smoke; a Nazarene, too, determined to keep chaste as he called a state of abstinence from women, and weekly indulgence in self-abuse which he tried to justify as inevitable.

The teaching of Jesus himself had little or no practical effect on him; he classed it all together as counsels of an impossible perfection, and like the vast majority of Americans, accepted a childish Pauline-German morality while despising the duty of forgiveness and scorning the Gospel of Love.

A few days after our first meeting, Willie proposed to me that I should lend him a thousand dollars and he would give me twenty-five per cent for the use of the money. When I exclaimed against the usurious rate, twelve per cent being the State limit, he told me he could lend a million dollars if he had it, at from three to five per cent a month on perfect security. "So you see," he wound up, "that I can easily afford to give you two hundred and fifty dollars a year for the use of your thousand: one can buy real estate here to pay fifty per cent a year; the country is only just beginning to be developed", and so forth and so on in wildest optimism: the end of it being that he got my thousand dollars, leaving me with barely five hundred, but as I could live in a good boardinghouse for four dollars a week, I reckoned that at the worst I had one carefree year before me and if Willie kept his promise, I would be free to do whatever I wanted to do for years to come.

It was written that I was to have another experience in Lawrence much more important than anything to do with my brother. "Coming events cast their shadows before", is a poetic proverb, singularly inept: great events arrive unheralded, were truer.

One evening I went to a political meeting at Liberty Hall near my hotel. Senator Ingalls was going to speak and a Congressman on the Granger movement, the first attempt of the Western farmers to react politically against the exploitation of Wall Street. The hall was packed: just behind me sat a man between two pretty grey-eyed girls. The man's face attracted me even at first sight: I should be able to picture him for even as I write his face comes before me as vividly as if the many long years that separate us, were but the momentary closing of my eyes.

At the end of this chapter I reproduce a perfect portrait of him and need only add the coloring and expression: the large eyes were hazel and set far apart under the white, over-hanging brow; the hair and whiskers were chestnut-brown tinged with auburn; but it was the eyes that drew and fascinated me for they were luminous as no other eyes that I have ever seen; frank too, and kind, kind always.

But his dress, a black frock coat, with low stand-up white collar and a narrow black silk tie excited my snobbish English contempt. Both the girls, sisters evidently, were making up to him for all they were worth, or so it seemed to my jaundiced envious eyes.

Senator Ingalls made the usual kind of speech: the farmers were right to combine; but the money-lords were powerful and after all farmers and bankers alike were Americans:—Americans first and last and all the time! (great cheering!) The Congressman followed with the same brand of patriotic piffle and then cries arose from all parts of the hall for Professor Smith! I heard eager whispering behind me and turning half round guessed that the good-looking young man was Professor Smith for his two girl-admirers were persuading him to go on the platform and fascinate the audience.

In a little while he went up amid great applause; a good figure of a man, rather tall, about five feet ten, slight with broad shoulders. He began to speak in a thin tenor voice: "there was a manifest conflict of interests," he said, "between the manufacturing Eastern States that demanded a high tariff on all imports and the farming West that wanted cheap goods and cheap rates of transport.

"In essence, it's a mere matter of arithmetic, a mathematical problem, demanding a compromise; for every country should establish its own manufacturing industries and be self-supporting. The obvious reform was indicated; the Federal government should take over the railways and run them for the farmers, while competition among American manufacturers would ultimately reduce prices."

No one in the hall seemed to understand this "obvious reform"; but the speech called forth a hurricane of cheers and I concluded that there were a great many students from the State University in the audience.

I don't know what possessed me but when Smith returned to his seat behind me between the two girls and they praised him to the skies, I got up and walked to the platform. I was greeted with a tempest of laughter and must have cut a ludicrous figure. I was in cowpuncher's dress as modified by Reece and Dell: I wore loose Bedford cord breeches, knee-high brown boots and a sort of buckskin shirt and jacket combined that tucked into my breeches. But rains and sun had worked their will on the buckskin which had shrunk down my neck and up my arms.

Spurred on by the laughter I went up the four steps to the platform and walked over to the Mayor who was Chairman:

"May I speak?" I asked:

"Sure", he replied "your name?"

"My name is Harris," I answered and the Mayor manifestly regarding me as a great joke announced that a Mr. Harris wished to address the meeting and he hoped the audience would give him a fair hearing even if his doctrines happened to be peculiar. As I faced them, the spectators shrieked with laughter: the house fairly rocked. I waited a full minute and then began: "How like Americans and Democrats", I said, "to judge a man by the clothes he wears and the amount of hair he has on his face or the dollars in his jeans."

There was instantaneous silence, the silence of surprise at least, and I went on to show what I had learned from Mill that open competition was the law of life, another name for the struggle for existence; that each country should concentrate its energies on producing the things it was best fitted to produce and trade these off against the products of other nations; this was the great economic law, the law of the territorial division of labor.

"Americans should produce corn and wheat and meat for the world", I said, and exchange these products for the cheapest English woolen goods and French silks and Irish linen. This would enrich the American farmer, develop all the waste American land and be a thousand times better for the whole country than taxing all consumers with high import duties to enrich a few Eastern manufacturers who were too inefficient to face the open competition of Europe. "The American farmers," I went on, "should organize with the laborers, for their interests are identical and fight the Eastern manufacturer who is nothing but a parasite living on the brains and work of better men."

And then, I wound up: "this common sense program won't please your Senators or your Congressmen who prefer cheap claptrap to thought, or your superfine Professors who believe the war of classes is 'a mere arithmetical problem' (and I imitated the Professor's thin voice), but it may nevertheless be accepted by the American farmer tired of being milked by the Yankee manufacturer and it should stand as the first chapter in the new Granger gospel."

I bowed to the Mayor and turned away but the audience broke into cheers and Senator Ingalls came over and shook my hand saying he hoped to know me better and the cheering went on till I had gotten back to my place and resumed my seat. A few minutes later and I was touched on the back by Professor Smith. As I turned round he said smiling "you gave me a good lesson: I'll never make a public speaker and what I said doubtless sounded inconsequent and absurd; but if you'd have a talk with me, I think I could convince you that my theory will hold water."

"I've no doubt you could," I broke in, heartily ashamed of having made fun of a man I didn't know; "I didn't grasp your meaning but I'd be glad to have a talk with you."

"Are you free tonight?" he went on: I nodded: "Then come with me to my rooms. These ladies live out of town and we'll put them in their buggy and then be free. This is Mrs.... he added presenting me to the stouter lady and this, her sister, Miss Stevens." I bowed and out we went, I keeping myself resolutely in the background till the sisters had driven away: then we set off together to Professor Smith's rooms, for our talk.

If I could give a complete account of that talk, this poor page would glow with wonder and admiration all merged in loving reverence. We talked or rather Smith talked for I soon found he knew infinitely more than I did, was able indeed to label my creed as that of Mill, "a bourgeois English economist" he called him with smiling disdain.

Ever memorable to me, sacred indeed, that first talk with the man who was destined to reshape my life and inspire it with some of his own high purpose. He introduced me to the communism of Marx and Engels and easily convinced me that land and its products, coal and oil, should belong to the whole community which should also manage all industries for the public benefit.

My breath was taken by his mere statement of the case and I thrilled to the passion in his voice and manner though even then I wasn't wholly convinced. Whatever topic we touched on, he illumined; he knew everything, it seemed to me, German and French and could talk Latin and Classic Greek as fluently as English. I had never imagined such scholarship and when I recited some verses of Swinburne as expressing my creed he knew them too and his Pantheistic Hymn to Hertha, as well. And he wore his knowledge lightly as the mere garment of his shining spirit! And how handsome he was, like a Sun-god! I had never seen anyone who could at all compare with him.

Day had dawned before we had done talking: then he told me he was the Professor of Greek in the State University and hoped I would come and study with him when the schools opened again in October. "To think of you as a cowboy" he said, "is impossible. Fancy a cowboy knowing books of Vergil and poems of Swinburne by heart; it's absurd: you must give your brains a chance and study."

“I’ve too little money” I said, beginning to regret my loan to my brother.

“I told you I am a Socialist,” Smith retorted smiling: “I have three or four thousand dollars in the Bank, take half of it and come to study” and his luminous eyes held me: then it was true, after all; my heart swelled, jubilant, there were noble souls in this world who took little thought of money and lived for better things than gold.

“I won’t take your money”, I said, with tears burning: “every herring should hang by its own head in these democratic days; but if you think enough of me to offer such help, I’ll promise to come though I fear you’ll be disappointed when you find how little I know; how ignorant I am. I’ve not been in school since I was fourteen.”

“Come, we’ll soon make up the time lost” he said. “By the bye where are you staying?” “The Eldridge House,” I replied.

He brought me to the door and we parted; as I turned to go I saw the tall slight figure and the radiant eyes and I went away into a new world that was the old, feeling as if I were treading on air.

Once more my eyes had been opened as on Overton Bridge to the beauties of nature; but now to the splendor of an unique spirit. What luck! I cried to myself to meet such a man! It really seemed to me as if some God were following me with divine gifts!

And then the thought came: This man has chosen and called you very much as Jesus called his disciples:—*Come, and I will make you fishers of men!* Already I was dedicate heart and soul to the new Gospel.

But even that meeting with Smith, wherein I reached the topmost height of golden hours, was set off, so to speak, by another happening of this wonder-week. At the next table to me in the dining-room I had already remarked once or twice a little, middle-aged, weary looking man who often began his breakfast with a glass of boiling water and followed it up with a baked apple drowned in rich cream. Brains, too, or sweetbreads he would eat for dinner and rice, not potatoes: when I looked surprise, he told me he had been up all night and had a weak digestion, Mayhew, he said, was his name and explained that if I ever wanted a game of faro or euchre or indeed anything else, he’d oblige me. I smiled; I could ride and shoot, I replied; but I was no good at cards.

The day after my talk with Smith, Mayhew and I were both late for supper: I sat long over a good meal and as he rose, he asked me if I would come across the street and see his “lay-out!” I went willingly enough, having nothing to do. The gambling saloon was on the first floor of a building nearly opposite the Eldridge House: the place was well-kept and neat, thanks to a colored bar-tender and colored waiter and a nigger of all work. The long room too was comfortably furnished and very brightly lit—altogether an attractive place.

As luck would have it, while he was showing me round, a lady came in; Mayhew after a word or two introduced me to her as his wife: Mrs. Mayhew was then a woman of perhaps twenty-eight or thirty, with tall, lissom slight figure and interesting rather than pretty face: her features were all good, her eyes even were large and blue-gray: she would have been lovely if her coloring had been more pronounced: give her golden hair or red or black and she would have been a beauty: she was always tastefully dressed and had appealing, ingratiating manners. I soon found that she loved books and reading and as Mayhew said he was going to be busy, I asked if I might see her home. She consented smiling and away we went. She lived in a pretty frame house standing alone in a street that ran parallel to Massachusetts Street, nearly opposite to a large and ugly church.

As she went up the steps to the door, I noticed that she had fine, neat ankles and I divined shapely limbs. While she was taking off her light cloak and hat, the lifting of her arms stretched her bodice and showed small round breasts: already my blood was lava and my mouth parched with desire.

"You look at me strangely!" she said swinging round from the long mirror with a challenge on her parted lips. I made some inane remark: I couldn't trust myself to speak frankly; but natural sympathy drew us together. I told her I was going to be a student and she wanted to know whether I could dance: I told her I could not, and she promised to teach me: "Lily Robins, a neighbor's girl, will play for us any afternoon. Do you know the steps?" she went on and when I said "No": she got up from the sofa, held up her dress and showed me the three polka steps which she said were the waltz steps too, only taken on a glide. "What pretty ankles! you have", I ventured; but she appeared not to hear me. We sat on and on and I learned that she was very lonely: Mr. Mayhew away every night and nearly all day and nothing to do in that little dead-and-alive place. "Will you let me come in for a talk sometimes?" I asked: "Whenever you wish", was her answer. As I rose to go and we were standing opposite to each other by the door, I said: "You know, Mrs. Mayhew, in Europe when a man brings a pretty woman home, she rewards him with a kiss—"

"Really?" she scoffed, smiling, "That's not a custom here."

"Are you less generous than they are?" I asked and the next moment I had taken her face in my hands and kissed her on the lips. She put her hands on my shoulders and left her eyes on mine: "We're going to be friends", she said, "I felt it when I saw you: don't stay away too long!"

"Will you see me tomorrow afternoon?" I asked: "I want that dance lesson!" "Surely" she replied, "I'll tell Lily in the morning." And once more our hands met: I tried to draw her to me for another kiss; but she held back with a smiling—"tomorrow afternoon!" "Tell me your name", I begged, "so that I may think of it." "Lorna" she replied, "you funny boy!" and I went my way with pulses hammering, blood aflame and hope in my heart.

Next morning I called again upon Smith; but the pretty servant, "Rose", she said her name was, told me that he was nearly always out at Judge Stevens' "five or six miles out," she thought it was; "they always come for him in a buggy", she added. So I said I'd write and make an appointment and I did write and asked him to let me see him next morning.

That same morning Willie recommended to me a pension kept by a Mrs. Gregory, an Englishwoman, the wife of an old Baptist clergyman, who would take good care of me for four dollars a week. Immediately I went with him to see her and was delighted to find that she lived only about a hundred yards from Mrs. Mayhew on the opposite side of the street. Mrs. Gregory was a large, motherly woman evidently a lady, who had founded this boardinghouse to provide for a rather feckless husband and two children, a big pretty girl, Kate and a lad, a couple of years younger. Mrs. Gregory was delighted with my English accent, I believe, and showed me special favor at once by giving me a large outside room with its own entrance and steps into the garden.

In an hour I had paid my bill at the Eldridge House and had moved in: I showed a shred of prudence by making Willie promise Mrs. Gregory that he would turn up each Saturday with the five dollars for my board; the dollar extra was for the big room.

In due course I shall tell how he kept his promise and discharged his debt to me. For the moment everything was easily, happily settled. I went out and ordered a decent suit of ordinary tweeds and dressed myself up in my best blue suit to call upon Mrs. Mayhew after lunch. The clock crawled but on the stroke of three, I was at her door: a colored maid admitted me.

"Mrs. Mayhew", she said in her pretty singing voice, "will be down right soon: I'll go call Miss Lily."

In five minutes Miss Lily appeared, a dark slip of a girl with shining black hair, wide laughing mouth, temperamental thick red lips and grey eyes fringed with black lashes: she had hardly time to speak to me when Mrs. Mayhew came in: "I hope you two'll be great friends", she said prettily; "you're both about the same age" she added.

In a few minutes Miss Lily was playing a waltz on the Steinway and with my arm round the slight, flexible waist of my inamorata I was trying to waltz.

But alas! after a turn or two I became giddy and in spite of all my resolution had to admit that I should never be able to dance.

"You have got very pale", Mrs. Mayhew said, "you must sit down on the sofa a little while." Slowly the giddiness left me: before I had entirely recovered Miss Lily with kindly words of sympathy had gone home and Mrs. Mayhew brought me in a cup of excellent coffee: I drank it down and was well at once.

"You should go in and lie down", said Mrs. Mayhew still full of pity, "see" and she opened a door, "there's the guest bedroom all ready." I saw my chance and went over to her: "if you'd come too", I whispered and then, "the coffee has made me quite well: won't you, Lorna, give me a kiss? You don't know how often I said your name last night, you dear!" and in a moment I had again taken her face and put my lips on hers. She gave me her lips this time and my kiss became a caress; but in a little while she drew away and said, "let's sit and talk, I want to know all you are doing." So I seated myself beside her on the sofa and told her all my news. She thought I would be comfortable with the Gregorys. "Mrs. Gregory is a good woman", she added, "and I hear the girl's engaged to a cousin: do you think her pretty?"

"I think no one pretty but you, Lorna", I said and I pressed her head down on the arm of the sofa and kissed her. Her lips grew hot: I was certain. At once I put my hand down on her sex; she struggled a little at first, which I took care should bring our bodies closer and when she ceased struggling I put my hands up her dress and began caressing her sex: it was hot and wet, as I knew it would be, and opened readily.

But in another moment she took the lead: "Some one might find us here," she whispered, "I've let the maid go: come up to my bedroom" and she took me upstairs. I begged her to undress: I wanted to see her figure; but she only said, "I have no corsets on, I don't often wear them in the house. Are you sure you love me, dear?" "You know I do!" was my answer. The next moment I lifted her on to the bed, drew up her clothes, opened her legs and was in her. There was no difficulty and in a moment or two I came; but went right on poking passionately; in a few minutes her breath went and came quickly and her eyes fluttered and she met my thrusts with sighs and nippings of her sex. My second orgasm took some time and all the while Lorna became more and more responsive, till suddenly she put her hands on my bottom and drew me to her forcibly while she moved her sex up and down awkwardly to meet my thrusts with a passion I had hardly imagined. Again and again I came and the longer the play lasted, the wilder was her excitement and delight. She kissed me hotly foraging and thrusting her tongue into my mouth. Finally she pulled up her chemise to get me further into her and at length with little sobs she suddenly got hysterical and panting wildly, burst into a storm of tears.

That stopped me: I withdrew my sex and took her in my arms and kissed her; at first she clung to me with choking sighs and streaming eyes, but as soon as she had won a little control, I went to the toilette and brought her a sponge of cold water and bathed her face and gave her some water to drink—that quieted her. But she would not let me leave her even to arrange my clothes.

"Oh, you great, strong dear," she cried, with her arms clasping me, "oh, who would have believed such intense pleasure possible: I never felt anything like it before: how could you keep on so long! Oh, how I love you, you wonder and delight!

"I am all yours," she added gravely, "you shall do what you like with me: I am your mistress, your slave, your plaything and you are my God and my love! Oh, Darling! oh!"

There was a pause while I smiled at her extravagant praise, then suddenly she sat up and got out of bed: "You wanted to see my figure", she exclaimed, "here it is, I can deny you nothing; I only hope it may please you" and in a moment or two she showed herself nude from head to stocking.

As I had guessed, her figure was slight and lissom, with narrow hips but she had a great bush of hair on her Mount of Venus and her breasts were not so round and firm as Jessie's: still she was very pretty and well-formed with the *fines attaches* (slender wrists and ankles) which the French are so apt to over-estimate. They think that small bones indicate a small sex; but I have found that the exceptions are very numerous, even if there is any such rule.

After I had kissed her breasts and navel, and praised her figure, she disappeared in the bathroom but was soon with me again on the sofa which we had left an hour or so before.

"Do you know" she began, "my husband assured me that only the strongest young man could go twice with a woman in one day? I believed him; aren't we women fools? You must have come a dozen times?"

"Not half that number", I replied smiling.

"Aren't you tired?" was her next question, "even I have a little headache" she added: "I never was so wrought up: at the end it was too intense: but you must be tired out." "No," I replied, "I feel no fatigue, indeed I feel the better for our joy ride!"

"But surely you're an exception?" she went on; "most men have finished in one short spasm and leave the woman utterly unsatisfied, just excited and no more."

"Youth", I said, "that, I believe, makes the chief difference."

"Is there any danger of a child?" she went on, "I ought to say 'hope'," she added bitterly, "for I'd love to have a child, your child" and she kissed me.

"When were you ill last?" I asked.

"About a fortnight ago", she replied, "I often thought that had something to do with it."

"Why?" I asked: "tell truth!" I warned her and she began: "I'll tell you anything; I thought the time had something to do with it for soon after I am well each month my 'pussy' that's what we call it, often burns and itches intolerably; but after a week or so I'm not bothered any more till next time. Why is that?" she added.

"Two things I ought to explain to you" I said, "your seed is brought down into your womb by the menstrual blood: it lives there a week or ten days and then dies and with its death your desires decrease and the chance of impregnation. But near the next monthly period, say within three days, there is a double danger again; for the excitement may bring your seed down before the usual time and in any case, my seed will live in your womb about three days, so if you wish to avoid pregnancy, wait for ten days after your monthly flow is finished and stop say four days before you expect it again, then the danger of getting a child is very slight."

"Oh, you wise boy!" she laughed, "don't you see you are skipping the time I most desire you, and that's not kind to either of us; is it?"

"There's still another way of evasion", I said, "get me to withdraw before I come the first time, or get up immediately and syringe yourself with water thoroughly: water kills my seed as soon as it touches it—"

"But how will that help if you go on half a dozen times more?" she asked.

"Doctors say," I replied, "that what comes from me afterwards is not virile enough to impregnate a woman: I'll explain the process to you if you like; but you can take it, the fact is as I state it."

"When did you learn all this?" she asked.

"It has been my most engrossing study," I laughed, "and by far the most pleasureful!"

"You dear, dear," she cried, "I must kiss you for that."

"Do you know you kiss wonderfully?" she went on reflectingly, "with a lingering touch of the inside of the lips and then the thrust of the tongue: that's what excited me so the first time" and she sighed as if delighted with the memory.

"You didn't seem excited," I said half reproachfully, "for when I wanted another kiss, you drew away and said 'tomorrow'! Why are women so coquettish, so perverse?" I added, remembering Lucille and Jessie.

"I think it is that we wish to be sure of being desired," she replied, "and a little too that we want to prolong the joy of it, the delight of being wanted, really wanted! It is so easy for us to give and so exquisite to feel a man's desire pursuing us! Ah how rare it is", she sighed passionately, "and how quickly lost! You'll soon tire of your mistress", she added, "now that I am all yours and thrill only for you" and she took my head in her hands and kissed me passionately, regretfully.

"You kiss better than I do, Lorna! Where did you acquire the art, Madame?" I asked, "I fear that you have been a naughty, naughty girl!"

"If you only knew the truth," she exclaimed, "if you only knew how girls long for a lover and burn and itch in vain and wonder why men are so stupid and cold and dull as not to see our desire.

"Don't we try all sorts of tricks? Aren't we haughty and withdrawn at one moment and affectionate, tender, loving at another? Don't we conceal the hook with every sort of bait only to watch the fish sniff at it and turn away. Ah, if you knew—I feel a traitor to my sex even in telling you—if you guessed how we angle for you and how clever we are, how full of wiles! There's an expression I once heard my husband use which describes us women exactly or nine out of ten of us. I wanted to know how he kept the office warm all night: he said, we damp down the furnaces and explained the process: that's it, I cried to myself, I'm a damped-down furnace: that's surely why I keep hot so long! Did you imagine", she asked, turning her flower-face all pale with passion half aside, "that I took off my hat that first day before the glass and turned slowly round with it held above my head, by chance? You dear innocent! I knew the movement would show my breasts and slim hips and did it deliberately hoping it would excite you and how I thrilled when I saw it did.

"Why did I show you the bed in that room?" she added, "and leave the door ajar when I came back here to the sofa, but to tempt you and how heart-glad I was to feel your desire in your kiss. I was giving myself before you pushed my head back on the sofa-arm and disarranged all my hair!" she added pouting and patting it with her hands to make sure it was in order.

"You were astonishingly masterful and quick," she went on: "how did you know that I wished you to touch me then! Most men would have gone on kissing and fooling, afraid to act decisively. You must have had a lot of experience? You naughty lad!"

"Shall I tell you the truth!" I said, "I will, just to encourage you to be frank with me. You are the first woman I have ever spent my seed in or had properly—"

"Call it improperly, for God's sake," she cried laughing aloud with joy, "you darling virgin, you! Oh! how I wish I was sixteen again and you were my first lover. You would have made me believe in God. Yet you are my first lover", she added quickly, "I have only learned the delight and ecstasy of love in your arms—"

Our love-talk lasted for hours till suddenly I guessed it was late and looked at my watch; it was nearly seven-thirty: I was late for supper which started at half-past six!

"I must go," I exclaimed, "or I'll get nothing to eat."

"I could give you supper," she added, "my lips too, that long for you and—and—but you know" she added regretfully, "he might come in and I want to know you better first before seeing you together: a young God and a man!—and the man in God's likeness, yet so poor an imitation!"

"Don't, don't," I said, "you'll make life harder for yourself—"

"Harder" she repeated with a sniff of contempt, "Kiss me, my love and go if you must. Shall I see you tomorrow? There!" she cried as with a curse, "I've given myself away: I can't help it, oh how I want you always: how I shall long for you and count the dull dreary hours! Go, go or I'll never let you"—and she kissed and clung to me to the door.

"Sweet—tomorrow", I said and tore off.

Of course it is manifest that my liaison with Mrs. Mayhew had little or nothing to do with love. It was demoniac youthful sex-urge in me and much the same hunger in her and as soon as the desire was satisfied my judgment of her was as impartial, cool as if she had always been indifferent to me. But with her I think there was a certain attachment and considerable tenderness. In intimate relations between the sexes it is rare indeed that the man gives as much to love as the woman.

Professor Byron. C. Smith: 1872.

SOME STUDY, MORE LOVE.

Chapter X.

Supper at the Gregory's was almost over when I entered the dining-room: Kate and her mother and father and the boy Tommy were seated at the end of the table, taking their meal: the dozen guests had all finished and disappeared. Mrs. Gregory hastened to rise and Kate got up to follow her mother into the neighbouring kitchen.

"Please don't get up!" I cried to the girl, "I'd never forgive myself for interrupting you: I'll wait on myself or on you", I added smiling, "if you wish anything—"

She looked at me with hard, indifferent eyes and sniffed scornfully: "If you'll sit there", she said, pointing to the other end of the table, "I'll bring you supper: do you take coffee or tea?"

"Coffee, please," I answered and took the seat indicated, at once making up my mind to be cold to her while winning the others. Soon the boy began asking me had I ever seen any Indians—"in warpaint and armed, I mean" he added eagerly.

"Yes and shot at them, too", I replied smiling. Tommy's eyes gleamed—"Oh tell us!" he panted and I knew I could always count on one good listener!

"I've lots to tell, Tommy," I said, "but now I must eat my supper at express rate or your sister'll be angry—" I added as Kate came in with some steaming food: she pulled a face and shrugged her shoulders with contempt.

"Where do you preach?" I asked the grey-haired father, "my brother says you're really eloquent—"

"Never eloquent," he replied deprecatingly, "but sometimes very earnest perhaps, especially when some event of the day comes to point the Gospel story—" he talked like a man of fair education and I could see he was pleased at being drawn to the front.

Then Kate brought me fresh coffee and Mrs. Gregory came in and continued her meal and the talk became interesting, thanks to Mr. Gregory who couldn't help saying how the fire in Chicago had stimulated Christianity in his hearers and given him a great text. I mentioned casually that I had been in the fire and told of Randolph Street Bridge and the hanging and what else I saw there and on the lakefront that unforgettable Monday morning.

At first Kate went in and out of the room removing dishes as if she were not concerned in the story, but when I told of the women and girls half-naked at the lakeside while the flames behind us reached the zenith in a red sheet that kept throwing flame-arrows ahead and started the ships burning on the water in front of us, she too stopped to listen.

At once I caught my cue, to be liked and admired by all the rest; but indifferent, cold to her. So I rose as if her standing enthralled had interrupted me and said:

"I'm sorry to keep you: I've talked too much, forgive me!" and betook myself to my room in spite of the protests and prayers to continue of all the rest. Kate just flushed; but said nothing.

She attracted me greatly: she was infinitely desirable, very good-looking and very young (only sixteen, her mother said later) and her great hazel eyes were almost as exciting as her pretty mouth or large hips and good height. She pleased me intimately but I resolved to win her altogether and felt I had begun well: at any rate she would think about me and my coldness.

I spent the evening in putting out my half dozen books, not forgetting my medical treatises, and then slept, the deep sleep of sex recuperation.

The next morning I called on Smith again where he lived with the Reverend Mr. Kellogg, who was the Professor of English History in the University, Smith said. Kellogg was a man of about forty, stout and well-kept, with a faded wife of about the same age. Rose, the pretty servant, let me in: I had a smile and warm word of thanks for her: she was astonishingly pretty, the prettiest girl I had seen in Lawrence: medium height and figure with quite lovely face and an exquisite rose-leaf skin! She smiled at me; evidently my admiration pleased her.

Smith, I found, had got books for me, Latin and Greek-English dictionaries, a Tacitus too and Xenophon's Memorabilia with a Greek grammar: I insisted on paying for them all and then he began to talk. Tacitus he just praised for his superb phrases and the great portrait of Tiberius—"perhaps the greatest historical portrait ever painted in words." I had a sort of picture of King Edward the Fourth in my romantic head, but didn't venture to trot it out. But soon, Smith passed to Xenophon and his portrait of Socrates as compared with that of Plato. I listened all ears while he read out a passage from Xenophon, painting Socrates with little human touches: I got him to translate every word literally and had a great lesson, resolving when I got home, I'd learn the whole page by heart. Smith was more than kind to me: he said I'd be able to enter the Junior Class and thus have only two years to graduation. If Willie gave me back even five hundred dollars, I'd be able to get through without care or work.

Then Smith told me how he had gone to Germany after his American University: how he had studied there and then worked in Athens at ancient

Greek for another year till he could talk classic Greek as easily as German. "There were a few dozen Professors and students" he said, "who met regularly and talked nothing but classic Greek: they were always trying to make the modern tongue just like the old." He gave me a translation of "Das Kapital" of Marx, and in fifty ways inspired and inspirited me to renewed effort.

I came back to the Gregorys for dinner and discussed in my own mind whether I should go to Mrs. Mayhew's as I had promised or work at Greek: I decided to work and then and there made a vow always to prefer work, a vow more honored in the breach, I fear, than in the observance. But at least I wrote to Mrs. Mayhew excusing myself and promising her the next afternoon. Then I set myself to learn by heart the two pages in the "Memorabilia."

That evening I sat near the end of the table; the head of it was taken by the University Professor of Physics, a dull pedant!

Every time Kate came near me I was ceremoniously polite: "Thank you very much! It is very kind of you!" and not a word more. As soon as I could, I went to my room to work.

Next day at three o'clock I knocked at Mrs. Mayhew's: she opened the door herself: I cried, "how kind of you" and once in the room drew her to me and kissed her time and time again: she seemed cold and numb.

For some moments she didn't speak, then: "I feel as if I had passed through fever", she said, putting her hands through her hair, lifting it in a gesture I was to know well in the days to come: "Never promise again if you don't come: I thought I should go mad: waiting is a horrible torture! Who kept you?—some girl?" and her eyes searched mine.

I excused myself; but her intensity chilled me. At the risk of alienating my girl-readers, I must confess this was the effect her passion had on me. When I kissed her, her lips were cold. But by the time we had got upstairs, she had thawed: she shut the door after us gravely and began: "See how ready I am for you!" and in a moment she had thrown back her robe and stood before me naked: she tossed the garment on a chair; it fell on the floor: she stooped to pick it up with her bottom to me: I kissed her soft bottom and caught her up by it with my hand on her sex. She turned her head over her shoulder:

"I've washed and scented myself for you, Sir: how do you like the perfume? and how do you like this bush of hair?" and she touched her Mount with a grimace; "I was so ashamed of it as a girl: I used to shave it off: that's what made it grow so thick, I believe: one day my mother saw it and made me stop shaving; oh, how ashamed of it I was: it's animal, ugly:—don't you hate it? Oh! tell the truth!" she cried, "or rather, don't; tell me you love it."

"I love it," I exclaimed, "because it's yours!" "Oh you dear lover," she smiled, "you always find the right word, the flattering salve for the sore!"

"Are you ready for me?" I asked, "ripe-ready or shall I kiss you first and caress pussy?"

"Whatever you do, will be right," she said, "you know I am rotten-ripe, soft and wet for you always!"

All this while I was taking off my clothes: now I too was naked.

"I want you to draw up your knees," I said: "I want to see the Holy of Holies, the shrine of my idolatry."

At once she did as I asked. Her legs and bottom were well-shaped without being statuesque; but her clitoris was much more than the average button: it stuck out fully half an inch and the inner lips of her vulva hung down a little below the outer lips. I knew I should see prettier pussies. Kate's was better shaped, I felt sure, and the heavy, madder-brown lips put me off a little.

The next moment I began caressing her red clitoris with my hot, stiff organ: Lorna sighed deeply once or twice and her eyes turned up; slowly I pushed my prick in to the full and drew it out again to the lips, then in again and I felt her warm love-juice gush as she drew up her knees even higher to let me further in: "Oh, it's divine", she sighed, "better even than the first time", and when my thrusts grew quick and hard as the orgasm shook me, she writhed down on my prick as I withdrew, as if she would hold it, and as my seed spirted into her, she bit my shoulder and held her legs tight as if to keep my sex in her. We lay a few moments bathed in bliss. Then as I began to move again to sharpen the sensation, she half rose on her arm: "Do you know", she said, "I dreamed yesterday of getting on you and doing it to you: do you mind, if I try—" "No, indeed!" I cried, "go to it: I am your prey!" She got up smiling and straddled kneeling across me and put my cock into her pussy and sank down on me with a deep sigh. She tried to move up and down on my organ and at once came up too high and had to use her hand to put my Tommy in again; then she sank down on it as far as possible: "I can sink down all right", she cried smiling at the double meaning, "but I cannot rise so well! What fools we women are, we can't master even the act of love; we are so awkward!"

"Your awkwardness, however, excites me," I said.

"Does it?" she cried, "then I'll do my best", and for some time she rose and sank rhythmically; but as her excitement grew, she just let herself lie on me and wiggled her bottom till we both came. She was flushed and hot and I couldn't help asking her a question:

"Does your excitement grow to a spasm of pleasure?" I asked, "or do you go on getting more and more excited continually?"

"I get more and more excited," she said, "till the other day with you for the first time in my life the pleasure became unbearably intense and I was hysterical, you wonder-lover!"

Since then I have read lascivious books in half a dozen languages and they all represent women coming to an orgasm in the act, as men do, followed by a period of content: which only shows that the books are all written by men and ignorant, insensitive men at that. The truth is hardly one married woman in a thousand is ever brought to her highest pitch of feeling: usually, just when she begins to feel, her husband goes to sleep. If the majority of husbands satisfied their wives occasionally, the Woman's Revolt would soon move to another purpose: women want above all a lover who loves to excite them to the top of their bent. As a rule men through economic conditions marry so late that they have already half exhausted their virile power before they marry. And when they marry young they are so ignorant and so self-centered that they imagine their wives must be satisfied when they are. Mrs. Mayhew told me that her husband had never excited her really. She denied that she had ever had any acute pleasure from his embraces.

"Shall I make you hysterical again?" I asked, out of boyish vanity, "I can, you know!"

"You mustn't tire yourself!" she warned, "my husband taught me long ago that when a woman tires a man, he gets a distaste for her and I want your love, your desire, dear, a thousand times more even that the delight you give me—"

"Don't be afraid", I broke in, "you are sweet, you couldn't tire me: turn sideways and put your left leg up, and I'll just let my sex caress your clitoris back and forth gently; every now and then I'll let it go right in until our hairs meet." I kept on this game perhaps half an hour until she first sighed and sighed and then made awkward movements with her pussy which I sought to divine and meet as she wished when suddenly she cried:

"Oh! Oh! hurt me, please! hurt me, or I'll bite you! Oh God, oh, oh"—panting, breathless till again the tears poured down!

"You darling!" she sobbed, "how you can love! Could you go on forever?"

For answer I put her hand on my sex: "Just as naughty as ever", she exclaimed, "and I am choking, breathless, exhausted! Oh, I'm sorry", she went on, "but we should get up, for I don't want my help to know or guess: niggers talk—"

I got up and went to the windows; one gave on the porch but the other directly on the garden. "What are you looking at?" she asked coming to me. "I was just looking for the best way to get out if ever we were surprised", I said, "if we leave this window open I can always drop into the garden and get away quickly."

"You would hurt yourself?", she cried.

"Not a bit of it", I answered, "I could drop half as far again without injury, the only thing is, I must have boots on and trousers, or those thorns of yours would give me gip!." … "You boy", she exclaimed laughing: "I think after your strength and passion, it is your boyishness I love best"—and she kissed me again and again.

"I must work", I warned her, "Smith has given me a lot to do." "Oh, my dear", she said, her eyes filling with tears, "that means you won't come tomorrow or", she added hastily, "even the day after?"

"I can't possibly", I declared, "I have a good week's work in front of me; but you know I'll come the first afternoon I can make myself free and I'll let you know the day before, sweet!" She looked at me with tearful eyes and quivering lips: "love is its own torment!" she sighed while I dressed and got away quickly.

The truth was I was already satiated: her passion held nothing new in it: she had taught me all she could and had nothing more in her, I thought; while Kate was prettier and much younger and a virgin. Why shouldn't I confess it? It was Kate's virginity attracted me irresistibly: I pictured her legs to myself, her hips and thighs and her sex: she wouldn't have a harsh bush of hairs; already I felt the silken softness of her triangle: would it be brown or have strands of gold in it like her hair?

The next few days passed in reading the book Smith had lent me, especially "Das Kapital", the second book of which, with its frank exposure of the English factory system, was simply enthralling: I read some of Tacitus, too, and Xenophon with a crib and learned a page of Greek every day by heart, and whenever I felt tired of work, I laid siege to Kate. That is, I continued my plan of campaign: one day I called her brother into my room and told him true stories of buffalo hunting and of fighting with Indians; another day I talked theology with the father or drew the dear mother out to tell of her girlish days in Cornwall: "I never thought I'd come down to work like this in my old age; but then children take all and give little; I was no better as a girl; I remember"—and I got a scene of her brief courtship!

I had won the whole household long before I said a word to Kate beyond the merest courtesies. A week or so passed like this till one day I held them all after dinner while I told the story of our raid into Mexico. I took care, of course, that Kate was out of the room. Towards the end of my tale, Kate came in: at once I hastened to the end abruptly and after excusing myself, went into the garden.

Half an hour later I saw she was in my room tidying up; I took thought and then went up the outside steps. As soon as I saw her, I pretended surprise: "I beg your pardon", I said, "I'll just get a book and go at once; please don't let me disturb you!" and I pretended to look for the book.

She turned sharply and looked at me fixedly: "Why do you treat me like this?" she burst out, shaking with indignation.

"Like what?" I repeated, pretending surprise. "You know quite well", she went on angrily, hastily: "at first I thought it was chance, unintentional; now I know you mean it. Whenever you're talking or telling a story, as soon as I come into the room you stop and hurry away as if you hated me. Why? Why?" she cried with quivering lips, "What have I done to make you dislike me so?" and the tears gathered in her lovely eyes.

I felt the moment had come: I put my hands on her shoulders and looked with my whole soul into her eyes: "Did you never guess, Kate, that it might be love, not hate?" I asked.

"No, no!" she cried, the tears falling, "love doesn't act like that!"

"Fear to miss love does, I can assure you", I cried, "I thought at first that you disliked me and already I had begun to care for you", (my arms went round her waist and I drew her to me) "to love you and want you. Kiss me, dear" and at once she gave me her lips while my hand got busy on her breasts and then went down of itself to her sex. Suddenly she looked at me gaily, brightly while heaving a big sigh of relief. "I'm glad, glad!" she said, "if you only knew how hurt I was and how I tortured myself; one moment I was angry, then I was sad. Yesterday I made up my mind to speak, but today I said to myself, I'll just be obstinate and cold as he is and now"—and of her own accord she put her arms round my neck and kissed me, "you are a dear, dear! Anyway, I love you!"

"You mustn't give me those bird-pecks!" I exclaimed, "those are not kisses: I want your lips to open and cling to mine" and I kissed her while my tongue darted into her mouth and I stroked her sex gently. She flushed, but at first didn't understand, then suddenly she blushed rosy red as her lips grew hot and she fairly ran from the room.

I exulted: I knew I had won: I must be very quiet and reserved and the bird would come to the lure; I felt exultingly certain!

Meanwhile I spent nearly every morning with Smith: golden hours! Always, always before we parted, he showed me some new beauty or revealed some new truth: he seemed to me the most wonderful creature in this strange, sunlit world. I used to hang entranced on his eloquent lips! (Strange! I was sixty-five before I found such a hero-worshipper as I was to Smith, who was then only four or five and twenty!) He made me know all the Greek dramatists: Aeschylus, Sophocles and Euripides and put them for me in a truer light than English or German scholars have set them yet. He knew that Sophocles was the greatest and from his lips I learned every chorus in the Oedipus Rex and Colonos before I had completely mastered the Greek grammar; indeed, it was the supreme beauty of the literature that forced me to learn the language. In teaching me the choruses, he was careful to point out that it was possible to keep the measure and yet mark the accent too: in fact, he made classic Greek a living language to me, as living as English. And he would not let me neglect Latin: in the first year with him I knew poems of Catullus by heart, almost as well as I knew Swinburne. Thanks to Professor Smith I had no difficulty in entering the Junior Class at the University; in fact, after my first three or four months' work I was easily the first in the class, which included Ned Stevens, the brother of Smith's inamorata. I soon discovered that Smith was heels over head in love with Kate Stevens, shot through the heart as Mercutio would say, with a fair girl's blue eye!

And small wonder, for Kate was lovely; a little above middle height with slight, rounded figure and most attractive face: the oval, a thought long, rather than round, with dainty, perfect features, lit up by a pair of superlative grey-blue eyes, eyes by turns delightful and reflective and appealing that mirrored a really extraordinary intelligence. She was in the Senior Class and afterwards for years held the position of Professor of Greek in the University. I shall have something to say of her in a later volume of this history, for I met her again in New York nearly fifty years later. But in 1872 or '73, her brother Ned, a handsome lad of eighteen who was in my class, interested me more. The only other member of the Senior Class of that time was a fine fellow, Ned Bancroft, who later came to France with me to study.

At this time, curiously enough, Kate Stevens was by way of being engaged to Ned Bancroft; but already it was plain that she was in love with Smith and my outspoken admiration of Smith helped her, I hope, as I am sure it helped him, to a better mutual understanding. Bancroft accepted the situation with extraordinary self-sacrifice, losing neither Smith's nor Kate's friendship: I have seldom seen nobler self-abnegation: indeed his high-mindedness in this crisis was what first won my admiration and showed me his other fine qualities.

Almost in the beginning I had serious disquietude: every little while Smith was ill and had to keep his bed for a day or two. There was no explanation of this illness which puzzled me and caused me a certain anxiety.

One day in mid-winter there was a new development. Smith was in doubt how to act and confided in me. He had found Professor Kellogg, in whose house he lived, trying to kiss the pretty help, Rose, entirely against her will: Smith was emphatic on this point, the girl was struggling angrily to free herself, when by chance he interrupted them.

I relieved Smith's solemn gravity a little by roaring with laughter: the idea of an old Professor and clergyman trying to win a young girl by force filled me with amusement: "What a fool the man must be!" was my English judgment; Smith took the American high moral tone at first.

"Think of his disloyalty to his wife in the same house", he cried, "and then the scandal if the girl talked and she's sure to talk!"

"Sure not to talk", I corrected, "girls are afraid of the effect of such revelations; besides a word from you asking her to shield Mrs. Kellogg will ensure her silence."

"Oh, I cannot advise her", cried Smith, "I will not be mixed up in it: I told Kellogg at the time, I must leave the house, yet I don't know where to go! It's too disgraceful of him! His wife is really a dear woman!"

For the first time I became conscious of a rooted difference between Smith and myself: his high moral condemnation on very insufficient data seemed to me childish; but no doubt many of my readers will think my tolerance a proof of my shameless libertinism! However I jumped at the opportunity of talking to Rose on such a scabrous matter and at the same time solved Smith's difficulty by proposing that he should come and take room and board with the Gregorys—a great stroke of practical diplomacy on my part, or so it appeared to me; for thereby I did the Gregorys, Smith and myself an immense, an incalculable service. Smith jumped at the idea, asked me to see about it at once and let him know and then rang for Rose.

She came half scared, half angry, on the defensive, I could see; so I spoke first, smiling: "Oh Rose", I said, "Professor Smith has been telling me of your trouble: but you ought not to be angry: for you are so pretty that no wonder a man wants to kiss you: you must blame your lovely eyes and mouth"—

Rose laughed outright: she had come expecting reproof and found sweet flattery.

"There's only one thing, Rose", I went on: "the story would hurt Mrs. Kellogg if it got out and she's not very strong, so you must say nothing about it, for her sake: that's what Professor Smith wanted to say to you", I added. "I'm not likely to tell", cried Rose: "I'll soon forget all about it: but I guess

I'd better get another job: he's liable to try again though I gave him a good hard slap", and she laughed merrily.

"I'm so glad for Mrs. Kellogg's sake", said Smith gravely, "and if I can help you to get another place, please call upon me."

"I guess I'll have no difficulty", said Rose flippantly with a shade of dislike of the Professor's solemnity: "Mrs. Kellogg will give me a good character" and the healthy young minx grinned; "besides I'm not sure but I'll go stay home a spell: I'm fed up with working and would like a holiday, and mother wants me—"

"Where do you live, Rose?" I asked with a keen eye for future opportunities; "On the other side of the river", she replied, "next door to Elder Conklin's, where your brother boards—" she added smiling.

When Rose went I begged Smith to pack his boxes for I would get him the best room at the Gregorys' and I assured him it was really large and comfortable and would hold all his books, etc., and off I went to make my promise good. On the way I set myself to think how I could turn the kindness I was doing the Gregorys to the advantage of my love. I decided to make Kate a partner in the good deed, or at least a herald of the good news. So when I got home I rang the bell in my room and as I had hoped, Kate answered it. When I heard her footsteps I was shaking, hot with desire and now I wish to describe a feeling I then first began to notice in myself. I longed to take possession of the girl, so to speak, abruptly, ravish her in fact, or at least thrust both hands up her dress at once and feel her bottom and sex altogether; but already I knew enough to realise certainly that girls prefer gentle and courteous approaches: why? Of the fact I'm sure. So I said, "Come in, Kate!" gravely; "I want to ask you whether the best bedroom is still free and if you'd like Professor Smith to have it, if I could get him to come here?"

"I'm sure Mother would be delighted", she exclaimed.

"You see", I went on, "I'm trying to serve you all I can, yet you don't even kiss me of your own accord": she smiled and so I drew her to the bed and lifted her up on it: I saw her glance and answered it: "The door is shut, dear", and half lying on her I began kissing her passionately while my hand went up her clothes to her sex. To my delight she wore no drawers, but at first she kept her legs tight together, frowning: "love denies nothing, Kate", I said gravely; slowly she drew her legs apart, half pouting, half smiling, and let me caress her sex. When her love-juice came I kissed her and stopped: "It's dangerous here", I said, "that door you came in by is open; but I must see your lovely limbs" and I turned up her dress. I hadn't exaggerated; she had limbs like a Greek statue and her triangle of brown hair lay in little silky curls on her belly and then—the sweetest cunny in the world: I bent down and kissed it.

In a moment Kate was on her feet, smoothing her dress down: "What a boy you are", she exclaimed, "but that's partly why I love you; oh, I hope you'll love me half as much. Say you will, Sir, and I'll do anything you wish!"

"I will", I replied, "but oh, I'm glad you want love: can you come to me to night? I want a couple of hours with you uninterrupted." "This afternoon", she said, "I'll say I'm going for a walk and I'll come to you, dear! They are all resting then or out and I shan't be missed."

I could only wait and think. One thing was fixed in me, I must have her, make her mine before Smith came: he was altogether too fascinating, I thought, to be trusted with such a pretty girl; but I was afraid she would bleed and I did not want to hurt her this first time, so I went out and bought a syringe and a pot of cold cream which I put beside my bed.

Oh, how that dinner lagged! Mrs. Gregory thanked me warmly for my kindness to them all (which seemed to me pleasantly ironical!) and Mr. Gregory followed her lead; but at length everyone had finished and I went to my room to prepare. First I locked the outside door and drew down the blinds: then I studied the bed and turned it back and arranged a towel along the edge: happily the bed was just about the right height! Then I loosened my trowsers, unbuttoned the front and pulled up my shirt: a little later Kate put her lovely face in at the door and slipped inside. I shot the bolt and began kissing her: girls are strange mortals: she had taken off her corsets just as I had put a towel handy. I lifted up her clothes and touched her sex, caressing it gently while kissing her; in a moment or two her love-milk came.

I lifted her up on the bed, pushed down my trowsers, anointed my prick with the cream and then parting her legs and getting her to pull her knees up, I drew her bottom to the edge of the bed: she frowned at that but I explained quickly, "It may give you a little pain, at first, dear; and I want to give you as little as possible" and I slipped the head of my cock gently, slowly into her. Even greased her pussy was very tight and at the very entrance, I felt the obstacle, her maidenhead in the way: I lay on her and kissed her and let her or Mother Nature help me.

As soon as Kate found that I was leaving it to her, she pushed forward boldly and the obstacle yielded: "O—O" she cried and then pushed forward again roughly and my organ went in her to the hilt and her clitoris must have felt my belly. Resolutely I refrained from thrusting or withdrawing for a minute or two and then drew out slowly to her lips and as I pushed Tommy gently in again, she leaned up and kissed me passionately. Slowly with extremest care I governed myself and pushed in and out with long, slow thrusts though

I longed, longed to plunge it in hard and quicken the strokes as much as possible; but I knew from Mrs. Mayhew that the long, gentle thrusts and slow withdrawals were the aptest to excite a woman's passion and I was determined to win Kate.

In two or three minutes she had again let down a flow of love-juice or so I believed and I kept right on with the love-game, knowing that the first experience is never forgotten by a girl and resolved to keep on to dinner-time if necessary to make her first love-joust ever memorable to her. Kate lasted longer than Mrs. Mayhew: I came ever so many times, passing ever more slowly from orgasm to orgasm before she began to move to me; but at length her breath began to get shorter and shorter and she held me to her violently, moving her pussy the while up and down harshly against my manroot. Suddenly she relaxed and fell back: there was no hysteria; but plainly I could feel the mouth of her womb fasten on my cock as if to suck it. That excited me fiercely and for the first time I indulged in quick, hard thrusts till a spasm of intensest pleasure shook me and my seed spirted or seemed to spirt for the sixth or seventh time.

When I had finished kissing and praising my lovely partner and drew away, I was horrified: the bed was a sheet of blood and some had gone on my pants: Kate's thighs and legs even were all incarnadined, making the lovely ivory white of her skin, one red. You may imagine how softly I used the towel on her legs and sex before I showed her the results of our love-passage. To my astonishment she was unaffected: "You must take the sheet away and burn it", she said, "or drop it in the river: I guess it won't be the first."

"Did it hurt very much", I asked.

"At first a good deal", she replied, "but soon the pleasure overpowered the smart and I would not even forget the pain: I love you so: I am not even afraid of consequences with you: I trust you absolutely and love to trust you and run whatever risks you wish."

"You darling!" I cried, "I don't believe there will be any consequences; but I want you to go to the basin and use this syringe: I'll tell you why afterwards." At once she went over to the basin: "I feel funny, weak", she said, "as if I were—I can't describe it—shaky on my legs. I'm glad now I don't wear drawers in summer: they'd get wet." Her ablutions completed and the sheet withdrawn and done up in paper, I shot back the bolt and we began our talk. I found her intelligent and kindly but ignorant and ill-read; still she was not prejudiced and was eager to know all about babies and how they were made. I told her what I had told Mrs. Mayhew and something more: how my seed was composed of tens of thousands of infinitesimal tadpole-shaped animalculae—Already in her vagina and womb these infinitely little things had a race: they could move nearly an inch in an hour and the strongest and quickest got up first to where her egg was waiting in the middle of her womb. My little tadpole, the first to arrive, thrust his head into her egg and thus having accomplished his work of impregnation, perished, love and death being twins.

The curious thing was that this indescribably small tadpole should be able to transmit all the qualities of all his progenitors in certain proportions; no such miracle was ever imagined by any religious teacher. More curious still the living foetus in the womb passes in nine months through all the chief changes that the human race has gone through in countless aeons of time in its progress from the tadpole to the man. Till the fifth month the foetus is practically a four-legged animal.

I told her that it was accepted today that the weeks occupied in the womb in any metamorphosis corresponded exactly to the ages it occupied in reality. Thus it was upright, a two-legged animal, ape and then man in the womb for the last three months and this corresponded nearly to one third of man's whole existence on this earth. Kate listened enthralled, I thought, till she asked me suddenly:

"But what makes one child a boy and another a girl?"

"The nearest we've come to a law on the matter", I said, "is contained in the so-called law of contraries: that is, if the man is stronger than the woman, the children will be mostly girls; if the woman is greatly younger or stronger, the progeny will be chiefly boys. This bears out the old English proverb: "Any weakling can make a boy, it takes a man to make a girl.""

Kate laughed and just then a knock came to the door. "Come in!" I cried and the colored maid came in with a note: "a lady's just been and left it", said Jenny. I saw it was from Mrs. Mayhew, so I crammed it into my pocket saying regretfully: "I must answer it soon." Kate excused herself and after a long, long kiss went to prepare supper while I read Mrs. Mayhew's note, which was short if not exactly sweet.

"Eight days and no Frank, and no news; you cannot want to kill me: come today if possible. Lorna."

I replied at once, saying I would come on the morrow, that I was installing Smith in my boardinghouse and was so busy I didn't know where to turn, but would be with her sure on the morrow and I signed "Your Frank."

That afternoon at five o'clock Smith came and I helped to arrange his books and make him comfy.

MY FIRST VENUS.

Venus toute entiére à sa proie attachèe.

Chapter XI.

I meant to write nothing but the truth in these pages; yet now I'm conscious that my memory has played a trick on me: it is an artist in what painters call foreshortening: events, that is, which took months to happen, it crushes together into days, passing, so to speak, from mountain top to mountain top of feeling, and so the effect of passion is heightened by the partial elimination of time. I can do nothing more than warn my readers that in reality some of the love-passages I shall describe were separated by weeks and sometimes by months, that the nuggets of gold were occasional "finds" in a desert.

After all, it cannot matter to my "gentle readers" and my good readers will have already divined the fact, that when you crush eighteen years into nine chapters, you must leave out all sorts of minor happenings while recording chiefly the important—fortunately these carry the message.

It was with my knowledge as with my passions: day after day I worked feverishly: whenever I met a passage such as the building of the bridge in Caesar, I refused to burden my memory with the dozens of new words because I thought, and still think, Latin comparatively unimportant: the nearest to a great man the Latins ever produced being Tacitus or Lucretius. No sensible person would take the trouble to master a language in order to gain acquaintance with the second-rate. But new words in Greek were precious to me like new words in English and I used to memorize every passage studded with them save choruses like that of the birds in Aristophanes, where he names birds unfamiliar to me in life.

Smith, I found, knew all such words in both languages. I asked him one day and he admitted that he had read everything in ancient Greek, following the example of Hermann, the famous German scholar, and believed he knew almost every word.

I did not desire any such pedantic perfection. I make no pretension to scholarship of any sort and indeed learning of any kind leaves me indifferent unless it leads to a fuller understanding of beauty or that widening of the spirit by sympathy that is another name for wisdom. But what I wish to emphasize here is that in the first year with Smith I learned by heart dozens of choruses from the Greek dramatists and the whole of the "Apologia" and "Crito" of Plato, having guessed then and still believe that the "Crito" is a model short story, more important than any of even Plato's speculations. Plato and Sophocles! it was worth while spending five years of hard labor to enter into their intimacy and make them sister-spirits of one's soul. Didn't Sophocles give me Antigone, the prototype of the new woman for all time, in her sacred rebellion against hindering laws and thwarting conventions, the eternal model of that dauntless assertion of love that is beyond and above sex, the very heart of the Divine!

And the Socrates of Plato led me to that high place where man becomes God, having learned obedience to law and the cheerful acceptance of Death; but even there I needed Antigone, the twin sister of Bazaroff, at least as much, realising intuitively that my life-work, too, would be chiefly in revolt and that the punishment Socrates suffered and Antigone dared, would almost certainly be mine; for I was fated to meet worse opponents; after all, Creon was only stupid whereas Sir Thomas Horridge was malevolent to boot and Woodrow Wilson unspeakable!

Again I am outrunning my story by half a century!

But in what I have written of Sophocles and Plato the reader will divine, I hope, my intense love and admiration for Smith who led me, as Vergil led Dante, into the ideal world that surrounds our earth as with illimitable spaces of purple sky, wind-swept and star-sown!

If I could tell what Smith's daily companionship now did for me, I would hardly need to write this book; for like all I have written, some of the best of it belongs as much to him as to me. In his presence for the first year and a half, I was merely a sponge, absorbing now this truth, now that, hardly conscious of an original impulse. Yet all the time, too, as will be seen, I was advising him and helping him from my knowledge of life. Our relation was really rather like that of a small, practical husband with some wise and infinitely learned Aspasia! I want to say here in contempt of probability that in all our years of intimacy, living together for over three years side by side, I never found a fault in him of character or of sympathy, save the one that drew him to his death.

Now I must leave him for the moment and turn again to Mrs. Mayhew. Of course I went to her that next afternoon even before three. She met me without a word so gravely that I did not even kiss her: but began explaining what Smith was to me and how I could not do enough for him who was everything to my mind as she was (God help me!) to my heart and body, and I kissed her cold lips while she shook her head half sadly.

"We have a sixth sense, we women, when we are in love", she began: "I feel a new influence in you; I scent danger in the air you bring with you: don't ask me to explain: I can't; but my heart is heavy and cold as death.... If you leave me, there'll be a catastrophe: the fall from such a height of happiness must be fatal.... If you can feel pleasure away from me, you no longer love me. I feel none except in having you, seeing you, thinking of you—none. Oh! why can't you love like a woman loves, No! like I love: it would be heaven; for you and you alone satisfy the insatiable; you leave me bathed in bliss, sighing with satisfaction, happy as the Queen of Heaven!"

"I have much to tell you, new things to say", I began in haste.

"Come upstairs," I broke in interrupting myself "I want you as you are now, with the color in your cheeks, the light in your eyes, the vibration in your voice, come!"

And she came like a sad sybil. "Who gave you the tact?" she began while we were undressing, "the tact to praise always?" I seized her and stood naked against her body to body: "What new thing have you to tell me?" I asked, lifting her into the bed and getting in beside her, cuddling up to her warmer body.

"There's always something new in my love," she cried, cupping my face with her slim hands and taking my lips with hers.

"Oh, how I desired you yesternoon, for I took the letter to your house myself and I heard you talking in your room perhaps with Smith", she added, sounding my eyes with hers; "I'm longing to believe it; but when I heard your voice, or imagined I did, I felt the lips of my sex open and shut and then it began to burn and itch intolerably. I was on the point of going in to you; but instead, turned and hurried away, raging at you and at myself—."

"I will not let you even talk such treason," I cried, separating her soft thighs, as I spoke, and sliding between them. In a moment my sex was in her and we were one body, while I drew it out slowly and then pushed it in again, her naked body straining to mine.

"Oh" she cried, "as you draw out, my heart follows your sex in fear of losing it and as you push in again, it opens wide in ecstasy and wants you all, all—" and she kissed me with hot lips.

"Here is something new," she exclaimed, "food for your vanity from my love! Mad as you make me with your love-thrusts, for at one moment I am hot and dry with desire, the next wet with passion, bathed in love, I could live with you all my life without having you, if you wished it, or if it would do you good. Do you believe me?"

"Yes," I replied, continuing the love-game; but occasionally withdrawing to rub her clitoris with my sex and then slowly burying him in her cunt again to the hilt.

"We women have no souls but love," she said faintly, her eyes dying as she spoke:

"I torture myself to think of some new pleasure for you, and yet you'll leave me, I feel you will, for some silly girl who can't feel a tithe of what I feel or give you what I give—." She began here to breathe quickly: "I've been thinking how to give you more pleasure; let me try. Your seed, darling, is dear to me: I don't want it in my sex; I want to feel you thrill and so I want your sex in my mouth, I want to drink your essence and I will—" and suiting the action to the word she slipped down in the bed and took my sex in her mouth and began rubbing it up and down till my seed spirted in long jets, filling her mouth while she swallowed it greedily.

"Now do I love you, Sir!" she exclaimed, drawing herself up on me again and nestling against me: "wait till some girl does that to you and you'll know she loves you to distraction or better still to self-destruction."

"Why do you talk of any other girl!" I chided her, "I don't imagine you going with any other man, why should you torment yourself just as causelessly?"

She shook her head: "My fears are prophetic", she sighed, "I'm willing to believe it hasn't happened yet though—Ah God, the torturing thought! the mere dread of your going with another drives me crazy; I could kill her, the bitch: why doesn't she get a man of her own? How dare she even look at you?" and she clasped me tightly to her. Nothing loath, I pushed my sex into her again and began the slow movement that excited her so quickly and me so gradually for even while using all my skill to give her the utmost pleasure, I could not help comparing and I realised surely enough that Kate's pussy was smaller and firmer and gave me infinitely more pleasure; still I kept on for her delight. And now again she began to pant and choke and as I continued ploughing her body and touching her womb with every slow thrust she began to cry inarticulately with little short cries growing higher in intensity till suddenly she squealed like a shot rabbit and then shrieked with laughter, breaking down in a storm of sighs and sobs and floods of tears.

As usual, her intensity chilled me a little; for her paroxysm aroused no corresponding heat in me, tending even to check my pleasure by the funny, irregular movements she made!

Suddenly I heard steps going away from the door, light stealing steps: who could it be! The servant? or—?

Lorna had heard them too, and though still panting and swallowing convulsively, she listened intently while her great eyes wandered in thought. I knew I could leave the riddle to her: it was my task to reassure and caress her.

I got up and went over to the open window for a breath of air and suddenly I saw Lily run quickly across the grass and disappear in the next house: so she was the listener! When I recalled Lorna's gasping cries, I smiled to myself.

If Lily tried to explain them to herself, she would have an uneasy hour, I guessed.

When Lorna had dressed, and she dressed quickly, and went downstairs hastily to convince herself, I think, that her darky had not spied on her, I waited in the sitting-room: I must warn Lorna that my "studies" would only allow me to give one day a week to our pleasures.

"Oh!" she cried, turning pale as I explained, "didn't I know it!"

"But Lorna," I pleaded, "didn't you say you could do without me altogether if 'twas for my good!"

"No, no, no! a thousand times no!" she cried, "I said if you were with me always, I could do without passion; but this starvation fare once a week! Go, go!" she cried, "or I'll say something I'll regret. Go!" and she pushed me out of the door and thinking it better in view of the future, I went.

The truth is, I was glad to get away: novelty is the soul of passion. There's an old English proverb: "fresh cunt, fresh courage." On my way home I thought oftener of the slim, dark figure of Lily than of the woman every hill and valley of whose body was now familiar to me, whereas Lily with her narrow hips and straight flanks must have a tiny sex I thought;—"D—n Lily" and I hastened to Smith.

We went down to supper together and I introduced Smith to Kate: they were just polite; but when she turned to me she scanned me curiously, her brows lifting in a gesture of "I know what I know" which was to become familiar to me in the sequel.

After supper I had a long talk with Smith in his room, a heart to heart talk which altered our relations.

I have already mentioned that Smith got ill every fortnight or so. I had no inkling of the cause, no notion of the scope of the malady. This evening he grew reminiscent and told me everything.

He had thought himself very strong, it appeared, till he went to Athens to study. There he worked prodigiously and almost at the beginning of his stay came to know a Greek girl of a good class who talked Greek with him and finally gave herself to him passionately. Being full of youthful vigor always quickened by vivid imaginings, he told me that he usually came the first time almost as soon as he entered and that in order to give his partner pleasure, he had to come two or three times and this drained and exhausted him. He admitted that he had abandoned himself to this fierce love-play day after day in and out of season. When he returned to the United States, he tried to put his Greek girl out of his head; but in spite of all he could do, he had love-dreams that came to an orgasm and ended in emissions of seed about once a fortnight. And after a year or so these fortnightly emissions gave him intense pains in the small of his back which lasted some twenty-four hours, evidently till some more seed had been secreted. I could not imagine how a fortnightly emission could weaken and distress a young man of Smith's vigor and health; but as soon as I had witnessed his suffering I set my wits to work and told him of the trick by which I had brought my wet-dreams to an end in the English school.

Smith at once consented to try my remedy and as the fortnight was about up, I went at once in search of whipcord, and tied up his unruly member for him night after night. For some days the remedy worked, then he went out and spent the afternoon and night at Judge Stevens' and he was ill again. Of course, there had been no connection: indeed, in my opinion, it would have been much better for Smith if there had been, but the propinquity of the girl he loved and, of course, the kissings that are always allowed to engaged couples by American custom, took place unchecked and when he went to sleep, his dreaming ended in an orgasm. The worst of it was that my remedy having prevented his dreaming from reaching a climax for eighteen or twenty days, he dreamed a second time and had a second wet dream, which brought him to misery and even intenser pain than usual.

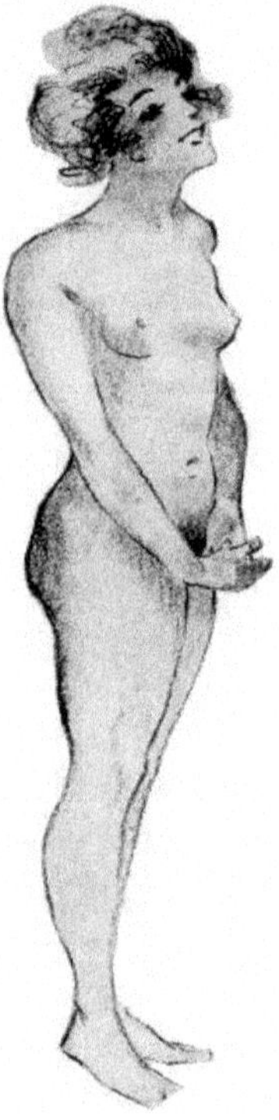

I combatted the evil with all the wit I possessed. I got Ned Stevens to lend the Professor a horse; I had Blue Devil out and we went riding two or three times a week. I got boxing gloves too and soon either Ned or I had a bout with Smith every day: gradually these exercises improved his general health; and when I could tie on the whipcord every night for a month or two, he put on weight and gained strength surprisingly.

The worst of it was that this improvement in health always led to a day or two spent with his betrothed, which undid all the good. I advised him to marry and then control himself rigorously; but he wanted to get well first and be his vigorous self again. I did all I knew to help him but for a long time I had no suspicion that an occasional wet-dream could have serious consequences. We used to make fun of them as schoolboys: how could I imagine—but as it is the finest, most highly strung natures that are most apt to suffer in this way, I will tell what happened step by step: suffice it to say here that he was in better health when staying with me at the Gregory's than he had been before and I continually hoped for a permanent improvement.

After our talk that first night in Gregory's, I went downstairs to the dining-room, hoping to find Kate alone: I was lucky: she had persuaded her mother, who was tired, to go to bed and was just finishing her tidying up.

"I want you so, Kate," I said, trying to kiss her: she drew her head aside: "That's why you've kept away all afternoon" I suppose; and she looked at me with sidelong glance. An inspiration came to me: "Kate", I exclaimed, "I had to be fitted for my new clothes!" "Forgive me", she cried at once, that excuse being valid: "I thought, I feared—oh I'm suspicious without reason, I know, am jealous without cause, there! I confess!" and the great hazel eyes turned on me full of love.

I played with her breasts, whispering "When am I to see you naked, Kate? I want to; when?" "You've seen most of me!" and she laughed joyously!

"All right," I said, turning away, "if you are resolved to make fun of me and be mean to me—"

"Mean to you!" she cried, catching me and swinging me round, "I could easier be mean to myself. I'm glad you want to see me, glad and proud, and tonight, if you'll leave your door open, I'll come to you: mean, oh—'and she gave her soul in a kiss.

"Isn't it risky?" I asked.

"I tried the stairs this afternoon," she glowed, "they don't creak: no one will hear, so don't sleep or I'll surprise you"—By way of sealing the compact, I put my hand up her clothes and caressed her sex; it was hot and soon opened to me.

"There now, Sir, go!" she smiled, "or you'll make me very naughty and I have a lot to do!"

"How do you mean 'naughty'," I said, "tell me what you feel? please!"

"I feel my heart beating", she said, "and, and—oh! wait till tonight and I'll try to tell you, dear!" and she pushed me out of the door.

For the first time in my life I notice here that the writer's art is not only inferior to reality in keenness of sensation and emotion; but also more same, monotonous even, because incapable of showing the tiny, yet ineffable differences of the same feeling which difference of personality brings with it. I seem to be repeating myself in describing Kate's love after Mrs. Mayhew's, making the girl's feelings a fainter replica of the woman's. In reality the two were completely different. Mrs. Mayhew's feelings long repressed flamed with the heat of an afternoon in July or August; while in Kate's one felt the freshness and cool of a summer morning, shot through with the suggestion of heat to come. And this comparison even is inept because it leaves out of the account, the effect of Kate's beauty, the great hazel eyes, the rosied skin, the superb figure. Besides there was a glamour of the spirit about Kate: Lorna Mayhew would never give me a new note that didn't spring from passion; in Kate I felt a spiritual personality and the thrill of undeveloped possibilities. And still using my utmost skill, I haven't shown my reader the enormous superiority of the girl and her more unselfish love. But I haven't finished yet.

Smith had given me "The Mill on the Floss" to read; I had never tried George Eliot before and I found that this book almost deserved Smith's praise. I had read till about one o'clock when my heart heard her; or was it some thrill of expectance? The next moment my door opened and she came in with the mane of hair about her shoulders and a long dressing gown reaching to her stockinged feet. I got up like a flash; but she had already closed the door and bolted it; I drew her to the bed and stopped her from throwing off the dressing-gown: "let me take off your stockings first", I whispered, "I want you all imprinted on me!"

The next moment, she stood there naked, the flickering flame of the candle throwing quaint arabesques of light and shade on her beautiful ivory body: I gazed and gazed: from the navel down she was perfect; I turned her round and the back too, the bottom even was faultless though large; but alas! the breasts were far too big for beauty, too soft to excite! I must think only of the bold curve of her hips, I reflected, the splendor of the firm thighs, the flesh of which had the hard outline of marble and her—sex? I put her on the bed and opened her thighs: her pussy was ideally perfect.

At once I wanted to get into her; but she pleaded: "please, dear, come into bed: I'm cold and want you." So in I got and began kissing her.

Soon she grew warm and I pulled off my nightshirt and my middle finger was caressing her sex that opened quickly: "E—E!" she said drawing in her breath quickly: "it still hurts." I put my sex gently against hers, moving it up and down slowly till she drew up her knees to let me in; but as soon as the head entered, her face puckered a little with pain and as I had had a long afternoon, I was the more inclined to forbear and accordingly I drew away and took place beside her:

"I cannot bear to hurt you," I said, "love's pleasure must be mutual."

"You're sweet!" she whispered, "I'm glad you stopped; for it shows you really care for me and not just for the pleasure!" and she kissed me lovingly.

"Kate, reward me," I said, "by telling me just what you felt when I first had you" and I put her hand on my hot stiff sex to encourage her.

"It's impossible," she said, flushing a little, "there was such a throng of new feelings; why, this evening waiting in bed for the time to pass and thinking of you, I felt a strange prickling sensation in the inside of my thighs that I never felt before and now"—and she hid her glowing face against my neck, "I feel it again!"

"Love is funny, isn't it?" she whispered the next moment: "now the pricking sensation is gone and the front part of my sex burns and itches, Oh! I must touch it!"

"Let me," I cried, and in a moment I was on her, working my organ up and down on her clitoris, the porch, so to speak, of Love's temple. A little later she herself sucked the head into her hot, dry pussy and then closed her legs as if in pain to stop me going further; but I began to rub my sex up and down on her tickler, letting it slide right in, every now and then, till she panted and her love-juice came and my weapon sheathed itself in her naturally. I soon began the very slow and gentle in-and-out movements which increased her excitement steadily while giving her more and more pleasure, till I came and immediately she lifted my chest up from her breasts with both hands and showed me her glowing face. "Stop, boy," she gasped, "please: my heart's fluttering so! I came too, you know, just with you" and indeed I felt her trembling all over convulsively.

I drew out and for safety's sake got her to use the syringe, having already explained its efficacy to her; she was adorably awkward and when she had finished I took her to bed again and held her to me, kissing her. "So you really love me, Kate!"

"Really," she said, "you don't know how much!"

"I'll try never to suspect anything or be jealous again," she went on, "it's a hateful feeling, isn't it? But I want to see your class-room: would you take me up once to the University?"

"Why, of course", I cried, "I should be only too glad; I'll take you tomorrow afternoon, or better still", I added, "come up the hill at four o'clock and I'll meet you at the entrance."

And so it was settled and Kate went back to her room as noiselessly as she had come.

The next afternoon I found her waiting in the University Hall ten minutes before the hour; for our lectures beginning at the hour always stopped after forty-five minutes to give us time to be punctual at any other class-room. After showing her everything of interest, we walked home together laughing and talking, when, a hundred yards from Mrs. Mayhew's, we met that lady, face to face. I don't know how I looked, for being a little shortsighted I hadn't recognized her till she was within ten yards of me; but her glance pierced me. She bowed with a look that took us both in, I lifted my hat and we passed on.

"Who's that?" exclaimed Kate, "what a strange look she gave us!"

"She's the wife of a gambler," I replied as indifferently as I could, "he gives me work now and then" I went on, strangely forecasting the future. Kate looked at me probing, then: "I don't mind; but I'm glad she's quite old!"

"As old as both of us put together!" I added traitorously, and we went on.

These love-passages with Mrs. Mayhew and Kate, plus my lessons and my talks with Smith, fairly represent my life's happenings for this whole year from seventeen to eighteen, with this solitary qualification that my afternoons with Lorna became less and less agreeable to me. But now I must relate happenings that again affected my life.

I hadn't been four months with the Gregorys when Kate told me that my brother Willie had ceased to pay my board for more than a fortnight; she added sweetly:

"It doesn't matter, dear, but I thought you ought to know and I'd hate any one to hurt you, so I took it on myself to tell you." I kissed her, said it was sweet of her, and went to find Willie; he made excuses voluble but not convincing and ended up by giving me a cheque while begging me to tell Mrs. Gregory that he, too, would come and board with her.

The incident set me thinking. I made Kate promise to tell me if he ever failed again to pay what was due and I used the happening to excuse myself to Lorna. I went to see her and told her that I must think at once of earning my living. I had still some five hundred dollars left but I wanted to be beforehand with need: besides it gave me a good excuse for not visiting her even weekly. "I must work!" I kept repeating though I was ashamed of the lie.

"Don't whip me, dear!" she pleaded; "my impotence to help you is painful enough; give me time to think. I know Mayhew is quite well off: give me a day or two, but come to me when you can. You see, I've no pride where you are concerned: I just beg like a dog for kind treatment for my love's sake. I wouldn't have believed that I could be so transformed. I was always so proud: my husband calls me 'proud and cold', me cold! It's true I shiver when I hear your voice, but it's the shivering of fever. When you came in just now unexpectedly and kissed me, waves of heat swept over me: my womb moved inside me. I never felt that till I had loved you and now, of course, my sex burns—I wish I were cold: a cold woman could rule the world—

"But no! I wouldn't change. Just as I never wished to be a man, never; though other girls used to say they would like to change their sex; I, never! And since I've been married, less than ever. What's a man? His love is over before ours begins—"

"Really?" I broke in grinning.

"Not you, my beloved!" she cried, "oh, not you; but then you are more than man! Come, don't let us waste time in talk. Now I have you, take me to our Heaven. I'm ready, 'ripe-ready' is your word: I go to our bed as to an altar. If I'm only to have you even less than once a week, don't come again for ten days: I shall be well again then and you can surely come to me a few days running: I want to reach the heights and hug the illusion, cramming one hot week with bliss and then death for a fortnight. What rags we women are! Come, dear, I will be your sheath and you shall be the sword and drive right into me—But I'll help you", she cried suddenly: "Was it that girl told you, you owed money for food? (I nodded and she glowed.) Oh, I'll help, never fear! I never liked that girl: she's brazen and conceited and—Oh! Why did you walk with her?"

"She wanted to see the University", I said, "and I could not well refuse her." "Oh, pay her" she cried, "but don't walk with her. She's a common thing, fancy her mentioning money to you, my dear!"

That same evening I got a note from Lorna, saying her husband wanted to see me.

I met the little man in the sitting-room and he proposed that I should come to his rooms every evening after supper and sit in a chair near the door reading; but with a Colt's revolver handy so that no one could rob him and get away with the plunder.

"I'd feel safer", he ended up, "and my wife tells me you're a sure shot and used to a wild life: what do you say? I'd give you sixty dollars a month and more than half the time you'd be free before midnight."

"It's very kind of you", I exclaimed with hot cheeks, "and very kind of Mrs. Mayhew too: I'll do it and I beg you to believe that no one will bother you and get away with a whole skin", and so it was settled.

Aren't women wonderful! In half a day she had solved my difficulty and I found the hours spent in Mayhew's gambling rooms were more valuable than I had dreamed. The average man reveals himself in gaming more than in love or drink and I was astonished to discover that many of the so-called best citizens had a flutter with Mayhew from time to time. I don't believe they had a fair deal, he won too constantly for that; but it was none of my business so long as the clients accepted the results: and he often showed kindness by giving back a few dollars after he had skinned a man of all he possessed.

Naturally the fact that I was working with her husband threw me more into Mrs. Mayhew's society: twice or so a week I had to spend the afternoon with her, and the constraint irked me. Kate, too, objected to my visits: she had too much pride to speak openly but one day she had seen me go in to Mrs. Mayhew's and I think divined the rest; for at first she was cold to me and drew away even from my kisses: "you've chilled me", she cried, "I don't think I shall ever love you again entirely." But when I got into her and really excited her, she suddenly kissed me fervently and her glorious eyes had heavy tears in them. "Why do you cry, dear?" I asked. "Because I cannot make you mine as I am all yours!" she cried. "Oh!" she went on, clutching me to her, "I think the pleasure is increased by the dreadful fear—and the hate—oh, love me and me only, love mine!" Of course, I promised fidelity; but I was surprised to feel that my desire for Kate, too, was beginning to cool.

The arrangement with the Mayhews came to an unexpected and untimely end. Mayhew now and then had a tussle with another gambler and after I had been with him about three months, a gambler from Denver had a great contest with him and afterwards proposed that they should join forces and Mayhew should come to Denver. "More money to be made there in a week", he declared, "than in Lawrence in a month." Finally he persuaded Mayhew, who was wise enough to say nothing to his wife till the whole arrangement was fixed. She raved but could do nothing save give in, and so we had to part. Mayhew gave me one hundred dollars as a bonus, and Lorna one unforgettable, astonishing afternoon which I must now try to describe.

I did not go near the Mayhews' the day after his gift, leaving Lorna to suppose that I looked upon everything as ended. But the day after that I got a word from her, an imperious:

"Come at once, I must see you!"

Of course I went though reluctantly.

As soon as I entered the room she rose from the sofa and came to me: "if I get you work in Denver, will you come out?"

"How could I?" I asked in absolute astonishment, "you know I'm bound here to the University and then I want to go into a law-office as well: besides I could not leave Smith: I've never known such a teacher: I don't believe his equal can be found anywhere."

She nodded her head: "I see", she sighed, "I suppose it's impossible; but I must see you", she cried, "if I haven't the hope, what do I say! the certainty of seeing you again, I shan't go. I'd rather kill myself! I'll be a servant and stay with you, my darling, and take care of you! I don't care what I do so long as we are together: I'm nearly crazed with fear that I shall lose you."

"It's all a question of money", I said quietly, for the idea of her staying behind scared me stiff: "if I can earn money, I'd love to go to Denver in my holidays. It must be gorgeous there in summer six thousand odd feet above sea-level: I'd delight in it."

"If I send you the money, you'll come?" she asked briefly.

I made a face: "I can't take money from—a love", (I said "love" instead of "woman": it was not so ugly) I went on, "but Smith says he can get me work and I have still a little: I'll come in the holidays."

"Holy days they'll be to me!" she said solemnly, and then with quick change of mood, "I'll make a beautiful room for our love in Denver; but you must come for Christmas, I could not wait till midsummer: oh, how I shall ache for you—ache!"

"Come upstairs", I coaxed and she came, and we went to bed: I found her mad with desire; but after I had brought her in an hour to hysteria and she lay in my arms crying, she suddenly said: "he promised to come home early this afternoon and I said I'd have a surprise for him. When he finds us together like this, it'll be a surprise, won't it?"

"But you're mad!" I cried, getting out of bed in a flash, "I shall never be able to visit you in Denver if we have a row here!"

"That's true", she said as if in a dream, "that's true: it's a pity: I'd love to have seen his foolish face stretched to wonder; but you're right. Hurry!" she cried and was out of the room in a twinkling.

When she returned, I was dressed.

"Go downstairs and wait for me", she commanded, "on our sofa. If he knocks, open the door to him; that'll be a surprise, though not so great a one as I had planned", she added, laughing shrilly.

"Are you going without kissing me?" she cried when I was at the door, "Well, go, it's all right, go! for if I felt your lips again, I might keep you."

I went downstairs and in a few moments she followed me. "I can't bear you to go!" she cried, "how partings hurt!" she whispered. "Why should we part again, love mine?" and she looked at me with rapt eyes.

"This life holds nothing worth having but love; let us make love deathless, you and I, going together to death. What do we lose? Nothing! This world is an empty shell! Come with me, love, and we'll meet Death together!"

"Oh, I want to do such a lot of things first", I exclaimed, "Death's empire is eternal; but this brief taste of life, the adventure of it, the change of it, the huge possibilities of it beckon me—I can't leave it." "The change!" she cried with dilating nostrils while her eyes darkened, "the change!"

"You are determined to misunderstand me," I cried, "is not every day a change?"

"I am weary", she cried, "and beaten: I can only beg you not to forget your promise to come—ah!" and she caught and kissed me on the mouth: "I shall die with your name on my lips", she said, and turned to bury her face in the sofa cushion. I went: what else was there to do?

I saw them off at the station: Lorna had made me promise to write often, and swore she would write every day and she did send me short notes daily for a fortnight: then came gaps ever lengthening: "Denver society was pleasant and a Mr. Wilson, a student, was assiduous: he comes every day", she wrote. Excuses finally, little hasty notes, and in two months her letters were formal, cold; in three months they had ceased altogether.

The break did not surprise me: I had taught her that youth was the first requisite in a lover for a woman of her type: she had doubtless put my precepts into practice: Mr. Wilson was probably as near the ideal as I was and very much nearer to hand.

The passions of the senses demand propinquity and satisfaction and nothing is more forgetful than pleasures of the flesh. If Mrs. Mayhew had given me little, I had given her even less of my better self.

HARD TIMES AND NEW LOVES

Chapter XII.

So far I had had more good fortune than falls to the lot of most youths starting in life; now I was to taste ill-luck and be tried as with fire. I had been so taken up with my own concerns that I had hardly given a thought to public affairs; now I was forced to take a wider view.

One day Kate told me that Willie was heavily in arrears: he had gone back to Deacon Conkling's to live on the other side of the Kaw River and I had naturally supposed that he had paid up everything before leaving. Now I found that he owed the Gregorys sixty dollars on his own account and more than that on mine.

I went across to him really enraged. If he had warned me, I should not have minded so much; but to leave the Gregorys to tell me, made me positively dislike him and I did not know then the full extent of his selfishness. Years later my sister told me that he had written time and again to my father and got money from him, alleging that it was for me and that I was studying and couldn't earn anything: "Willie kept us poor, Frank", she said, and I could only bow my head; but if I had known this fact at the time, it would have changed all my relations with Willie.

As it was, I found him in the depths. Carried away by his optimism, he had bought real estate in 1871 and 1872, mortgaged it for more than he gave and as the boom continued, he had repeated this game time and again till on paper and in paper he reckoned he had made a hundred thousand dollars. This he had told me and I was glad of it for his sake, unfeignedly glad.

It was easy to see that the boom and inflation period had been based at first on the extraordinary growth of the country through the immigration and trade that had followed the Civil War. But the Franco-German war had wasted wealth prodigiously, deranged trade too, and diverted commerce into new channels. France and then England first felt the shock: London had to call in monies lent to American railways and other enterprises. Bit by bit even American optimism was overcome for immigration in 1871 and 1872 fell off greatly and the foreign calls for cash exhausted our banks. The crash came in 1873; nothing like it was seen again in these States till the slump of 1907 which led to the founding of the Federal Reserve Bank.

Willie's fortune melted almost in a moment: this mortgage and that, had to be met and could only be met by forced sales with no buyers except at minimum values. When I talked to him, he was almost in despair; no money: no property: all lost; the product of three years' hard work and successful speculation all swept away. Could I help him? If not, he was ruined. He told me then he had drawn all he could from my father: naturally I promised to help him; but first I had to pay the Gregorys and to my astonishment he begged me to let him have the money instead. "Mrs. Gregory and all of 'em like you", he pleaded, "they can wait, I cannot; I know of a purchase that could be made that would make me rich again!"

I realised then that he was selfish through and through, conscienceless in egotistic greed. I gave up my faint hope that he would ever repay me: henceforth he was a stranger to me and one that I did not even respect, though he had some fine, ingratiating qualities.

I left him to walk across the river and in a few blocks met Rose. She looked prettier than ever and I turned and walked with her, praising her beauty to the skies and indeed she deserved it; short green sleeves, I remember, set off her exquisite, plump, white arms. I promised her some books and made her say she would read them; indeed I was astonished by the warmth of her gratitude: she told me it was sweet of me, gave me her eyes and we parted the best of friends, with just a hint of warmer relationship in the future.

That evening I paid the Gregorys, Willie's debt and my own and—did not send him the balance of what I possessed as I had promised; but instead, a letter telling him I had preferred to cancel his debt to the Gregorys.

Next day he came and assured me he had promised monies on the strength of my promise, had bought a hundred crates, too, of chickens to ship to Denver and had already an offer from the Mayor of Denver at double what he had given. I read the letters and wire he showed me and let him have four hundred dollars, which drained me and kept me poor for months; indeed, till I brought off the deal with Dingwall which I am about to relate which put me on my feet again in comfort.

I should now tell of Willie's misadventure with his car-load of chickens: it suffices here to say that he was cheated by his purchaser and that I never saw a dollar of all I had loaned him.

Looking back I understand that it was probably the slump of 1873 that induced the Mayhews to go to Denver; but after they left, I was at a loose end for some months. I could not get work though I tried everything: I was met everywhere with the excuse: "hard times: hard times!" At length I took a place as waiter in the Eldridge House, the only job I could find that left most of the forenoon free for the University. Smith disliked this new departure of mine and told me he would soon find me a better post, and Mrs. Gregory was disgusted and resentful—partly out of snobbishness, I think. From this time on I felt her against me and gradually she undermined my influence with Kate: I soon knew I had fallen in public esteem too, but not for long.

One day in the fall Smith introduced me to a Mr. Rankin, the cashier of the First National Bank, who handed over to me at once the letting of Liberty Hall, the one hall in the town large enough to accommodate a thousand people: it had a stage, too, and so could be used for theatrical performances. I gave up my work in the Eldridge House and instead used to sit in the box-office of the Hall from two every afternoon till seven, and did my best to let it advantageously to the advance agents of the various travelling shows or lecturers. I received sixty dollars a month for this work and one day got an experience which has modified my whole life, for it taught me how money is made in this world and can be made by any intelligent man.

One afternoon the advance agent of the Hatherly Minstrels came into my room and threw down his card.

"This old one-hoss shay of a town", he cried, "should wear grave-clothes."

"What's the matter!" I asked. "Matter!" he repeated scornfully, "I don't believe there's a place in the hull God d—d town big enough to show our double-crown Bills! Not one: not a place. And I meant to spend ten thousand dollars here in advertising the great Hatherly Minstrels, the best show on earth: they'll be here for a hull fortnight and by God, you won't take my money: you don't want money in this dead-and-alive hole!"

The fellow amused me: he was so convinced and outspoken that I took to him. As luck would have it I had been at the University till late that day and had not gone to the Gregory's for dinner: I was healthily hungry: I asked Mr. Dingwall whether he had dined?

"No, Sir", was his reply, "Can one dine in this place?"

"I guess so", I replied, "if you'll do me the honor of being my guest, I'll take you to a good porterhouse steak at least" and I took him across to the Eldridge House, a short distance away, leaving a young friend, Will Thomson, a doctor's son whom I knew, in my place.

I gave Dingwall the best dinner I could and drew him out: he was, indeed, "a live wire" as he phrased it and suddenly inspired by his optimism the idea came to me that if he would deposit the ten thousand dollars he had talked of, I could put up hoardings on all the vacant lots in Massachusetts Street and make a good thing out of exhibiting the bills of the various travelling shows that visited Lawrence. It wasn't the first time I had been asked to help advertise this or that entertainment. I put forward my idea timidly, yet Dingwall took it up at once: "if you can find good security, or a good surety", he said, "I'll leave five thousand dollars with you: I've no right to, but I like you and I'll risk it."

I took him across to Mr. Rankin, the banker, who listened to me benevolently and finally said:

"Yes", he'd go surety that I'd exhibit a thousand bills for a fortnight all down the chief street on hoardings to be erected at once, on condition that Mr. Dingwall paid five thousand dollars in advance, and he gave Mr. Dingwall a letter to that effect and then told me pleasantly he held five thousand and some odd dollars at my service.

Dingwall took the next train west, leaving me to put up hoardings in a month, after getting first of all the permission from the lot-owners. To cut a long story short, I got the permission from a hundred lot-owners in a week through my brother Willie, who as an estate agent knew them all. Then I made a contract with a little English carpenter and put the hoardings up and got the bills all posted three days before the date agreed upon. Hatherly's Minstrels had a great fortnight and everyone was content. From that time on, I drew about fifty dollars a week as my profit from letting the hoardings, in spite of the slump.

Suddenly Smith got a bad cold: Lawrence is nearly a thousand feet above sea-level and in winter can be as icy as the Pole. He began to cough, a nasty, little, dry hacking cough: I persuaded him to see a doctor and then to have a consultation, the result being that the specialists all diagnosed tuberculosis and recommended immediate change to the milder east. For some reason or other, I believe because an editorial post on the "Press" in Philadelphia was offered to him, he left Lawrence hastily and took up his residence in the Quaker City.

His departure had notable results for me. First of all, the spiritual effect astonished me. As soon as he went, I began going over all he had taught me, especially in economics and metaphysics: bit by bit I came to the conclusion that his Marxian communism was only half the truth and probably the least important half: his Hegelianism, too, which I have hardly mentioned, was pure moonshine in my opinion: extremely beautiful at moments, as the moon is when silvering purple clouds: "history is the development of the Spirit in time: Nature is the projection of the idea in space", sounds wonderful; but it's moon-shiney, and not very enlightening.

In the first three months of Smith's absence, my own individuality sprang upright, like a sapling that has long been bent almost to breaking, so to speak, by a superincumbent weight and I began to grow with a sort of renewed youth. Now for the first time, when about nineteen years of age, I came to self-consciousness as Frank Harris and began to deal with life in my own way and under this name, Frank.

As soon as I returned from the Eldridge House to lodge with the Gregorys again, Kate showed herself just as kind to me as ever; she would come to my bedroom twice or thrice a week and was always welcome; but again and again I felt that her mother was intent on keeping us apart as much as possible and at length she arranged that Kate should pay a visit to some English friends who were settled in Kansas City. Kate postponed the visit several times: but at length she had to yield to her mother's entreaties and advice. By this time my hoardings were bringing me in a good deal and so I proposed to accompany Kate and spend the whole night with her in some Kansas City hotel.

We got to the hotel about ten and bold as brass I registered as Mr. and Mrs. William Wallace and went up to our room with Kate's luggage, my heart beating in my throat: Kate, too, was "all of a quiver" as she confessed to me a little later; but what a night we had! Kate resolved to show me all her love and gave herself to me passionately; but she never took the initiative, I noticed, as Mrs. Mayhew used to do.

At first I kissed her and talked a little; but as soon as she had arranged her things, I began to undress her: when her chemise fell, all glowing with my caressings she asked: "You really like that?" and she put her hand over her sex, standing there naked like a Greek Venus. "Naturally", I exclaimed, "and these too" and I kissed and sucked her nipples till they grew rosy-red.

"Is it possible to do it—standing up?" she asked in some confusion. "Of course", I replied, "let's try! But what put that into your head?"

"I saw a man and girl once behind the Church near our house!" she whispered, "and I wondered how—" and she blushed rosily. As I got into her, I felt difficulty: her pussy was really small and this time seemed hot and dry: I felt her wince and at once withdrew: "does it still hurt, Kate?" I asked.

"A little at first," she replied; "but I don't mind", she hastened to add, "I like the pain!"

By way of answer I slipped my arms around her under her bottom and carried her to the bed: "I will not hurt you tonight", I said, "I'll make you give down your love-juice first and then there'll be no pain." A few kisses and she sighed: "I'm wet now", and I got into bed and put my sex against hers. "I'm going to leave everything to you", I said, "but please don't hurt yourself." She put her hand down to my sex and guided it in sighing a little with satisfaction as bit by bit it slipped home.

After the first ecstasy I got her to use the syringe while I watched her curiously. When she came back to bed, "No danger now", I cried, "no danger, my love is queen!"

"You darling lover!" she cried, her eyes wide as if in wonder, "my sex throbs and itches and oh! I feel prickings on the inside of my thighs: I want you dreadfully, Frank", and she stretched out as she spoke, drawing up her knees.

I got on top of her and softly, slowly let my sex slide into her and then began the love-play. When my second orgasm came, I indulged myself with quick, short strokes, though I knew that she preferred the long, slow movement, for I was resolved to give her every sensation this golden night. When she felt me begin again the long slow movement she loved, she sighed two or three times and putting her hands on my buttocks drew me close; but otherwise made little sign of feeling for perhaps half an hour. I kept right on: the slow movement now gave me but little pleasure: it was rather a task than a joy; but I was resolved to give her a feast. I don't know how long the bout lasted: but once I withdrew and began rubbing her clitoris and the front of her sex, and panting she nodded her head and rubbed herself ecstatically against my sex, and after I had begun the slow movement again: "please, Frank!" she gasped, "I can't stand more: I'm going crazy—choking!"

Strange to say, her words excited me more than the act: I felt my spasm coming and roughly, savagely I thrust in my sex at the same time kneeling between her legs so as to be able to play back and forth on her tickler as well. "I'll ravish you!" I cried and gave myself to the keen delight. As my seed spirted, she didn't speak, but lay there still and white; I jumped out of the bed, got a spongeful of cold water and used it on her forehead. At once to my joy she opened her eyes: "I'm sorry", she gasped, and took a drink of water, "but I was so tired, I must have slept. You dear heart!" When I had put down the sponge and glass, I slipped into her again and in a little while she became hysterical: "I can't help crying, Frank love", she sighed, "I'm so happy, dear! You'll always love me? Won't you? sweet!" Naturally I reassured her with promises of enduring affection and many kisses; finally I put my left arm round her neck and so fell asleep with my head on her soft breast.

In the morning we ran another course, though sooth to say, Kate was more curious than passionate.

"I want to study you!" she said and took my sex in her hands and then my balls: "What are they for?" she asked and I had to explain that that was where my seed was secreted: she made a face, so I added, "You have a similar manufactory, my dear; but it's inside you, the ovaries they are called, and it takes them a month to make one egg whereas my balls make millions of tadpoles in an hour. I often wonder why?"

After getting Kate an excellent breakfast, I put her in a cab and she reached her friend's house just at the proper time; but the girl-friend could never understand how they had missed each other at the station.

I returned to Lawrence the same day, wondering what Fortune had in store for me! I was soon to find out that life could be disagreeable.

The University of Kansas had been established by the first Western outwanderers and like most pioneers they had brains and courage and accordingly they put in the statutes that there should be no religious teaching of any kind in the University, still less should religion ever be exalted into a test or qualification.

But in due course Yankees from New England swarmed out to prevent Kansas from being made into a slave-state and these Yankees were all fanatical so-called Christians belonging to every known sect; but all distinguished or rather deformed by an intolerant bigotry in matters of religion and sex. Their honesty was by no means so pronounced: each sect had to have its own professor; thus history got an Episcopalian clergyman who knew no history, and Latin a Baptist who, when Smith greeted him in Latin, could only blush and beg him not to expose his shameful ignorance; the lady who taught French was a joke but a good Methodist, I believe, and so forth and so on: education degraded by sectarian jealousies.

As soon as Professor Smith left the University, the Faculty passed a resolution establishing "College Chapel" in imitation of an English University custom. At once I wrote to the Faculty protesting and citing the Statutes of the Founders. The Faculty did not answer my letter; but instituted roll-call instead of chapel and when they got all the students assembled for roll-call, they had the doors locked and began prayers, ending with a hymn.

After the roll-call I got up and walked to the door and tried in vain to open it. Fortunately the door on this side the hall was only a makeshift structure of thin wooden planks. I stepped back a pace or two and appealed again to the Professors seated on the platform: when they paid no heed, I ran and jumped with my foot against the lock; it sprang and the door flew open with a crash.

Next day by an unanimous vote of the Faculty, I was expelled from the University and was free to turn all my attention to law. Judge Stevens told me he would bring action on my behalf against the Faculty if I wished and felt sure he'd get damages and reinstate me. But the University without Smith meant less than nothing to me and why should I waste time fighting brainless bigots? I little knew then that that would be the main work of my life; but this first time I left my enemies the victory and the field, as I probably shall at long last.

I made up my mind to study law and as a beginning induced Barker of Barker & Sommerfeld to let me study in his law office. I don't remember how I got to know them; but Barker, an immensely fat man, was a famous advocate and very kind to me for no apparent reason. Sommerfeld was a tall, fair, German-looking Jew, peculiarly inarticulate, almost tongue-tied, indeed, in English; but an excellent lawyer and a kindly, honest man who commanded the respect of all the Germans and Jews in Douglas County partly because his fat little father had been one of the earliest settlers in Lawrence and one of the most successful tradesmen. He kept a general provision store and had been kind to all his compatriots in their early struggling days.

It was an admirable partnership: Sommerfeld had the clients and prepared the briefs; while Barker did the talking in court with a sort of invincible good humor which I never saw equalled save in the notorious Englishman, Bottomley. Barker before a jury used to exude good-nature and commonsense and thus gain even bad cases. Sommerfeld, I'll tell more about in due time.

A little later I got depressing news from Smith: his cough had not diminished and he missed our companionship: there was a hopelessness in the letter which hurt my very heart: but what could I do? I could only keep on working hard at law, while using every spare moment to increase my income by adding to my hoardings in two senses.

One evening I almost ran into Lily. Kate was still away in Kansas City, so I stopped eagerly enough to have a talk, for Lily had always interested me. After the first greetings she told me she was going home: "they are all out, I believe", she added. At once I offered to accompany her and she consented. It was early in summer but already warm, and when we went into the parlor and Lily took a seat on the sofa, her thin white dress defined her slim figure seductively.

"What do you do?" she asked mischievously, "now that dear Mrs. Mayhew's gone? You must miss her!" she added suggestively.

"I do," I confessed boldly; "I wonder if you'd have pluck enough to tell me the truth?" I went on.

"Pluck?" She wrinkled her forehead and pursed her large mouth; "Courage, I mean", I said.

"Oh, I have courage!" she rejoined.

"Did you ever come upstairs to Mrs. Mayhew's bedroom", I asked, "when I had gone up for a book?" The black eyes danced and she laughed knowingly.

"Mrs. Mayhew said that she had taken you upstairs to bathe your poor head after dancing", she retorted disdainfully, "but I don't care: it's nothing to do with me what you do!"

"It has too," I went on, carrying the war into her country. "How?" she asked.

"Why, the first day you went away and left me though I was really ill", I said, "so I naturally believed that you disliked me though I thought you lovely!"

"I'm not lovely," she said, "my mouth's too big and I'm too slight."

"Don't malign yourself," I replied earnestly, "that's just why you are seductive and excite a man."

"Really?" she cried, and so the talk went on while I cudgeled my brains for an opportunity but found none and all the while was in fear lest her father and mother should return. At length angry with myself, I got up to go on some pretext and she accompanied me to the stoop. I said "Good-bye" on the top step and then jumped down by the side with a prayer in my heart that she'd come a step or two down and she did. There she stood, her hips on a level with my mouth; in a moment my hands went up her dress, the right to her sex, the left to her bottom behind to hold her: the thrill as I touched her half-fledged sex was almost painful in intensity. Her first movement brought her sitting down on the step above me and at once my finger was busy in her slit.

"How dare you!" she cried, but not angrily, "take your hand away!"

"Oh, how lovely your sex is!" I exclaimed as if astounded, "Oh, I must see it and have you, you miracle of beauty!" and my left hand drew down her head for a long kiss while my middle finger still continued its caress. Of a sudden her lips grew hot and at once I whispered.

"Won't you love me, dear? I want you so: I'm burning and itching with desire (I knew she was!) Please, I won't hurt you and I'll take care; please, love, no one will know", and the end of it was that right there on the porch I drew her to me and put my sex against hers and began the rubbing of her tickler and front part of her sex that I knew would excite her. In a moment she came and her love-dew wet my sex and excited me terribly; but I kept on frigging her with my manroot while restraining myself from coming by thinking of other things, till she kissed me of her own accord and suddenly moving forward pushed my prick right into her pussy.

To my astonishment, there was no obstacle, no maidenhead to break through, though her sex itself was astonishingly small and tight. I didn't scruple then to let my seed come, only withdrawing to the lips and rubbing her clitoris the while, and as soon as my spirting ceased, my root glided again into her and continued the slow in-and-out movement till she panted with her head on my shoulder and asked me to stop. I did as she wished, for I knew I had won another wonderful mistress.

We went into the house again for she insisted I should meet her father and mother, and while we were waiting she showed me her lovely tiny breasts, scarcely larger than small apples, and I became aware of something childish in her mind which matched the childish outlines of her lovely, half-formed hips and pussy.

"I thought that you were in love with Mrs. Mayhew," she confessed, "and I couldn't make out why she made such funny noises; but now I know", she added, "you naughty dear; for I felt my heart fluttering just now and I was nearly choking—"

I don't know why; but that ravishing of Lily made her dear to me: I resolved to see her naked and to make her thrill to ecstasy as soon as possible, and then and there we made a meeting-place on the far side of the church, whence I knew I could bring her to my room at the Gregory's in a minute, and then I went home, for it was late and I didn't particularly want to meet her folks.

The next night I met Lily by the church and took her to my room: she laughed aloud with delight as we entered; for indeed she was almost like a boy of bold, adventurous spirit. She confessed to me that my challenge of her pluck had pleased her intimately:

"I never took a 'dare'!" she cried in her American slang, tossing her head.

"I'll give you two," I whispered, "right now: the first is, I dare you to strip naked as I'm going to do, and I'll tell you the other when we're in bed." Again she tossed her little blue-black head: "pooh!" she cried, "I'll be undressed first", and she was. Her beauty made my pulses hammer and parched my mouth. No one could help admiring her: she was very slight, with tiny breasts, as I have said, flat belly and straight flanks and hips: her triangle was only brushed in, so to speak, with fluffy soft hairs, and as I held her naked body against mine, the look and feel of her exasperated my desire. I still admired Kate's riper, richer, more luscious outlines; her figure was nearer my boyish ideal; but Lily represented a type of adolescence destined to grow on me mightily. In fact as my youthful virility decreased, my love of opulent feminine charms diminished, and I grew more and more to love slender, youthful outlines with the signs of sex rather indicated than pronounced. What an all-devouring appetite Rubens confesses with the great, hanging breasts and uncouth fat pink bottoms of his Venuses!

I lifted Lily on to the bed and separated her legs to study her pussy. She made a face at me; but as I rubbed my hot sex against her little button that I could hardly see, she smiled and lay back contentedly. In a minute or two her love-juice came and I got into bed on her and slipped my root into her small cunt: even when the lips were wide open it was closed to the eye and this and her slim nakedness excited me uncontrollably. I continued the slow movements for a few minutes; but once she moved her sex quickly down on mine as I drew out to the lips, and gave me an intense thrill: I felt my seed coming and I let myself go in short, quick thrusts that soon brought on my spasm of pleasure and I lifted her little body against mine and crushed my lips on hers: she was strangely tantalizing, exciting like strong drink.

I took her out of bed and used the syringe in her, explaining its purpose, and then went to bed again and gave her the time of her life! Lying between her legs but side by side an hour later, I dared her to tell me how she had lost her maidenhead. I had to tell her first what it was. She maintained stoutly that no "feller" had ever touched her except me and I believed her, for she admitted having caressed herself ever since she was ten: at first she could not even get her forefinger into her pussy she told me. "What are you now?" I asked. "I shall be sixteen next April", was her reply.

About eleven o'clock she dressed and went home, after making another appointment with me.

The haste of this narrative has many unforeseen drawbacks: it makes it appear as if I had had conquest after conquest and little or no difficulty in my efforts to win love. In reality my half dozen victories were spread out over nearly as many years, and time and again I met rebuffs and refusals quite sufficient to keep even my conceit in decent bounds. But I want to emphasize the fact that success in love, like success in every department of life, falls usually to the tough man unwearied in pursuit. Chaucer was right when he makes his Old Wyfe of Bath confess:

And by a close attendance and attention

Are we caught, more or less the truth to mention.

It is not the handsomest man or the most virile who has most success with women, though both qualities smooth the way; but that man who pursues them most assiduously, flatters them most constantly and cleverly, and always insists on taking the girl's "No" for consent, her reproofs for endearments and even a little crossness for a new charm.

Above all, it is necessary to push forward after every refusal, for as soon as a girl refuses, she is apt to regret and may grant then what she expressly denied the moment before. Yet I could give dozens of instances where assiduity and flattery, love-looks and words were all ineffective, so much so that I should never say with Shakespeare: "he's not a man who cannot win a woman." I have generally found, too, that the easiest to win were the best worth winning for me, for women have finer senses for suitability in love than any man.

Now for an example of one of my many failures which took place when I was still a student and had fair opportunity to succeed.

It was a custom in the University for every professor to lecture for forty-five minutes, thus leaving each student fifteen minutes at least free to go back to his private class-room to prepare for the next lecture. All the students took turns to use these classrooms for their private pleasure. For example, from 11:45 to noon each day I was supposed to be working in the Junior Class-room and no student would interfere with me or molest me in any way.

One day, a girl Fresher, Grace Weldon by name, the daughter of the owner of the biggest department store in Lawrence, came to Smith when Miss Stevens and I were with him, about the translation of a phrase or two in Xenophon.

"Explain it to Miss Weldon, Frank!" said Smith and in a few moments I had made the passage clear to her. She thanked me prettily and I said, "If you ever want anything I can do, I'll be happy to make it clear to you, Miss Weldon; I'm in the Junior class-room from 11:45 to noon always."

She thanked me and a day or two later came to me in the class-room with another puzzle and so our acquaintance ripened. Almost at once she let me kiss her; but as soon as I tried to put my hand up her clothes, she stopped me. We were friends for nearly a year, close friends, and I remember trying all I knew one Saturday when I spent the whole day with her in our class-room, till dusk came and I could not get her to yield.

The curious thing was I could not even soothe the smart to my vanity with the belief that she was physically cold: on the contrary she was very passionate; but she had simply made up her mind and would not change.

That Saturday in the class-room she told me if she yielded she would hate me: I could see no sense in this, even though I was to find out later what a terrible weapon the Confessional is as used by Irish Catholic Priests. To commit a sin is easy; to confess it to your priest is for many women an absolute deterrent.

A few days later, I think, I got a letter from Smith that determined me to go to Philadelphia as soon as my hoardings provided me with sufficient money. I wrote and told him I'd come and cheered him up: I had not long to wait.

Early that fall Bradlaugh came to lecture in Liberty Hall on the French Revolution—a giant of a man with a great head, rough-hewn, irregular features and stentorian voice: no better figure of a rebel could be imagined. I knew he had been an English private soldier for a dozen years; but I soon found that in spite of his passionate revolt against the Christian religion and all its cheap moralistic conventions, he was a convinced individualist and saw nothing wrong in the despotism of Money which had already established itself in Britain, though condemned by Carlyle at the end of his "French Revolution" as the vilest of all tyrannies.

Bradlaugh's speech taught me that a notorious and popular man, earnest and gifted, too, and intellectually honest might be fifty years before his time in one respect and fifty years behind the best opinion of the age in another province of thought. In the great conflict of our day between the "Haves" and the "Have-nots", Bradlaugh played no part whatever: he wasted his great powers in a vain attack on the rotten branches of the Christian tree, while he should have assimilated the spirit of Jesus and used it to gild his loyalty to truth.

About this time Kate wrote that she would not be back for some weeks: she declared she was feeling another woman; I felt tempted to write, "So am I, stay as long as you please"; but instead I wrote an affectionate, tempting letter; for I had a real affection for her, I discovered.

When she returned a few weeks later, I felt as if she were new and unknown and I had to win her again; but as soon as my hand touched her sex, the strangeness disappeared and she gave herself to me with renewed zest.

I teased her to tell me just what she felt and at length she consented. "Begin with the first time" I begged, "and then tell what you felt in Kansas City."

"It will be very hard", she said, "I'd rather write it for you." "That'll do just as well", I replied, and here is the story she sent me the next day.

"I think the first time you had me," she began "I felt more curiosity than desire: I had so often tried to picture it all to myself. When I saw your sex, I was astonished, for it looked very big to me and I wondered whether you could really get it into my sex which I knew was just big enough for my finger to go in. Still I did want to feel your sex pushing into me, and your kisses and the touch of your hand on my sex made me even more eager. When you slipped the head of your sex into mine, it hurt dreadfully; it was almost like a knife cutting into me, but the pain for some reason seemed to excite me and I pushed forward so as to get you further in me; I think that's what broke my maidenhead. At first I was disappointed because I felt no thrill, only the pain; but when my sex became all wet and open and yours could slip in and out easily, I began to feel real pleasure. I liked the slow movement best; it excited me to feel the head of your sex just touching the lips of mine and when you pushed in slowly all the way, it gave me a gasp of breathless delight; when you drew your sex out, I wanted to hold it in me. And the longer you kept on, the more pleasure you gave me. For hours afterwards my sex was sensitive; if I rubbed it ever so gently, it would begin to itch and burn.

"But that night in the hotel at Kansas City I really wanted you and the pleasure you gave me then was much keener than the first time. You kissed and caressed me for a few minutes and I soon felt my love-dew coming and the button of my sex began to throb. As you thrust your shaft in and out of me, I felt such a strange sort of pleasure: every little nerve on the inside of my thighs and belly seemed to thrill and quiver: it was almost a feeling of pain. At first the sensation was not so intense, but when you stopped and made me wash, I was shaken by quick, short spasms in my thighs and my sex was burning and throbbing; I wanted you more than ever.

"When you began the slow movement again, I felt the same sensations in my thighs and belly, only more keenly, and as you kept on, the pleasure became so intense that I could scarcely bear it. Suddenly you rubbed your sex against mine and my button began to throb: I could almost feel it move. Then you began to move your sex quickly in and out of me; in a moment I was breathless with emotion and I felt so faint and exhausted that I suppose I fell asleep for a few minutes, for I knew nothing more till I felt the cold water trickling down my face. When you began again, you made me cry; perhaps because I was all dissolved in feeling and too, too happy. Ah, love is divine: isn't it?"

Kate was really of the highest woman-type, mother and mistress in one. She used to come down and spend the night with me oftener than ever and on one of these occasions she found a new word for her passion: she declared she felt her womb move in yearning for me when I talked my best or recited poetry to her in what I had christened her Holy Week. Kate, it was, who taught me first that women could be even more moved and excited by words than by deeds: once, I remember, when I had talked sentimentally, she embraced me of her own accord and we had each other with wet eyes.

Another effect of Smith's absence was important; for it threw me a good deal with Miss Stevens. I soon found that she had inherited the best of her father's brains and much of his strength of character. If she had married Smith, she might have done something noteworthy: as it was, she was very attractive and well-read as a girl and would have made Smith, I am sure, a most excellent wife.

Once and once only I tried to hint to her that her sweetness to Smith might do him harm physically; but the suspicion of reproof made her angry and she evidently couldn't or wouldn't understand what I meant without a physical explanation, which she would certainly have resented. I had to leave her to what she would have called her daimon; for she was as prettily pedantic as Tennyson's Princess, or any other mid-Victorian heroine.

Her brother Ned, too, I came to know pretty well. He was a tall, handsome youth with fine grey eyes: a good athlete, but of commonplace mind.

The father was the most interesting of the whole family, were it only for his prodigious conceit. He was of noble appearance: a large, handsome head with silver grey hairs setting off a portly figure well above middle height. In spite of his assumption of superiority, I felt him hide-bound in thought; for he accepted all the familiar American conventions, believing or rather knowing that the American people, "the good old New England stock in particular, were the salt of the earth, the best breed to be seen anywhere...."

It showed his brains that he tried to find a reason for this belief. "English oak is good", he remarked one day sententiously, "but American hickory is tougher still. Reasonable, too, this belief of mine", he added, "for the last glacial period skinned all the good soil off of New England and made it bitterly hard to get a living and the English who came out for conscience sake were the pick of the Old Country and they were forced for generations to scratch a living out of the poorest kind of soil with the worst climate in the world, and hostile Indians all round to sharpen their combativeness and weed out the weaklings and wastrels."

There was a certain amount of truth in his contention; but this was the nearest to an original thought I ever heard him express and his intense patriotic fervor moved me to doubt his intelligence.

I was delighted to find that Smith rated him just as I did: "a first-rate lawyer, I believe", was his judgment, "a sensible, kindly man."

"A little above middle height", I interpreted and Smith added smiling, "and considerably above average weight: he would never have done anything notable in literature or thought."

As the year wore on, Smith's letters called for me more and more insistently and at length I went to join him in Philadelphia.

NEW EXPERIENCES.

Emerson, Walt Whitman, Bret Harte.

Chapter XIII.

Smith met me at the station: he was thinner than ever and the wretched little cough shook him very often in spite of some lozenges that the doctor had given him to suck: I began to be alarmed about him and I soon came to the belief that the damp climate of the Quaker City was worse for him than the thin, dry Kansas air. But he believed in his doctors!

He boarded with a pleasant Puritan family in whose house he had also got me a room and at once we resumed the old life. But now I kept constant watch on him and insisted on rigorous self-restraint, tying up his unruly organ every night carefully with thread, which was still more efficient (and painful) than the whipcord. I also put a lump of ice near his bed so that he could end at once any thrill of sex. But now he didn't improve quickly: it was a month before I could find any of the old vigor in him; but soon afterwards the cough diminished and he began to be his bright self again.

One of our first evenings I described to him the Bradlaugh lecture in much the same terms I have used in this narrative. Smith said: "Why don't you write it? You ought to: the 'Press' would take it. You've given me an extraordinary, life-like portrait of a great man, blind, so to speak, in one eye, a sort of Cyclops. If he had been a Communist, how much greater he'd have been."

I ventured to disagree and we were soon at it, hammer and tongs. I wanted to see both principles realised in life, individualism and Socialism, the centrifugal as well as the centripetal force and was convinced that the problem was how to bring these opposites to a balance which would ensure an approximation to justice and make for the happiness of all.

Smith on the other hand argued at first as an out-and-out Communist and follower of Marx; but he was too fair-minded to shut his eyes for long to the obvious. Soon he began congratulating me on my insight, declaring I had written a new chapter in economics.

His conversion made me feel that I was at long last his equal as a thinker, in any field where his scholarship didn't give him too great an advantage: I was no longer a pupil but an equal and his quick recognition of the fact increased, I believe, our mutual affection. Though infinitely better read he put me forward in every company with the rarest generosity, asserting that I had discovered new laws in sociology. For months we lived very happily together but his Hegelianism defied all my attacks: it corresponded too intimately with the profound idealism of his own character.

As soon as I had written out the Bradlaugh story, Smith took me down to the "Press" office and introduced me to the chief editor, a Captain Forney: indeed the paper then was usually called "Forney's Press" though already some spoke of it as "The Philadelphia Press." Forney liked my portrait of Bradlaugh and engaged me as a reporter on the staff and occasional descriptive writer at fifty dollars a week, which enabled me to save all the money coming to me from Lawrence.

One day Smith talked to me of Emerson and confessed he had got an introduction to him and had sent it on to the philosopher with a request for an interview. He wished me to accompany him to Concord: I consented, but without any enthusiasm: Emerson was then an unknown name to me; Smith read me some of his poetry and praised it highly though I could get little or nothing out of it. When young men now show me a similar indifference, my own experience makes it easy for me to excuse them. They know not what they do! is the explanation and excuse for all of us.

One bright fall day Smith and I went over to Concord and next day visited Emerson. He received us in the most pleasant, courteous way: made us sit and composed himself to listen. Smith went off at score, telling him how greatly he had influenced his life and helped him with brave encouragement: the old man smiled benignantly and nodded his head, ejaculating from time to time: "Yes, yes!" Gradually Smith warmed to his work and wanted to know why Emerson had never expressed his views on sociology or on the relations between Capital and Labor. Once or twice the old gentleman cupped his ear with his hand; but all he said was: "Yes, Yes! or I think so" with the same benevolent smile.

I guessed at once that he was deaf; but Smith had no inkling of the fact for he went on probing, probing while Emerson answered pleasant nothings quite irrelevantly. I studied the great man as closely as I could. He looked about five feet nine or ten in height, very thin, attenuated even, and very scrupulously dressed: his head was narrow though long, his face bony; a long, high, somewhat beaked nose was the feature of his countenance:—a good conceit of himself, I concluded, and considerable will-power, for the chin was well-defined and large; but I got nothing more than this and from his clear steadfast gray eyes, an intense impression of kindness and good will, and why shouldn't I say it? of sweetness even, as of a soul lifted high above earth's carking cares and stragglings.

"A nice old fellow", I said to myself, "but deaf as a post."

Many years later his deafness became to me the symbol and explanation of his genius. He had always lived "the life removed" and kept himself unspotted from the world: that explains both his narrowness of sympathy and the height to which he grew! His narrow, pleasantly smiling face comes back to me whenever I hear his name mentioned.

But at the time I was indignant with his deafness and out of temper with Smith because he didn't notice it and seemed somehow to make himself cheap. When we went away, I cried: "The old fool is as deaf as a post!" "Ah, that was the explanation then of his stereotyped smile and peculiar answers", cried Smith, "how did you divine it?"

"He put his hand to his ear more than once", I replied.

"So he did", Smith exclaimed, "how foolish of me not to have drawn the obvious inference!"

It was in this fall, I believe, that the Gregorys went off to Colorado. I felt the loss of Kate a good deal at first; but she had made no deep impression on my mind and the new life in Philadelphia and my journalistic work left me but little time for regrets and as she never wrote to me, following doubtless her mother's advice, she soon drifted out of my memory. Moreover, Lily was quite as interesting a lover and Lily too had begun to pall on me. The truth is, the fever of desire in youth is a passing malady that intimacy quickly cures. Besides, I was already in pursuit of a girl in Philadelphia who kept me a long time at arm's length, and when she yielded I found her figure commonplace and her sex so large and loose that she deserves no place in this chronicle. She was modest, if you please, and no wonder. I have always since thought, that modesty is the proper fig-leaf of ugliness.

In the spring of this year 1875, I had to return to Lawrence on business connected with my hoardings. In several cases the owners of the lots refused to allow me to keep up the hoardings unless they had a reasonable share in the profits. Finally I called them all together and came to an amicable agreement to divide twenty-five percent of my profit among them, year by year.

I had also to go through my examination and get admitted to the Bar. I had already taken out my first naturalization papers and Judge Bassett of the District Court appointed the lawyers Barker and Hutchings to examine me. The examination was a mere form: they each asked me three simple questions: I answered them and we adjourned to the Eldridge House for supper and they drank my health in champagne. I was notified by Judge Bassett that I had passed the examination and told to present myself for admission on the 15th of June, I think, 1875.

To my surprise the court was half full. Judge Stevens even was present, whom I had never seen in court before. About eleven the Judge informed the audience that I had passed a satisfactory examination, had taken out my first papers in due form and unless some lawyer wished first to put questions to me to test my capacity, he proposed to call me within the Bar. To my astonishment Judge Stevens rose:

"With the permission of the Court", he said, "I'd like to put some questions to this candidate who comes to us with high University commendation." (No one had heard of my expulsion though he knew of it.) He then began a series of questions which soon plumbed the depths of my abysmal ignorance. I didn't know what an action of account was at old English common law: I don't know now, nor do I want to. I had read Blackstone carefully and a book on Roman law; Chitty on Evidence, too, and someone on Contracts—half a dozen books and that was all. For the first two hours Judge Stevens just exposed my ignorances: it was a very warm morning and my conceit was rubbed raw when Judge Bassett proposed an adjournment for dinner. Stevens consented and we all rose. To my surprise Barker and Hutchings and half a dozen other lawyers came round to encourage me: "Stevens is just showing off", said Hutchings, "I myself couldn't have answered half his questions!" Even Judge Bassett sent for me to his room and practically told me I had nothing to fear, so I returned at two o'clock, resolved to do my best and at all costs to keep smiling.

The examination continued in a crowded court till four o'clock and then Judge Stevens sat down. I had done better in this session; but my examiner had caught me in a trap on a moot point in the law of evidence and I could have kicked myself. But Hutchings rose as the senior of my two examiners who had been appointed by the Court, and said simply that now he repeated the opinion he had already had the honor to convey to Judge Bassett, that I was a fit and proper person to practice law in the State of Kansas.

"Judge Stevens", he added, "has shown us how widely read he is in English common law; but some of us knew that before and in any case his erudition should not be made a purgatory to candidates: it looks", he went on, "as if he wished to punish Mr. Harris for his superiority to all his classmates in the University.

"Impartial persons in this audience will admit", he concluded, "that Mr. Harris has come brilliantly out of an exceedingly severe test and I have the pleasant task of proposing, your Honor, that he now be admitted within the Bar, though he may not be able to practice till he becomes a full citizen two years hence."

Everyone expected that Barker would second this proposal; but while he was rising, Judge Stevens began to speak.

"I desire", he said, "to second that proposal; and I think I ought to explain why I subjected Mr. Harris to a severe examination in open court. Since I came to Kansas from the State of New York twenty-five years ago, I have been asked a score of times to examine one candidate or another. I always refused: I did not wish to punish Western candidates by putting them against our Eastern standards. But here at long last appears a candidate who has won honor in the University to whom, therefore, a stiff examination in open court can only be a vindication, and accordingly I examined Mr. Harris as if he had been in the State of New York; for surely Kansas too has come of age and its inhabitants cannot wish to be humored as inferiors.

"This whole affair", he went on, "reminds me of a story told in the east of a dog-fancier. The father lived by breeding and training bull-dogs. One day he got an extraordinarily promising pup and the father and son used to hunker down, shake their arms at the pup and thus encourage him to seize hold of their coat-sleeves and hang on. While engaged in this game once, the bull-pup, grown bold by constant praise, sprang up and seized the father by the nose. Instinctively the old man began to choke him off but the son exclaimed:

"'Don't, father, don't, for God's sake! it may be hard on you, but it'll be the making of the pup'. So my examination, I thought, might be hard on Mr. Harris; but it would be the making of him."

The Court roared and I applauded merrily. Judge Stevens continued: "I desire, however, to show myself not an enemy but a friend of Mr. Harris whom I have known for some years. Mr. Hutchings evidently thinks that Mr. Harris must wait two years in order to become a citizen of the United States. I am glad from my reading of the Statute laws of my country to be able to assure him that Mr. Harris need not wait a day. The law says that if a minor has lived three years in any state, he may on coming of age choose to become a citizen of the United States, and if Mr. Harris chooses to be one of us, he can be admitted at once as a citizen and if your Honor approve, be allowed also to practice law tomorrow."

He sat down amid great applause, in which I joined most heartily. So on that day I was admitted to practice law as a full-fledged citizen. Unluckily for me, when I asked the Clerk of the Court for my full papers, he gave me the certificate of my admission to practice law in Lawrence, saying that as this could only be given to a citizen, it in itself was sufficient.

Forty odd years later the government of Woodrow Wilson refused to accept this plain proof of my citizenship and thus put me to much trouble by forcing me to get naturalized again!

But at the moment in Lawrence I was all cock-a-hoop and forthwith took a room on the same first floor where Barker & Sommerfeld had their offices, and put out my shingle.

I have told this story of my examination at great length because I think it shows as in a glass the amenities and deep kindness of the American character.

A couple of days later I was again in Philadelphia.

Towards the end of this year 1875, I believe, or the beginning of 1876, Smith drew my attention to an announcement that Walt Whitman, the poet, was going to speak in Philadelphia on Thomas Paine, the notorious infidel, who according to Washington had done more to secure the independence of the United States than any other man. Smith determined to go to the meeting and if Whitman could rehabilitate Paine against the venomous attacks of Christian clergymen who had asserted without contradiction that Paine was a notorious drunkard and of the loosest character, he would induce Forney to let him write an exhaustive and forceful defence of Paine in "The Press."

I felt pretty sure that such an article would never appear but I would not pour cold water on Smith's enthusiasm. The day came, one of those villainous days common enough in Philadelphia in every winter: the temperature was about zero with snow falling whenever the driving wind permitted. In the afternoon Smith finally determined that he must not risk it and asked me to go in his stead. I consented willingly and he spent some hours in reading to me the best of Whitman's poetry, laying especial stress, I remember, on "When lilacs last in the dooryard bloomed." He assured me again and again that Whitman and Poe were the two greatest poets these States had ever produced and he hoped I would be very nice to the great man.

Nothing could be more depressing than the aspect of the Hall that night: ill-lit and half-heated, with perhaps thirty persons scattered about in a space that would have accommodated a thousand. Such was the reception America accorded to one of its greatest spirits, though that view of the matter did not strike me for many a year.

I took my seat in the middle of the first row, pulled out my notebook and made ready. In a few minutes Whitman came on the platform from the left: he walked slowly, stiffly, which made me grin for I did not then know that he had had a stroke of paralysis and I thought his peculiar walk, a mere pose. Besides, his clothes were astonishingly ill-fitting and ill-suited to his figure. He must have been nearly six feet in height and strongly made, yet he wore a short jacket which cocked up behind in the perkiest way. Looked at from the front, his white collar was wide open and discovered a tuft of grey hairs, while his trousers that corkscrewed about his legs had parted company with his vest and disclosed a margin of dingy white shirt. His appearance filled me—poor little English snob that I was—with contempt: he recalled to my memory irresistibly an old Cochin-China rooster I had seen when a boy; it stalked across the farm-yard with the same slow, stiff gait and carried a stubby tail cocked up behind.

Yet a second look showed me Whitman as a fine figure of a man with something arresting in the perfect simplicity and sincerity of voice and manner. He arranged his notes in complete silence and began to speak very slowly, often pausing for a better word or to consult his papers, sometimes hesitating and repeating himself—clearly an unpracticed speaker who disdained any semblance of oratory. He told us simply that in his youth he had met and got to know very well a certain Colonel in the army who had known Thomas Paine intimately. This Colonel had assured him more than once that all the accusations against Paine's habits and character were false—a mere outcome of Christian bigotry. Paine would drink a glass or two of wine at dinner like all well-bred men of that day; but he was very moderate and in the last ten years of his life the Colonel asserted that Paine never once drank to excess. The Colonel cleared Paine, too, of looseness of morals in much the same decisive way and finally spoke of him as invariably well-conducted, of witty speech and a vast fund of information, a most interesting and agreeable companion. And the Colonel was an unimpeachable witness, Whitman assured us, a man of the highest honor and most scrupulous veracity.

Whitman spoke with such uncommon slowness that I was easily able to take down the chief sentences in longhand: he was manifestly determined to say just what he had to say, neither more nor less—which made an impression of singular sincerity and truthfulness.

When he had finished, I went up on the platform to see him near at hand; and draw him out if possible. I showed him my card of the "Press" and asked him if he would kindly sign and thus authenticate the sentences on Paine he had used in his address.

"Aye, aye!" was all he said; but he read the half dozen sentences carefully, here and there correcting a word.

I thanked him and said Professor Smith, an Editor of the "Press", had sent me to get a word-for-word report of his speech for he purposed writing an article in the "Press" on Paine, whom he greatly admired.

"Aye, aye!" ejaculated Whitman from time to time while his clear grey eyes absorbed all that I said. I went on to assure him that Smith had a profound admiration for him (Whitman), thought him the greatest American poet and regretted deeply that he was not well enough to come out that night and make his personal acquaintance.

"I'm sorry, too", said Whitman slowly, "for your friend Smith must have something large in him to be so interested in Paine and in me." Perfectly simple and honest Walt Whitman appeared to me, even in his self-estimate—an authentic great man!

I had nothing more to say, so hastened home to show Smith Whitman's boyish signature and to give him a description of the man. The impression Whitman left on me was one of transparent simplicity and sincerity: not a mannerism in him, not a trace of affectation, a man simply sure of himself, most careful in speech; but careless of appearances and curiously, significantly free of all afterthoughts or regrets: a new type of personality which, strangely enough, has grown upon me more and more with the passing of the years and now seems to me to represent the very best in America, the large unruffled soul of that great people manifestly called and chosen to exert an increasingly important influence on the destinies of mankind. I would die happy if I could believe that America's influence would be anything like as manful and true and clear-eyed as Whitman's in guiding humanity; but alas!—

It would be difficult to convey to European readers any just notion of the horror and disgust with which Walt Whitman was regarded at that time in the United States on account merely of the sex-poems in "Leaves of Grass." The poems to which objection could be taken, don't constitute five per cent of the book and my objection to them is that in any normal man, love and desire take up a much larger proportion of life than five per cent. Moreover the expression of passion is tame in the extreme: nothing in the "Leaves of Grass" can compare with half a dozen passages in the Song of Solomon: think of the following verse:

"I sleep but my heart waketh: it is the voice of
my beloved that knocketh, saying, Open to me, my
sister, my love, my dove, my undefiled: for my
head is filled with dew and my locks with the drops
of the night....

"My beloved put his hand in by the hole of
the door and my bowels were moved for him."

And then the phrases: "her lips are like a thread of scarlet" ... "her love like an army with banners"; but American puritanism is more timid even than its purblind teachers.

It was commonly said at the time that Whitman had led a life of extraordinary self-indulgence: rumor attributed to him half a dozen illegitimate children and perverse tastes to boot. I think such statements exaggerated or worse: they are no more to be trusted than the stories of Paine's drunkenness. At any rate, Horace Traubel later declared to me that Whitman's life was singularly clean and his own letter to John Addington Symonds must be held to have disproved the charge of homo-sexuality. But I dare swear he loved more than once not wisely but too well, or he would not have risked the reprobation of the "unco guid." In any case, it is to his honor that he dared to write plainly in America of the joys of sexual intercourse. Emerson, as Whitman himself tells us, did his utmost all one long afternoon to dissuade him from publishing the sex-poems; but fortunately all his arguments served only to confirm Whitman in his purpose. From certain querulous complaints later, it is plain that Whitman was too ignorant to gauge the atrocious results to himself and his reputation of his daring; but the same ignorance that allowed him to use scores of vile neologisms, in this one instance stood him in good stead. It was right of him to speak plainly of sex; accordingly he set down the main facts, disdainful of the best opinion of his time. And he was justified; in the long run, it will be plain to all that he thus put the seal of the Highest upon his judgment. What can we think and what will the future think of Emerson's condemnation of Rabelais whom he dared to liken to a dirty little boy who scribbles indecencies in public places and then runs away and his contemptuous estimate of Shakespeare as a ribald playwright, when in good sooth he was "the reconciler" whom Emerson wanted to acclaim and had not the brains to recognize.

Whitman was the first of great men to write frankly about sex and five hundred years hence, that will be his singular and supreme distinction.

Smith seemed permanently better though, of course, for the moment disappointed because his careful eulogy of Paine never appeared in the "Press", so one day I told him I'd have to return to Lawrence to go on with my law work, though Thompson, the doctor's son, kept all my personal affairs in good order and informed me of every happening. Smith at this time seemed to agree with me, though not enthusiastically, and I was on the point of starting when I got a letter from Willie, telling me that my eldest brother Vernon was in a New York hospital, having just tried to commit suicide and I should go to see him.

I went at once and found Vernon in a ward in bed: the surgeon told me that he had tried to shoot himself and that the ball had struck the jaw-bone at such an angle that it went all round his head and was taken out just above his left ear: "it stunned him and that was all; he can go out almost any day now." The first glance showed me the old Vernon: he cried:

"Still a failure, you see, Joe: could not even kill myself though I tried!" I told him I had renamed myself, Frank; he nodded amicably smiling.

I cheered him up as well as I could, got lodgings for him, took him out of hospital, found work for him too and after a fortnight saw that I could safely leave him. He told me that he regretted having taken so much money from my father, "your share, I'm afraid, and Nita's; but why did he give it me? He might just as well have refused me years ago as let me strip him; but I was a fool and always shall be about money: happy go lucky, I can take no thought for the morrow."

That fortnight showed me that Vernon had only the veneer of a gentleman; at heart he was as selfish as Willie but without Willie's power of work. I had over-estimated him wildly as a boy, thought him noble and well-read; but Smith's real nobility, culture and idealism showed me that Vernon was hardly silver-gilt. He had nice manners and good temper and that was about all.

I stopped at Philadelphia on my way to Lawrence just to tell Smith all I owed him, which the association with Vernon had made clear to me. We had a great night and then for the first time he advised me to go to Europe to study and make myself a teacher and guide of men. I assured him he overestimated me, because I had an excellent verbal memory; but he declared that I had unmistakeable originality and singular fairness of judgment, and above all, a driving power of will that he had never seen equalled: "Whatever you make up your mind to do", he concluded, "you will assuredly accomplish, for you are inclined to underrate yourself." At the time I laughed, saying he didn't even guess at my unlimited conceit, but his words and counsel sank into my mind and in due course exercised a decisive, shaping influence on my life.

I returned to Lawrence, put up a sofa-bed in my law-room and went to the Eldridge House nearby for my meals. I read law assiduously and soon had a few clients, "hard cases" for the most part, sent to me, I found out, by Judge Stevens and Barker, eager to foist nuisances on a beginner.

An old mulatto woman kept our offices tidy and clean for a few dollars monthly from each of us, and one night I was awakened by her groans and cries: she lived in a garret up two flights of stairs and was evidently suffering from indigestion and very much frightened, as colored folk are apt to be when anything ails them: "I'm gwine to die!" she told me a dozen times. I treated her with whisky and warm water, heated on my little gas-heater and sat with her till at length she fell asleep. She declared next day I had saved her life and she'd never forget it "Nebber, fo sure!" I laughed at her and forgot all about it.

Every afternoon I went over to Liberty Hall for an hour or so to keep in touch with events, though I left the main work to Will Thompson. One day I was delighted to find that Bret Harte was coming to lecture for us: his subject "The Argonauts of '49": I got some of his books from the bookstore kept by a lame man named Crew, I think, on Massachusetts Street, and read him carefully. His poetry did not make much impression on me, mere verse, I thought it; but "The Outcasts of Poker Flat" and other stories seemed to me almost masterpieces in spite of their romantic coloring and tinge of melodrama. Especially the description of Oakhurst, the gambler, stuck in my mind: it will be remembered that when crossing the "divide", Oakhurst advised the party of outcasts to keep on travelling till they reached a place of safety. But he did not press his point: he decided it was hopeless and then came Bret Harte's extraordinary painting phrase: "life to Oakhurst was at best an uncertain sort of game and he recognized the usual percentage in favor of the dealer." There is more humor and insight in the one sentence than in all the ridiculously overpraised works of Mark Twain.

One afternoon I was alone in the box-office of Liberty Hall when Rose came in, as pretty as ever. I was delighted to renew our acquaintance and more delighted still to find that she would like tickets for Bret Harte's lecture. "I didn't know that you cared for reading, Rose?" I said, a little surprised.

"Professor Smith and you would make anybody read," she cried, "at any rate you started me." I gave her the tickets and engaged to take her for a buggy-ride next day. I felt sure Rose liked me; but she soon surprised me by showing a stronger virtue than I usually encountered.

She kissed me when I asked her in the buggy but told me at the same time that she didn't care much for kissing: "all men", she said, "are after a girl for the same thing; it's sickening; they all want kisses and try to touch you and say they love you; but they can't love and I don't want their kisses."

"Rose, Rose," I said, "you mustn't be too hard on us: we're different from you girls and that's all."

"How do you mean?" she asked. "I mean that mere desire", I said, "just the wish to kiss and enjoy you, strikes the man first; but behind that lust is often a good deal of affection, and sometimes a deep and sacred tenderness comes to flower; whereas the girl begins with the liking and affection and learns to enjoy the kissing and caressing afterwards."

"I see", she rejoined quietly, "I think I understand: I'm glad to believe that."

Her unexpected depth and sincerity impressed me and I continued:

"We men may be so hungry that we will eat very poor fruit greedily because it's at hand; but that doesn't prove that we don't prefer good and sweet and nourishing food when we can get it." She let her eyes dwell on mine: "I see", she said, "I see!"

And then I went on tell her how lovely she was and how she had made a deathless impression on me and I ventured to hope she liked me a little and would yet be good to me and come to care for me, and I was infinitely pleased to find that this was the right sort of talk and I did my best in the new strain. Three or four times a week I took her out in a buggy and in a little while I had taught her how to kiss and won her to confess that she cared for me, loved me indeed and bit by bit she allowed me the little familiarities of love.

One day I took her out early for a picnic and said, "I'll play Turk and you must treat me" and I stretched myself out on a rug under a tree. She entered into the spirit of the game with zest, brought me food and at length, as she stood close beside me, I couldn't control myself; I put my hand up her dress on her firm legs and sex. Next moment I was kneeling beside her: "Love me, Rose", I begged, "I want you so: I'm hungry for you, dear!"

She looked at me gravely with wide-open eyes: "I love you too", she said, "but oh! I'm afraid: be patient with me!" she added like a little girl. I was patient but persistent and I went on caressing her till her hot lips told me that I had really excited her.

My fingers informed me that she had a perfect sex and her legs were wonderfully firm and tempting, and in her yielding there was the thrill of a conscious yielding out of affection for me, which I find it hard to express. I soon persuaded her to come next day to my office. She came about four o'clock and I kissed and caressed her and at length in the dusk got her to strip. She had the best figure I had ever seen and that made me like her more than I would have believed possible; but I soon found when I got into her that she was not nearly as passionate as Kate even, to say nothing of Lily. She was a cool mistress but would have made a wonderful wife, being all self-sacrifice and tender, thoughtful affection: I have still a very warm corner in my heart for that lovely child-woman and am rather ashamed of having seduced her, for she was never meant to be a plaything or pastime.

But incurably changeable, I had Lily a day or two afterwards and sent Rose a collection of books instead of calling on her. Still I took her out every week till I left Lawrence and grew to esteem her more and more.

Lily, on the other hand, was a born "daughter of the game" to use Shakespeare's phrase and tried to become more and more proficient at it: she wanted to know when and how she gave me most pleasure and really did her best to excite me. Besides, she soon developed a taste in hats and dresses and when I paid for a new outfit, she would dance with delight. She was an entertaining, light companion too and often found odd little naughty phrases that amused me. Her pet aversion was Mrs. Mayhew: she called her always "the Pirate", because she said Lorna only liked "stolen goods" and wanted every man "to walk the plank into her bedroom." Lily insisted that Lorna could cry whenever she wished; but had no real affection in her and her husband filled Lily with contempt: "a well-matched pair", she exclaimed one day, "a mare and a mule, and the mare, as men say, in heat—all wet", and she wrinkled her little nose in disgust.

At the Bret Harte lecture both Rose and Lily had seats and they both understood that I would go and talk with the great man afterwards.

I expected to get a great deal from the lecture and Harte's advance agent had arranged that the hero of the evening should receive me in the Eldridge House after the address.

I was to call for him at the Hotel and take him across to the Hall. When I called, a middle-sized man came to meet me with a rather good-looking, pleasant smile and introspective, musing eyes. Harte was in evening dress that suited his slight figure and as he seemed disinclined to talk, I took him across to the Hall at once and hastened round to the front to note ~~his~~ entrance. He walked quite simply to the desk, arranged his notes methodically and began in a plain, conversational tone, "The Argonauts" and he repeated it, "The Argonauts of '49."

I noticed that there was no American nasal twang in his accent; but with the best of will, I can give no account of the lecture, just as I can give no portrait of the man. I recall only one phrase but think it probably the best: referring to the old-timers crossing the Great Plains, he said, "I am going to tell you of a new Crusade, a Crusade without a cross, an exodus without a prophet!"

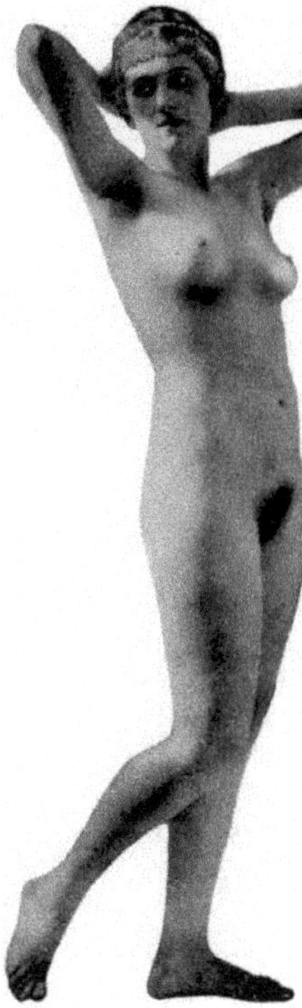

I met him ten years later in London when I had more self-confidence and much deeper understanding both of talent and genius; but I could never get anything of value out of Bret Harte, in spite of the fact that I had then and still keep a good deal of admiration for his undoubted talent. In London later I did my best to draw him out, to get him to say what he thought of life, death and the undiscovered country; but he either murmured commonplaces or withdrew into his shell of complete but apparently thoughtful silence.

The monotonous work and passionate interludes of my life were suddenly arrested by a totally unexpected happening. One day Barker came into my little office and stood there hiccoughing from time to time: "did I know any remedy for hiccoughs?" I only knew a drink of cold water usually stopped it.

"I've drunk every sort of thing," he said, "but I reckon I'll give it best and go home and if it continues, send for the doctor!" I could only acquiesce: next day I heard he was worse and in bed. A week later Sommerfeld told him I ought to call on poor Barker for he was seriously ill.

That same afternoon I called and was horrified at the change: the constant hiccoughing had shaken all the unwieldy mass of flesh from his bones; the skin of his face was flaccid, the bony outline showing under the thin folds. I pretended to think he was better and attempted to congratulate him; but he did not try even to deceive himself. "If they can't stop it, it'll stop me", he said, "but no one ever heard of a man dying of hiccoughs and I'm not forty yet."

The news came a few days later that he was dead—that great fat man!

His death changed my whole life, though I didn't dream at the time it could have any effect upon me. One day I was in court arguing a case before Judge Bassett. Though I liked the man, he exasperated me that day by taking what I thought was a wrong view. I put my point in every light I could; but he wouldn't come round and finally gave the case against me. When I had collected my papers and looked up, he was smiling:

"I shall take this case to the Supreme Court at my own expense", I explained bitterly, "and have your decision reversed."

"If you want to waste your time and money," he remarked pleasantly, "I can't hinder you."

I went out of the court and suddenly found Sommerfeld beside me:

"You fought that case very well", he said, "and you'll win it in the Supreme Court, but you shouldn't have told Bassett so, in his own—'domain'", I suggested, and he nodded.

When we got to our floor and I turned towards my office, he said, "Won't you come in and smoke a cigar, I'd like a talk—"

Sommerfeld's cigars were uniformly excellent and I followed him very willingly into his big, quiet office at the back that looked over some empty lots. I was not a bit curious; for a talk with Sommerfeld usually meant a rather silent smoke. This time, however, he had something to say and said it very abruptly:

"Barker's gone," he remarked in the air, and then: "Why shouldn't you come in here and take his place?"

"As your partner?" I exclaimed. "Sure", he replied, "I'll make out the briefs in the cases as I did for Barker and you'll argue them in court. For instance", he added in his slow way, "there is a decision of the Supreme Court of the State of Ohio that decides your case today almost in your words, and if you had cited it, you'd have convinced Bassett", and he turned and read out the report.

"The State of Ohio," he went on, "is one of the four States, as you know, (I didn't know it) that have adopted the New York Code—New York, Ohio, Kansas and California"—he proceeded, "the four States in a line across the continent; no one of these high courts will contradict the other. So you can be sure of your verdict—well, what do you say?" he concluded.

"I shall be delighted," I replied at once, "indeed I am proud to work with you: I could have wished no better fortune."

He held out his hand silently and the thing was settled.

Sommerfeld smoked a while in silence and then remarked casually, "I used to give Barker a hundred dollars a week for his household expenses: will that suit you?"

"Perfectly, perfectly", I cried, "I only hope I shall earn it and justify your good opinion—"

"You are a better advocate than Barker even now," he said, "but you have one—drawback"—he hesitated.

"Please go on," I cried, "don't be afraid, I can stand any criticism and profit by it—I hope."

"Your accent is a little English, isn't it?" he said, "and that prejudices both judge and jury against you, especially the jury: if you had Barker's accent, you'd be the best pleader in the State—"

"I'll get the accent," I exclaimed, "you're dead right: I had already felt the need of it; but I was obstinate, now I'll get it: you may bet on that, get it within a week" and I did.

There was a lawyer in the town named Hoysradt who had had a fierce quarrel with my brother Willie. He had the most pronounced Western American accent I had ever heard and I set myself the task every morning and evening of imitating Hoysradt's accent and manner of speech. I made it a rule too, to use the slow Western enunciation in ordinary speech and in a week, no one would have taken me for any one but an American.

Sommerfeld was delighted and told me he had fuller confidence in me than ever and from that time on our accord was perfect, for the better I knew him, the more highly I esteemed him: he was indeed able, hardworking, truthful and honest—a compact of all the virtues, but so modest and inarticulate that he was often his own worst enemy.

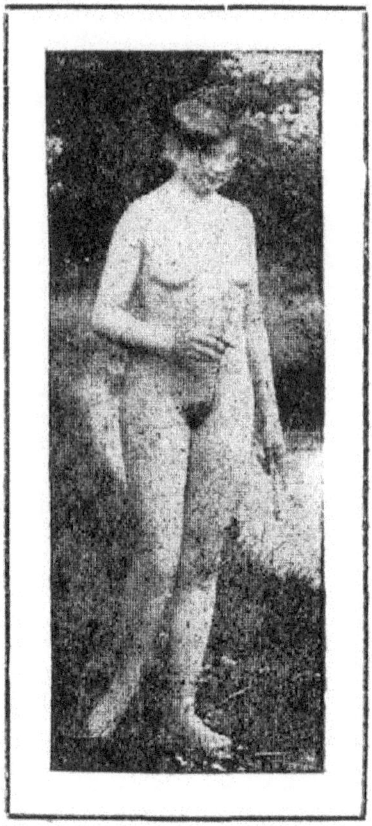

WORK AND SOPHY.

Chapter XIV.

Now began for me a most delightful time. Sommerfeld relieved me of nearly all the office work: I had only to get up the speeches, for he prepared the cases for me. My income was so large that I only slept in my office-room for convenience sake, or rather for my lechery's sake.

I kept a buggy and horse at a livery stable and used to drive Lily or Rose out nearly every day. As Rose lived on the other side of the river, it was easy to keep the two separate and indeed neither of them ever dreamed of the other's existence. I had a very soft spot in my heart for Rose: her beauty of face and form always excited and pleased me and her mind, too, grew quickly through our talks and the books I gave her. I'll never forget her joy when I first bought a small bookcase and sent it to her home one morning, full of the books I thought she would like and ought to read.

In the evening she came straight to my office, told me it was the very thing she had most wanted and she let me study her beauties one by one; but when I turned her round and kissed her bottom, she wanted me to stop: "You can't possibly like or admire that", was her verdict.

"Indeed I do," I cried; but I confessed to myself that she was right; her bottom was adorably dimpled; but it was a little too fat, and the line underneath it was not perfect. One of her breasts, too, was prettier than the other, though both were small and stuck out boldly; my critical sense could find no fault with her triangle or her sex; the lips of it were perfect, very small and rose-red and her clitoris was like a tiny, tiny button. I often wished it were half an inch long like Mrs. Mayhew's. Only once in our intercourse did I try to bring her to ecstasy and only half succeeded; consequently I used simply to have her, just to enjoy myself and only now and then went on to a second orgasm so as really to warm her to the love-play; Rose was anything but sensual, though invariably sweet and an excellent companion. How she could be so affectionate though sexually cold was always a puzzle to me.

Lily, as I have said, was totally different: a merry little grig and born child of Venus: now and then she gave me a really poignant sensation. She was always deriding Mrs. Mayhew; but curiously enough, she was very like her in many intimate ways—a sort of understudy of the older and more passionate woman, with a child's mischievous gaiety to boot and a childish joy in living.

But a great and new sensation was now to come into my life. One evening a girl without a hat on and without knocking came into my office. Sommerfeld had gone home for the night and I was just putting my things straight before going out; she took my breath; she was astoundingly good-looking, very dark with great, black eyes and slight, girlish figure: "I'm Topsy", she announced and stood there smiling, as if the mere name told enough.

"Come in", I said, "and take a seat: I've heard of you!" and I had.

She was a privileged character in the town: she rode on the street-cars and railroads too without paying; those who challenged her were all "pore white trash", she said, and some man was always eager to pay for her: she never hesitated to go up to any man and ask him for a dollar or even five dollars—and invariably got what she wanted: her beauty was as compelling to men as her scornful aloofness. I had often heard of her as "that d—d pretty nigger girl!" but I could see no trace of any negro characteristic in her pure loveliness.

She took the seat and said with a faint Southern accent I found pleasing, "You' name Harris?"

"That's my name", I replied smiling: "You here instead Barker?" she went on: "he sure deserved to die hiccuppin': pore white trash!"

"What's your real name?" I asked.

"They call me 'Topsy'," she replied, "but ma' real true name is Sophy, Sophy Beveridge: you was very kind to my mother who lives upstairs: yes", she went on defiantly, "she's my mother and a mighty good mother too and don't you fergit it!" she added, tossing her head in contempt of my astonishment.

"Your father must have been white!" I couldn't help remarking for I couldn't couple Topsy with the old octaroon, do what I would. She nodded, "he was white all right: that is, his skin was!" and she got up and wandered about the office as if it belonged to her. "I'll call you, 'Sophy'," I said; for I felt a passionate revolt of injured pride in her. She smiled at me with pleasure.

I didn't know what to do. I must not go with a colored girl: though I could see no sign of black blood in Sophy and certainly she was astonishingly good-looking even in her simple sprigged gown. As she moved about I could not but remark the lithe panther-like grace of her and her little breasts stuck out against the thin cotton garment with a most provocative allurement: my mouth was parching when she swung round on me; "You ondressing me", she said smiling, "and I'se glad, 'cause my mother likes you and I loves her—sure pop!"

There was something childish, direct, innocent even about her frankness that fascinated me and her good looks made sunshine in the darkening room.

"I like you, Sophy", I said, "but anyone would have done as much for your mother as I did. She was ill!"

"Hoo!" she snorted indignantly, "most white folk would have let her die right there on the stairs: I know them: they'd have been angry with her for groaning: I hate 'em!" and her great eyes glowered.

She came over to me in a flash:

"If you'd been American, I couldn't never have come to you, never! I'd rather have died, or saved and stole and paid you—" the scorn in her voice was bitter with hate: evidently the negro question had a side I had never realised.

"But you're different", she went on, "an' I just came—" and she paused, lifting her great eyes to mine, with an unspoken offer in their lingering regard.

"I'm glad", I said lamely, staving off the temptation, "and I hope you'll come again soon and we'll be great friends—eh, Sophy?" and I held out my hand smiling; but she pouted and looked at me with reproach or appeal or disappointment in her eyes. I could not resist: I took her hand and drew her to me and kissed her on the lips, slipping my right hand the while up to her left breast: it was as firm as india-rubber: at once I felt my sex stand and throb: resolve and desire fought in me, but I was accustomed to make my will supreme:

"You are the loveliest girl in Lawrence", I said, "but I must really go now: I have an appointment and I'm late."

She smiled enigmatically as I seized my hat and went, not stopping even to shut or lock the office door.

As I walked up the street, my thoughts and feelings were all in a whirl: "Did I want her? Should I have her? Would she come again?

"Oh Hell! women are the very devil and he's not so black as he's painted! Black?"

That night I was awakened by a loud knocking at my office door; I sprang up and opened without thinking and at once Sophy came in laughing.

"What is it?" I cried half asleep still.

"I'se tired waiting", she answered cheekily, "and anyways I just came." I was about to remonstrate with her when she cried: "You go right to bed" and she took my head in her hands and kissed me. My wish to resist died out of me. "Come quickly!" I said getting into bed and watching her as she stripped. In a hand's turn she had undressed to her chemise: "I reckon this'll do", she said coquettishly.

"Please take it off", I cried and the next moment she was in my arms naked. As I touched her sex, she wound her arms round my neck and kissed me greedily with hot lips. To my astonishment her sex was well-formed and very small: I had always heard that negroes had far larger genitals than white people; but the lips of Sophy's sex were thick and firm, "Have you ever been had, Sophy?" I asked.

"No, sir!" she replied, "I liked you because you never came after me and you was so kind and I thot that I'd be sure to do it sometime, so I'd rather let you have me than anyone else: I don't like colored men", she added, "and the white men all look down on me and despise me and I—I love you", she whispered, burying her face on my neck.

"It'll hurt you at first, Sophy, I'm afraid"; but she stilled all scruples with "Shucks, I don't care: if I gives you pleasure, I'se satisfied" and she opened her legs, stretching herself as I got on her. The next moment my sex was caressing her clitoris and of herself she drew up her knees and suddenly with one movement brought my sex into hers and against the maiden barrier. Sophy had no hesitation: she moved her body lithely against me and the next moment I had forced the passage and was in her. I waited a little while and then began the love-game. At once Sophy followed my movements, lifting her sex up to me as I pushed in and depressing it to hold me as I withdrew. Even when I quickened, she kept time and so gave me the most intense pleasure, thrill on thrill, and as I came and my seed spirted into her, the muscle inside her vagina gripped my sex, heightening the sensation to an acute pang; she even kissed me more passionately than any other girl, licking the inside of my lips with her hot tongue. When I went on again with the slow in-and-out movements, she followed in perfect time and her trick of bending her sex down on mine as I withdrew and gripping it at the same time excited me madly: soon, of her own accord, she quickened while gripping and thrilling me till again we both spent together in an ecstasy.

"You're a perfect wonder!" I cried to her then, panting in my turn, "but how did you learn so quickly?"

"I loves you", she said, "so I do whatever I think you'd like and then I likes that too, see?" And her lovely face glowed against mine.

I got up to show her the use of the syringe and found we were in a bath of blood. In a moment she had stripped the sheet off: "I'll wash that in the morning" she said laughing while doubling it into a ball and throwing it in the corner. I turned the gas on full: never was there a more seductive figure. Her skin was darkish, it is true; but not darker than that of an ordinary Italian or Spanish girl, and her form had a curious attraction for me: her breasts, small and firm as elastic, stood out provocatively; her hips, however, were narrower than even Lily's though the cheeks of her bottom were full; her legs too were well-rounded, not a trace of the sticks of the negro; her feet even were slender and high-arched.

"You are the loveliest girl I've ever seen!" I cried as I helped to put in the syringe and wash her sex.

"You're mah man!" she said proudly, "an' I want to show you that I can love better than any white trash; they only gives themselves airs!"

"You are white", I cried, "don't be absurd!" She shook her little head: "if you knew!" she said, "when I was a girl, a child, old white men, the best in town, used to say dirty words to me in the street and try to touch me—the beasts!" I gasped: I had had no idea of such contempt and persecution.

When we were back in bed together: "tell me, Sophy dear, how you learned to move with me in time as you do and give me such thrills!"

"Hoo!" she cried, gurgling with pleased joy, "that's easy to tell. I was scared you didn't like me, so this afternoon I went to wise ole niggah woman and ask her how to make man love you really! She told me to go right to bed with you and do that", and she smiled.

"Nothing more?" I asked: her eyes opened brightly, "Shu!" she cried, "if you want to do love again, I show you!" The next moment I was in her and now she kept even better time than at first and somehow or other the thick, firm lips of her sex seemed to excite me more than anyone had ever excited me. Instinctively the lust grew in me and I quickened and as I came to the short, hard strokes, she suddenly slipped her legs together under me and closing them tightly held my sex as in a firm grip and then began "milking" me—no other word conveys the meaning—with extraordinary skill and speed, so that in a moment I was gasping and choking with the intensity of the sensation and my seed came in hot jets while she continued the milking movement, tireless, indefatigable!

"What a marvel you are!" I exclaimed as soon as I got breath enough to speak, "the best bedfellow I've ever had, wonderful, you dear, you!"

All glowing with my praise, she wound her arms about my neck and mounted me as Lorna Mayhew had done once; but now what a difference! Lorna was so intent on gratifying her own lust that she often forgot my feelings altogether and her movements were awkward in the extreme; but Sophy thought only of me and, whereas Lorna was always slipping my sex out of her sheath, Sophy in some way seated herself on me and then began rocking her body back and forth while lifting it a little at each churning movement, so that my sex in the grip of her firm, thick lips had a sort of double movement. When she felt me coming as I soon did, she twirled half round on my organ half a dozen times with a new movement and then began rocking herself again, so that my seed was dragged out of me, so to speak, giving me indescribably acute, almost painful sensations. I was breathless thrilling with her every movement.

"Had you any pleasure, Sophy?" I asked as soon as we were lying side by side again.

"Shuah!" she said smiling, "you're very strong, and you—" she asked, "was you pleased?"

"Great God!" I cried, "I felt as if all the hairs of my head were travelling down my backbone like an army! You are extraordinary, you dear!"

"Keep me with you, Frank", she whispered, "if you want me, I'll do anything, everything for you: I never hoped to have such a lover as you. Oh, this child's real glad her breasties and sex please you. You taught me that word, instead of the nasty word all white folk use; 'sex' is good word, very good!" and she crowed with delight. "What do colored people call it?" I asked: "Coozie", she replied smiling, Coozie! good word too, very good!

Long years later I heard an American story which recalled Sophy's performance vividly.

An engineer with a pretty daughter had an assistant who showed extraordinary qualities as a machinist and was quiet and well behaved to boot. The father introduced his helper to his daughter and the match was soon arranged. After the marriage, however, the son-in-law drew away and 'twas in vain that the father-in-law tried to guess the reason of the estrangement. At length he asked his son-in-law boldly for the reason: "I meant right, Bill", he began earnestly, "but if I've made a mistake I'll be sorry: waren't the goods accordin' to specification? Warn't she a virgin?"

"It don't matter nothin'!" replied Bill, frowning.

"Treat me fair, Bill", cried the father, "war she a virgin?"

"How can I tell?" exclaimed Bill, "all I can say is, I never know'd a virgin before that had that cinder-shifting movement."

Sophy was the first to show me the "cinder-shifting" movement and she surely was a virgin!

As a mistress Sophy was perfection perfected and the long lines and slight curves of her lovely body came to have a special attraction for me as the very highest of the pleasure-giving type.

Lily first and then Rose were astonished and perhaps a little hurt at the sudden cooling off of my passion for them. From time to time I took Rose out or sent her books and I had Lily anywhere, any when; but neither of them could compare with Sophy as a bedfellow and her talk even fascinated me more, the better I knew her. She had learned life from the streets, from the animal side first; but it was astonishing how quickly she grew in understanding: love is the only magical teacher! In a fortnight her speech was better than Lily's; in a month she talked as well as any of the American girls I had had; her desire of knowledge and her sponge-like ease of acquirement were always surprising me. She had a lovelier figure than even Rose and ten times the seduction even of Lily: she never hesitated to take my sex in her hand and caress it; she was a child of nature, bold with an animal's boldness and had besides a thousand endearing familiarities. I had only to hint a wish for her to gratify it. Sophy was the pearl of all the girls I met in this first stage of my development and I only wish I could convey to the reader a suggestion even of her quaint, enthralling caresses. My admiration of Sophy cleansed me of any possible disdain I might otherwise have had of the negro people, and I am glad of it; for else I might have closed my heart against the Hindu and so missed the best part of my life's experiences.

I have had a great artist make the sketch of her back which I reproduce at the end of this chapter: it conveys something of the strange vigor and nerve-force of her lovely firm body.

But it was written that as soon as I reached ease and content, the Fates would reshuffle the cards and deal me another hand.

First of all, there came a letter from Smith, telling me how he had got a bad wetting one night and had caught a severe cold. The cough then had returned and he was losing weight and heart. He had come to the conclusion, too, that I had reached, that the moist air of Philadelphia was doing him harm and the doctors now were beginning to urge him to go to Denver, Colorado: all the foremost specialists agreeing that mountain air was the best for his lung-weakness. If I couldn't come to him, I must wire him and he'd stop in Lawrence to see me on his way West, he had much to say—

A couple of days later he was in the Eldridge House and I went to see him. His appearance shocked me: he had grown spectre thin and the great eyes seemed to burn like lamps in his white face. I knew at once that he was doomed and could scarcely control my tears.

We passed the whole day together and when he heard how I spent my days in casual reading and occasional speaking and my Topsy-turvey nights, he urged me to throw up the law and go to Europe to make myself a real scholar and thinker. But I could not give up Sophy and my ultra-pleasant life. So I resisted, told him he overrated me: I'd easily be the best advocate in the State, I said, and make a lot of money and then I'd go back and do Europe and study as well.

He warned me that I must choose between God and Mammon; I retorted lightly that Mammon and my senses gave me much that God denied: "I'll serve both", I cried, but he shook his head.

"I'm finished, Frank", he declared at length, "but I'd regret life less if I knew that you would take up the work I once hoped to accomplish, won't you?"

I couldn't resist his appeal: "All right", I said, after choking down my tears, "give me a few months and I'll go, round the world first and then to Germany to study."

He drew me to him and kissed me on the forehead: I felt it as a sort of consecration.

A day or so afterwards he took train for Denver and I felt as if the sun had gone out of my life.

I had little to do in Lawrence at this time except read at large and I began to spend a couple of hours every day in the town library. Mrs. Trask, the librarian, was the widow of one of the early settlers who had been brutally murdered during the Quantrell raid when Missourian bandits "shot up" the little town of Lawrence in a last attempt to turn Kansas into a slave-owning state.

Mrs. Trask was a rather pretty little woman who had been made librarian to compensate her in some sort for the loss of her husband. She was well-read in American literature and I often took her advice as to my choice of books. She liked me, I think, for she was invariably kind to me and I owe her many pleasant hours and some instruction.

After Smith had gone West I spent more and more time in the library for my law-work was becoming easier to me every hour. One day about a month after Smith had left, I went into the library and could find nothing enticing to read. Mrs. Trask happened to be passing and I asked her: "What am I to read?"

"Have you read any of that?" she replied pointing to Bohn's edition of Emerson in two volumes. "He's good!"

"I saw him in Concord", I said, "but he was deaf and made little impression on me."

"He's the greatest American thinker", she retorted, "and you ought to read him."

Automatically I took down the volume and it opened of itself at the last page of Emerson's advice to the scholars of Dartmouth College. Every word is still printed on my memory: I can see the left-hand page and read again that divine message: I make no excuse for quoting it almost word for word:

"Gentlemen, I have ventured to offer you these considerations upon the scholar's place and hope, because I thought that standing, as many of you now do, on the threshold of this College, girt and ready to go and assume tasks, public and private, in your country, you would not be sorry to be admonished of those primary duties of the intellect whereof you will seldom hear from the lips of your new companions. You will hear every day the maxims of a low prudence. You will hear that the first duty is to get land and money, place and name. 'What is this Truth you seek? what is this beauty!' men will ask, with derision. If nevertheless God have called any of you to explore truth and beauty, be bold, be firm, be true. When you shall say, 'As others do, so will I: I renounce, I am sorry for it, my early visions; I must eat the good of the land and let learning and romantic expectations go, until a more convenient season';—then dies the man in you; then once more perish the buds of art, and poetry, and science, as they have died already in a thousand thousand men. The hour of that choice is the crisis of your history, and see that you hold yourself fast by the intellect. It is this domineering temper of the sensual world that creates the extreme need of the priests of science.... Be content with a little light, so it be your own. Explore, and explore. Be neither chided nor flattered out of your position of perpetual inquiry. Neither dogmatize, nor accept another's dogmatism. Why should you renounce your right to traverse the star-lit deserts of truth, for the premature comforts of an acre, house, and barn? Truth also has its roof, and bed, and board. Make yourself necessary to the world, and mankind will give you bread, and if not store of it, yet such as shall not take away your property in all men's affections, in art, in nature, and in hope."

The truth of it shocked me: "then perish the buds of art and poetry and science in you as they have perished already in a thousand, thousand men!" That explained why it was that there was no Shakespeare, no Bacon, no Swinburne in America where, according to population and wealth there should be dozens.

There flashed on me the realization of the truth, that just because wealth was easy to get here, it exercised an incomparable attraction and in its pursuit "perished a thousand, thousand" gifted spirits who might have steered humanity to new and nobler accomplishment.

The question imposed itself: "Was I too to sink to fatness? wallow in sensuality, degrade myself for a nerve-thrill?"

"No!" I cried to myself, "ten thousand times, no! No! I'll go and seek the star-lit deserts of Truth or die on the way!"

I closed the book and with it and the second volume of it in my hand went to Mrs. Trask.

"I want to buy this book", I said, "it has a message for me that I must never forget!"

"I'm glad", said the little lady smiling, "what is it?"

I read her a part of the passage: "I see", she exclaimed, "but why do you want the books?"

"I want to take them with me", I said, "I mean to leave Lawrence at once and go to Germany to study!"

"Good gracious!" she cried, "how can you do that? I thought you were a partner of Sommerfeld's; you can't go at once!"

"I must", I said, "the ground burns under my feet: if I don't go now, I shall never go: I'll be out of Lawrence tomorrow!"

Mrs. Trask threw up her hands and remonstrated with me: such quick decisions were dangerous; "why should I be in such a hurry?"

I repeated time and again: "If I don't go at once, I shall never go: 'the ignoble pleasures' will grow sweeter and sweeter to me and I shall sink gradually and drown in the mud-honey of life."

Finally seeing I was adamant and my mind fixed: she sold me the books at full price with some demur, then she added:

"I almost wish I had never recommended Emerson to you!" and the dear lady looked distressed, almost on the verge of tears.

"Never regret that!" I cried, "I shall remember you as long as I live because of that and always be grateful to you. Professor Smith told me I ought to go; but it needed the word of Emerson to give me the last push! The buds of poetry and science and art shall not perish in me as they have 'perished already in a thousand, thousand men!' Thanks to you!" I added warmly, "all my best heart-thanks: you have been to me the messenger of high fortune."

I clasped her hands, wished to kiss her, but foolishly feared to hurt her and so contented myself with a long kiss on her hand and went out at once to find Sommerfeld.

He was in the office and forthwith I told him the whole story, how Smith had tried to persuade me and how I had resisted till this page of Emerson had convinced me: "I am sorry to leave you in the lurch," I explained; but "I must go and go at once."

He told me it was madness: I could study German right there in Lawrence; he would help me with it gladly. "You mustn't throw away a livelihood just for a word", he cried, "it is madness, I never heard a more insane decision!"

We argued for hours: I couldn't convince him any more than he could persuade me; he tried his best to get me to stay two years at any rate and then go with full pockets: "you can easily spare two years", he cried, but I retorted, "not even two days: I'm frightened of myself."

When he found that I wanted the money to go round the world with first, he saw a chance of delay and said I must give him some time to find out what was coming to me; I told him I trusted him utterly (as indeed I did) and could only give him the Saturday and Sunday, for I'd go on the Monday at the latest. He gave in at last and was very kind.

I got a dress and little hat for Lily and lots of books beside a chinchilla cape for Rose and broke the news to Lily next morning, keeping the afternoon for Rose. To my astonishment I had most trouble with Lily: she would not hear any reason: "There is no reason in it", she cried again and again, and then she broke down in a storm of tears: "What will become of me?" she sobbed, "I always hoped you'd marry me!" she confessed at last, "and now you go away for nothing, nothing—on a wild-goose chase—to study", she added in a tone of absolute disdain, "just as if you couldn't study here!"

"I'm too young to marry, Lily," I said, "and—"

"You were not too young to make me love you", she broke in, "and now what shall I do? Even Mamma said that we ought to be engaged and I want you so,—oh! oh!" and again the tears fell in a shower.

I could not help saying at last that I would think it all over and let her know and away I went to Rose. Rose heard me out in complete silence and then with her eyes on mine in lingering affection, she said:

"Do you know, I've been afraid often of some decision like this. I said to myself a dozen times, 'why should he stay here? the wider world calls him' and if I feel inclined to hate my work because it prevents my studying, what must it be for him in that horrible court, fighting day after day? I always knew I should lose you, dear!" she added, "but you were the first to help me to think and read, so I must not complain. Do you go soon?"

"On Monday," I replied, and her dear eyes grew sombre and her lips quivered. "You'll write?" she asked, "please do, Frank! No matter what happens I shall never forget you: you've helped me, encouraged me more than I can say. Did I tell you, I've got a place in Crew's bookstore? When I said I had learned to love books from you, he was glad and said 'if you get to know them as well as he did, or half as well, you'll be invaluable'; so you see, I am following in your footsteps, as you are following in Smith's."

"If you knew how glad I am that I've really helped and not hurt you, Rose?" I said sadly, for Lily's accusing voice was still in my ears.

"You couldn't hurt anyone," she exclaimed, almost as if she divined my remorse, "you are so gentle and kind and understanding."

Her words were balm to me and she walked with me to the bridge where I told her she would hear from me on the morrow. I wanted to know what she would think of the books and cape. The last thing I saw of her was her hand raised as if in benediction.

I kept the Sunday morning for Sommerfeld and my friend Will Thompson and the rest of the day for Sophy.

Sommerfeld came to the office before nine and told me the firm owed me three thousand dollars: I didn't wish to take it; could not believe he had meant to go halves with me but he insisted and paid me.

"I don't agree with your sudden determination," he said, "perhaps because it was sudden; but I've no doubt you'll do well at anything you take up. Let me hear from you now and again and if you ever need a friend, you know where to find me!"

As we shook hands I realised that parting could be as painful as the tearing asunder of flesh.

Will Thompson, I found, was eager to take over the hoardings and my position in Liberty Hall; he had brought his father with him and after much bargaining I conveyed everything I could, over to him for three thousand five hundred dollars, and so after four year's work I had just the money I had had in Chicago four years earlier!

I dined in the Eldridge House and then went back to the office to meet Sophy who was destined to surprise me more even than Lily or Rose: "I'm coming with you," she announced coolly, "if you're not ashamed to have me along; you goin' Frisco,—so far anyway—" she pleaded divining my surprise and unwillingness.

"Of course, I'll be delighted," I said, "but—" I simply could not refuse her.

She gurgled with joy and drew out her purse: "I've four hundred dollars", she said proudly, "and that'll take this child a long way."

I made her put the money away and promise me she wouldn't spend a cent of her money while we were together and then I told her how I wished to dress her when we got to Denver, for I wanted to stop there for a couple of days to see Smith who had written approving of everything I did and adding, to my heart's joy, that he was much better.

On the Monday morning Sophy and I started westwards: she had had the tact to go to the depot first so that no one in Lawrence ever coupled our names. Sommerfeld and Judge Bassett saw me off at the depot and wished me "all luck!" And so the second stage of my life came to an end.

Sophy was a lively sweet companion; after leaving Topeka, she came boldly into my compartment and did not leave me again. May I confess it? I'd rather she had stayed in Lawrence; I wanted the adventure of being alone and there was a girl in the train whose long eyes held mine as I passed her seat, and I passed it often: I'd have spoken to her if Sophy had not been with me.

When we got to Denver, I called on Smith, leaving Sophy in the hotel. I found him better, but divined that the cursed disease was only taking breath, so to speak, before the final assault. He came back with me to my hotel and as soon as he saw Sophy, he declared I must go back with him, he had forgotten to give me something I must have. I smiled at Sophy to whom Smith was very courteous-kind and accompanied him. As soon as we were in the street, Smith began in horror:

"Frank, she's a colored girl: you must leave her at once or you'll make dreadful trouble for yourself later." "How did you know she was colored?" I asked. "Look at her nails!" he cried, "and her eyes: no Southerner would be in doubt for a moment. You must leave her at once, please!"

"We are going to part at Frisco", I said. And when he pressed me to send her back at once, I refused. I would not put such shame upon her and even now I'm sure I was right in that resolve.

Smith was sorry but kind to me and so we parted forever.

He had done more for me than any other man and now after fifty years I can only confess my incommensurable debt to him and the hot tears come into my eyes now as they came when our hands met for the last time: he was the dearest, sweetest, noblest spirit of a man I have met in this earthly pilgrimage. *Ave atque vale.*

As the time drew on to the day when the boat was to start, Sophy grew thoughtful. I got her a pretty corn-colored dress that set off her beauty as golden sunlight a lovely woodland, and when she thanked and hugged me, I wanted to put my hand up her clothes for she had made a mischievous, naughty remark that amused me and reminded me we had driven all the previous day and I had not had her. To my surprise she stopped me: "I've not washed since we came in", she explained.

"Do you wash so often?" "Shuah," she replied, fixing me.

"Why?" I asked, searching her regard.

"Because I'm afraid of nigger-smell," she flung out passionately—

"What nonsense!" I exclaimed.

"'Tain't either", she contradicted me angrily, "My mother took me once to negro-church and I near choked: I never went again; I just couldn't: when they get hot, they stink—pah!" and she shook her head and made a face in utter disgust and contempt.

"That's why you goin' to leave me", she added after a long pause, with tears in her voice; "if it wasn't for that damned nigger blood in me, I'd never leave you: I'd just go on with you as servant or anything: ah God, how I love you and how lonely this Topsy'll be!" and the tears ran down her quivering face. "If I were only all white or all black," she sobbed: "I'm so unhappy!" My heart bled for her.

If it had not been for the memory of Smith's disdain, I would have given in and taken her with me. As it was, I could only do my best to console her by saying: "a couple of years, Sophy, and I'll return; they'll pass quickly: I'll write you often, dear!"

But Sophy knew better and when the last night came, she surpassed herself. It was warm and we went early to bed: "it's my night!" she said: "you just let me show you, you dear! I don't want you to go after any whitish girl in those Islands till you get to China and you won't go with those yellow, slit-eyed girls—that's why I love you so, because you keep yourself for those you like:—but you're naughty to like so many—ma man!" and she kissed me with passion: she let me have her almost without response, but after the first orgasm she gripped my sex and milked me, and afterwards mounting me made me thrill again and again till I was speechless and like children we fell asleep in each other's arms, weeping for the parting on the morrow.

I said "Good-bye!" at the hotel and went on board the steamer by myself: my eyes set on the Golden Gate into the great Pacific and the hopes and hazards of the new life. At length I was to see the world: what would I find in it? I had no idea then that I should find little or much in exact measure to what I brought and it is now the saddest part of these Confessions that on this first trip round the world, I was so untutored, so thoughtless that I got practically nothing out of my long journeying.

Like Odysseus I saw many cities of men; but scenes seldom enrich the spirit: yet one or two places made a distinct impression on me, young and hard though I was: Sidney Bay and Heights, Hong Kong, too; but above all, the old Chinese gate leading into the Chinese City of Shanghai so close to the European town and so astonishingly different. Kioto, too, imprinted itself on my memory and the Japanese men and girls that ran naked out of their hot baths in order to see whether I was really white all over.

But I learned nothing worth recalling till I came to Table Bay and saw the long line of Table Mountain four thousand feet above me, a cliff cutting the sky with an incomparable effect of dignity and grandeur. I stayed in Cape Town a month or so, and by good luck I got to know Jan Hofmeyr there who taught me what good fellows the Boers really were and how highly the English Premier Gladstone was esteemed for giving freedom to them after Majuba: "we look on him with reverence" said my friend, Hofmeyr, "as the embodied conscience of England"; but alas! England could not stomach Majuba and had to spend blood and treasure later to demonstrate the manhood of the Boers to the world. But thank God, England then gave freedom and self-government again to South Africa and so atoned for her shameful "Concentration Camps." Thanks to Jan Hofmeyr I got to know and esteem the South African Boer even on this first short acquaintance.

When I went round the world for the second time twenty years later, I tried to find the Hofmeyrs of every country and so learned all manner of things worthful and strange that I shall tell of, I hope, at the end of my next volume. For the only short cut to knowledge is through intercourse with wise and gifted men.

Now I must confess something of my first six months of madness and pleasure in Paris and then speak of England again and Thomas Carlyle and his incomparable influence upon me and so lead you, gentle render, to my later prentice years in Germany and Greece.

There in Athens I learned new sex-secrets which may perchance interest even the Philistines though they can be learned in Paris as well, and will be set forth simply in the second volume of these "Confessions", which will tell the whole "art of love" as understood in Europe and perhaps contain my second voyage round the world and the further instruction in the great art which I received from the Adepts of the East—unimaginable refinements, for they have studied the body as deeply as the soul.

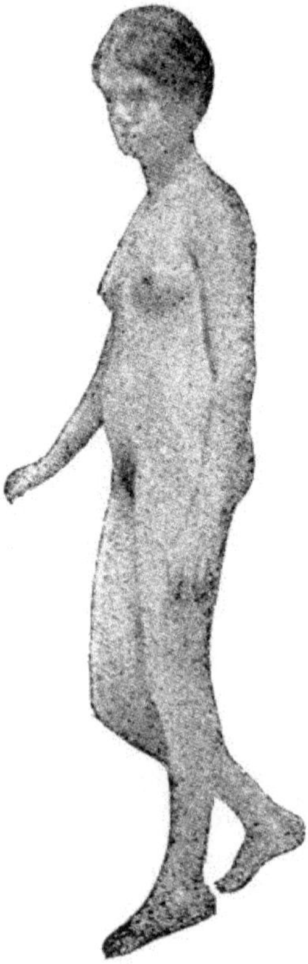

EUROPE AND THE CARLYLES.

Chapter XV.

I returned to Europe touching at Bombay and getting just a whiff of the intoxicating perfume of that wonder-land with its noble, though sad, spiritual teaching which is now beginning through the Rig Veda to inform the best European thought.

I stopped too at Alexandria and ran up to Cairo for a week to see the great Mosques: I admired their splendid rhetoric; but fell in love with the desert and its Pyramids and above all with the Sphinx and her eternal questioning of sense and outward things. Thus by easy, memorable stages that included Genoa and Florence and their storied palaces and churches and galleries, I came at length to Paris.

I distrust first impressions of great places or events or men. Who could describe the deathless fascination of the mere name and first view of Paris to the young student or artist of another race! If he has read and thought, he will be in a fever; tears in his eyes, heart thrilling with joyful expectancy, he will wander into that world of wonders!

I got to the station early one summer morning and sent my baggage at once by fiacre to the Hotel Meurice in the rue Rivoli; the same old hotel that Lever the novelist had praised, and then I got into a little Victoria and drove to the Place de la Bastille. The obvious café life of the people did not appeal to me; but when I saw the Glory springing from the Column of July, tears flooded my eyes, for I recalled Carlyle's description of the taking of the prison.

I paid the cocher and wandered up the rue Rivoli, past the Louvre, past the blackened walls with the sightless windows of the Tuileries palace—a regret in their desolate appeal, and so to the Place de la Gréve with its memories of the guillotine and the great revolution, now merged in the Place de la Concorde. Just opposite I could distinguish the gilt dome of the Church of the Invalides where the body of Napoleon lies as he desired: "On the banks of the Seine, in the midst of that French people I have loved so passionately!"

And there were the horses of Marly ramping at the entrance to the Champs Elysées and at the far end of the long hill, the Arch! The words came to my lips:

Up the long dim road where thundered

The army of Italy onward

By the great pale arch of the Star.

It was the deep historic sense of this great people that first won me and their loving admiration of their poets and artists and guides. I can never describe the thrill it gave me to find on a small house a marble plaque recording the fact that poor de Musset had once lived there, and another on the house wherein he died. Oh, how right the French are to have a Place Malherbe, and Avenue Victor Hugo, an Avenue de la Grande Armée too, and an Avenue de L'Imperatrice as well, though it has since been changed prosaically into the Avenue du Bois de Boulogne.

From the Place de la Concorde I crossed the Seine and walked down the quays to the left, and soon passed the Conciergerie and Ste Chapelle with its gorgeous painted glass-windows of a thousand, years ago and there before me on the Ile de la Cité, the twin towers of Notre Dame caught my eyes and breath and finally, early in the afternoon I turned up the Boul' Mich and passed the Sorbonne and then somehow or other lost myself in the old rue St. Jacques that Dumas père and other romance-writers had described for me a thousand times.

I little tired at length having left the Luxemburg gardens far behind with their statues which I promised myself soon to study more closely, I turned into a little wine-shop restaurant kept by a portly and pleasant lady whose name I soon learned was Marguerite. After a most excellent meal I engaged a large room on the first floor looking on the street, for forty francs a month, and if a friend came to live with me, why Marguerite promised with a large smile to put in another bed for an additional ten francs monthly and supply us besides with coffee in the morning and whatever meals we wanted at most reasonable prices: there I lived gaudy, golden days for some three heavenly weeks.

I threw myself on French like a glutton and this was my method, which I don't recommend but simply record, though it brought me to understand everything said by the end of the first week. I first spent five whole days on the grammar, learning all the verbs, especially the auxiliary and irregular verbs by heart, till I knew them as I knew my Alphabet. I then read Hugo's Hernani with a dictionary in another long day of eighteen hours and the next evening went to the gallery in the Comédie Française to see the play acted by Sarah Bernhardt as Doña Sol and Mounet Sully as Hernani. For a while the rapid speech and strange accent puzzled me; but after the first act I began to understand what was said on the stage and after the second act I caught every word and to my delight when I came out into the streets, I understood everything said to me. After that golden night with Sarah's grave, *traînante* voice in my ears, I made rapid because unconscious progress.

Next day in the restaurant I picked up a dirty torn copy of Madame Bovary that lacked the first eighty pages. I took it to my room and swallowed it in a couple of breathless hours, realising at once that it was a masterwork; but marking a hundred and fifty new words to turn out in my pocket dictionary afterwards. I learned these words carefully by heart and have never given myself any trouble about French since.

What I know of it and I know it fairly well now, has come from reading and speaking it for thirty odd years. I still make mistakes in it chiefly of gender, I regret to say, and my accent is that of a foreigner, but taking it by and large I know it and its literature and speak it better than most foreigners and that suffices me.

After some three weeks Ned Bancroft came from the States to live with me. He was never particularly sympathetic to me and I cannot account for our companionship save by the fact that I was peculiarly heedless and full of human, unreflecting kindness. I have said little of Ned Bancroft who was in love with Kate Stevens before she fell for Professor Smith; but I have just recorded the unselfish way he withdrew while keeping intact his friendship both for Smith and the girl: I thought that very fine of him.

He left Lawrence and the University shortly after we first met and by "pull" obtained a good position on the railroad at Columbus, Ohio.

He was always writing to me to come to visit him and on my return from Philadelphia, in 1875 I think, I stopped at Columbus and spent a couple of days with him. As soon as he heard that I had gone to Europe and had reached Paris, he wrote to me that he wished I had asked him to come with me and so I wrote setting forth my purpose and at once he threw up his good prospects of riches and honor and came to me in Paris. We lived together for some six months: he was a tall, strong fellow, with pale face and gray eyes; a good student, an honorable, kindly, very intelligent man; but we envisaged life from totally different sides and the longer we were together, the less we understood each other.

In everything we were antipodes; he should have been an Englishman for he was a born aristocrat with imperious, expensive tastes, while I had really become a Western American, careless of dress or food or position, intent only on acquiring knowledge and, if possible, wisdom in order to reach greatness.

The first evening we dined at Marguerite's and spent the night talking and swapping news. The very next afternoon Ned would go into Paris and we dined in a swell restaurant on the Grand Boulevard. A few tables away a tall, splendid-looking brunette of perhaps thirty was dining with two men: I soon saw that Ned and she were exchanging looks and making signs. He told me he intended to go home with her: I remonstrated but he was as obstinate as Charlie, and when I told him of the risks he said he'd never do it again; but this time he couldn't get out of it. "I'll pay the bill at once", I said, "and let's go!" but he would not, desire was alight in him and a feeling of false shame hindered him from taking my advice. Half an hour later the lady made a sign and he went out with the party and when she entered her Victoria, he got in with her; the pair on the sidewalk, he said, bursting into laughter as he and the woman drove away together.

Next morning he was back with me early, only saying that he had enjoyed himself hugely and was not even afraid. Her rooms were lovely, he declared; he had to give her a hundred francs: the bath and toilette arrangements were those of a queen: there was no danger. And he treated me to as wild a theory as Charlie had cherished: told me that the great *cocottes* who make heaps of money took as much care of themselves as gentlemen. "Go with a common prostitute and you'll catch something; go with a real topnotcher and she's sure to be all right!" And perfectly at ease he went to work with a will.

Bancroft's way of learning French even was totally different from mine: he went at the grammar and syntax and mastered them: he could write excellent French at the end of four months; but spoke it very haltingly and with a ferocious American accent. When I told him I was going to hear Taine lecture on the Philosophy of Art and the Ideal in Art, he laughed at me; but I believe I got more from Taine than he got from his more exact knowledge of French. When I came to know Taine and was able to call on him and talk to him, Bancroft too wanted to know him. I brought them together; but clearly Taine was not impressed, for Ned out of false shame hardly opened his mouth. But I learned a good deal from Taine and one illustration of his abides with me as giving a true and vivid conception of art and its ideal. In a lecture he pointed out to his students that a lion was not a running beast; but a great jaw set on four powerful springs of short, massive legs. The artist, he went on, seizing the *idea* of the animal may exaggerate the size and strength of the jaw a little, emphasize too the springing power in his loins and legs and the tearing strength of his front paws and claws; but if he lengthened his legs or diminished his jaw, he would denaturalize the true *idea* of the beast and would produce an abortion. The ideal, however, should only be indicated. Taine's talks, too, on literature and the importance of the environment even on great men, all made a profound impression on me. After listening to him for some time I began to see my way up more clearly. I shall never forget, too, some of his thought-inspiring words. Talking one day of the convent of Monte Casino, where a hundred generations of students, freed from all the sordid cares of existence, had given night and day to study and thought and had preserved besides the priceless manuscripts of long past ages and so paved the way for a Renascence of learning and thought, he added gravely:

"I wonder whether Science will ever do as much for her votaries as Religion has done for hers: in other words, I wonder will there ever be a laic Monte Casino!"

Taine was a great teacher and I owe him much kindly encouragement and even enlightenment.

I add this last word, because his French freedom of speech came as pure spring water to my thirsty soul. A dozen of us were grouped about him one day, talking when one student with a remarkable gift for vague thought and highfalutin' rhetoric, wanted to know what Taine thought of the idea that all the worlds and planets and solar systems were turning round one axis and moving to some divine fulfillment (accomplissement). Taine, who always disliked windy rhetoric, remarked quietly: "The only axis in my knowledge round which everything moves to some accomplishment is a woman's cunt (le con d'une femme)." They laughed, but not as if the bold word had astonished them. He used it when it was needed, as I have often heard Anatole France use it since, and no one thought anything of it.

In spite of the gorgeous installation of his brunette, Ned at the end of a week found out how blessed are those described in Holy Writ, who fished all night and caught nothing. He had caught a dreadful gonorrhea and was forbidden spirits or wine or coffee till he got well. Exercise, too, was only to be taken in small doses, so it happened that when I went out, he had to stay at home and the outlook on the rue St. Jacques was anything but exhilarating. This naturally increased his desire to get about and see things, and as soon as he began to understand spoken French and to speak it a little, he chafed against the confinement and a room without a bath; he longed for the centre, for the opera and the Boulevards, and nothing would do but we should take rooms in the heart of Paris: he would borrow money from his folks, he said.

Like a fool I was willing and so we took rooms one day in a quiet street just behind the Madeleine, at ten times the price we were paying Marguerite. I soon found that my money was melting; but the life was very pleasant. We often drove in the Bois, went frequently to the Opera, the theatres and music-halls and appraised, too, the great restaurants, the Café Anglais and the Trois Frères as if we had been millionaires.

As luck would have it, Ned's venereal disease and the doctors became a heavy additional expense that I could ill afford. Suddenly one day I realised that I had only six hundred dollars in the bank: at once I made up my mind to stop and make a fresh start. I told my resolution to Bancroft: he asked me to wait: "he had written to his people for money", he said, "he would soon pay his debt to me"; but that wasn't what I wanted: I felt that I had got off the right road because of him and was angry with myself for having wasted my substance in profligate living and worst of all in silly luxury and brainless showing off.

I declared I was ill and was going to England at once; I must make a new start and accumulate some more money and a few mornings later I bade

Bancroft "Good-bye" and crossed the Channel and went on to my sister and father in Tenby, arriving there in a severe shivering fit with a bad headache and every symptom of ague.

I was indeed ill and played out: I had taken double doses of life and literature, had swallowed all the chief French writers from Rabelais and Montaigne to Flaubert, Zola and Balzac, passing by Pascal and Vauvenargues, Renan and Hugo, a glutton's feast for six months. Then, too, I had nosed out this artist's studio and that; had spent hours watching Rodin at work and more hours comparing this painter's model with that: these breasts and hips with those.

My love of plastic beauty nearly brought me to grief at least once and perhaps I had better record the incident, though it rather hurt my vanity at the time. One day I called at Manet's old studio which was rented now by an American painter named Alexander. He had real power as a craftsman but only a moderate brain and was always trying by beauty or something remarkable in his model to make up for his own want of originality. On this visit I noticed an extraordinary sketch of a young girl standing where childhood and womanhood meet: she had cut her hair short and her chestnut-dark eyes lent her a startling distinction.

"You like it?" asked Alexander. "She has the most perfect figure I have ever seen!"

"I like it", I replied; "I wonder whether the magic is in the model or in your brush?" "You'll soon see", he retorted, a little piqued, "she's due here already" and almost as he spoke she came in with quick, alert step. She was below medium height; but evidently already a woman. Without a word she went behind the screens to undress, when Alexander said: "Well?" I had to think a moment or two before answering.

"God and you have conspired together!" I exclaimed, and indeed his brush had surpassed itself. He had caught and rendered a childish innocence in expression that I had not remarked and he had blocked in the features with superb *brio*:

"It is your best work to date", I went on, "and almost anyone would have signed it."

At this moment the model emerged with a sheet about her and probably because of my praise Alexander introduced me to Mlle. Jeanne and said I was a distinguished American writer. She nodded to me saucily, flashing white teeth at me, mounted the estrade, threw off the sheet and took up her pose—all in a moment. I was carried off my feet; the more I looked, the more perfections I discovered. For the first time I saw a figure that I could find no fault with. Needless to say I told her so in my best French with a hundred similes. Alexander also I conciliated by begging him to do no more to the sketch but sell it to me and do another. Finally he took four hundred and fifty francs for it and in an hour had made another sketch.

My purchase had convinced Mlle. Jeanne that I was a young millionaire and when I asked her if I might accompany her to her home, she consented more than readily. As a matter of fact, I took her for a drive in the Bois de Boulogne and from there to dinner in a private room at the Café Anglais. During the meal I had got to like her: she lived with her mother, Alexander had told me; though by no means prudish, still less virginal, she was not a *coureuse.* I thought I might risk connection; but when I got her to take off her clothes and began to caress her sex, she drew away and said quite as a matter of course: "Why not *faire minette*?"

When I asked her what she meant, she told me frankly: "We women do not get excited in a moment as you men do; why not kiss and tongue me there for a few minutes, then I shall have enjoyed myself and shall be ready...."

I'm afraid I made rather a face for she remarked coolly: "Just as you like, you know. I prefer in a meal the *hors d'oeuvres* to the *pièce de résistance* like a good many other women: indeed I often content myself with the *hors d'oeuvres* and don't take any more. Surely you understand that a woman goes on getting more and more excited for an hour or two and no man is capable of bringing her to the highest pitch of enjoyment while pleasing himself."

"I'm able", I said stubbornly, "I can go on all night if you please me, so we should skip appetizers."

"No, no!" she replied, laughing, "let us have a banquet then, but begin with lips and tongue!"

The delay, the bandying to and fro of argument and above all, the idea of kissing and tonguing her sex, had brought me to coolness and reason. Was I not just as foolish as Bancroft if I yielded to the—an unknown girl.

I replied finally, "No, little lady, your charms are not for me", and I took my seat again at the table and poured myself out some wine. I had the ordinary American or English youth's repugnance to what seemed like degradation, never guessing that Jeanne was giving me the second lesson in the noble art of seduction, of which my sister had taught me long ago the rudiments.

The next time I was offered *minette*, I had grown wiser and made no scruples; but that's another story. The fact is that in my first visit to Paris I kept perfectly chaste, thanks in part to the example of Ned's blunder; thanks, too, to my dislike of going with any girl sexually whom I didn't really care for, and I didn't care for Jeanne: she was too imperious and imperiousness in a girl is the quality I most dislike, perhaps because I suffer from an overdose of the humor. At any rate, it was not sexual indulgence that broke my health in

Paris; but my passionate desire to learn that had cut down my hours of sleep and exasperated my nerves: I took cold and had a dreadful recurrence of malaria. I wanted rest and time to take breath and think.

The little house in a side-street in the lovely Welsh watering-place was exactly the haven of rest I needed. I soon got well and strong and for the first time learned to know my father. He came for long walks with me, though he was over sixty. After his terrible accident seven years before (he slipped and fell thirty feet into a dry-dock while his ship was being repaired), one side of his hair and moustache had turned white while the other remained jet black. I was astonished first by his vigor: he thought nothing of a ten-mile walk and on one of our excursions I asked him why he had not given me the nomination I wanted as midshipman.

He was curiously silent and waved the subject aside with: "The Navy for you? No!" and he shook his head. A few days afterwards, however, he came back to the subject of his own accord.

"You asked me", he began, "why I didn't send you the nomination for the midshipman's examination. Now I'll tell you. To get on in the British Navy and make a career in it, you should either be well-born or well-off: you were neither. For a youth without position or money, there are only two possible roads up: servility or silence, and you were incapable of both."

"Oh, Governor, how true and how wise of you!" I cried, "but why, why didn't you tell me? I'd have understood then as well as now and thought the more of you for thwarting me."

"You forget", he went on, "that I had trained myself in the other road of silence: it is difficult for me even now to express myself", and he went on with bitterness in voice and accent:

"They drove me to silence: if you knew what I endured before I got my first step as lieutenant. If it hadn't been that I was determined to marry your mother, I could never have swallowed the countless humiliations of my brainless superiors! What would have happened to you I saw as in a glass. You were extraordinarily quick, impulsive and high-tempered: don't you know that brains and energy and will-power are hated by all the wastrels and in this world they are everywhere in the vast majority. Some lieutenant or captain would have taken an instantaneous dislike to you that would have grown on every manifestation of your superiority: he would have laid traps for you of insubordination and insolence probably for months and then in some port where he was powerful, he would have brought you before a court-martial and you would have been dismissed from the Navy in disgrace and perhaps your whole life ruined. The British Navy is the worst place in the world for genius."

That scene began my reconciliation with my father; one more experience completed it.

I got wet through on one of our walks and next day had lumbago; I went to a pleasant Welsh doctor I had become acquainted with and he gave me a bottle of belladonna mixture for external use: "I have not got a proper poison bottle", he added, "and I've no business to give you this" (it is forbidden to dispense poisons in Great Britain save in rough octagonal bottles which betray the nature of their contents to the touch). "I'll not drink it", I said laughing. "Well, if you do", he said, "don't send for me, for there's more than enough here to kill a dozen men!" I took the bottle and curiously enough, we talked belladonna and its effects for some minutes. Richards, (that was his name) promised to send me a black draught the same evening and he assured me that my lumbago would soon be cured and he was right: but the cure was not effected as he thought it would be.

My sister had a girl of all work at this time called Eliza, Eliza Gibby, if I remember rightly. Lizzie, as we called her, was a slight, red-haired girl of perhaps eighteen with really large chestnut-brown eyes and a cheeky pug nose, and freckled neck and arms. I really don't know what induced me first to make up to her; but soon I was kissing her; when I wanted to touch her sex however, she drew away confiding to me that she was afraid of the possible consequences. I explained to her immediately that I would withdraw after the first spasm, and then there would be no more risk. She trusted me and one night she came to my room in her night-dress. I took it off with many kisses and was really astounded by her ivory white skin and almost perfect girlish form. I laid her on the edge of my bed, put her knees comfortably under my arm-pits and began to rub her clitoris: in a moment the brown eyes turned up and I ventured to slip in the head of my sex; to my surprise there was no maidenhead to break through and soon my sex had slipt into the tightest cunt I had ever met. Very soon I played Onan and like that Biblical hero "spilt my seed upon the ground"—which in my case was a carpet.

I then got into bed with her and practiced the whole art of love as I understood it at that time. A couple of hours of it brought me four or five orgasms and Lizzie a couple of dozen, to judge by hurried breathings, inarticulate cries and long kissings that soon became mouthings.

Lizzie was what most men would have thought a perfect bedfellow; but I missed Sophy's science and Sophy's passionate determination to give me the utmost thrill conceivable. Still in a dozen pleasant nights we became great friends and I began to notice that by working in and out very slowly I could after the first orgasm go on indefinitely without spending again. Alas! I had no idea at the time that this control simply marked the first decrease of my sexual power. If I had only known, I would have cut out all the Lizzies that infested my life and reserved myself for the love that was soon to oust the mere sex-urge.

Next door to us lived a doctor's widow with two daughters, the eldest a medium-sized girl with large head and good grey eyes, hardly to be called pretty though all girls were pretty enough to excite me for the next ten years or more. This eldest girl was called Molly—a pet name for Maria. Her sister Kathleen was far more attractive physically: she was rather tall and slight, with a lithe grace of figure that was intensely provocative. Yet though I noted all Kathleen's feline witchery, I fell prone for Molly. She seemed to me both intelligent and witty: she had read widely too and knew both French and German; she was as far above all the American girls I had met in knowledge of books and art as she was inferior to the best of them in bodily beauty. For the first time my mind was excited and interested and I thought I was in love and one late afternoon or early evening on Castle Hill I told her I loved her and we became engaged. Oh, the sweet folly of it all! When she asked me how we should live, what I intended to do, I had no answer ready save the perfect self-confidence of the man who had already proved himself in the struggle of life. Fortunately for me, that didn't seem very convincing to her:

she admitted that she was three years older than I was and if she had said four, she would have been nearer the truth, and she was quite certain I would not find it so easy to win in England as in America: she underrated both my brains and my strength of will. She confided to me that she had a hundred a year of her own: but that, of course, was wholly inadequate. So though she kissed me freely and allowed me a score of little privacies, she was resolved not to give herself completely. Her distrust of my ability and her delightfully piquant reserve heightened my passion and once I won her consent to an immediate marriage. At her best Molly was astonishingly intelligent and frank. One night alone together in our sitting-room which my father and sister left to us, I tried my best to get her to give herself to me. But she shook her head: "it would not be right, dear, till we are married", she persisted.

"Suppose we were on a desert island", I said, "and no marriage possible?" "My darling!" she said kissing me on the mouth and laughing aloud, "don't you know, I should yield then without your urging: you dear! I want you, Sir, perhaps more than you want me." But she wore closed drawers and I didn't know how to unbutton them at the sides and though she grew intensely and quickly excited, I could not break down the final barrier. In any case, before I could win, Fate used her shears decisively.

One morning I reproached Lizzie for not bringing me up a black draught Doctor Richards had promised to send me. "It's on the mantle-piece in the dining-room", I said, "but don't trouble, I'll get it myself", and I ran down as I was. An evening or two later I left the belladonna mixture the doctor had made up for me on the chimney piece! Like the black draught it was dark brown in color and in a similar bottle.

Next morning Lizzie woke me and offered me a glassful of dark liquid: "Your medicine" she said and half asleep still, I told her to leave the breakfast tray on the table by my bed and then drained the glass she offered to me. The taste awoke me: the drink had made my whole mouth and throat dry: I sprang out of bed and went to the looking-glass, yes! yes! the pupils of my eyes were unnaturally distended: had she given me the whole draught of belladonna instead of a black draught? I still heard her on the stairs but why waste time in asking her. I went over to the table, poured out cup after cup of tea and drained them: then I ran down to the dining-room where my sister and father were at breakfast. I poured out their tea and drank cups full of it in silence: then I asked my sister to get me mustard and warm water and met my father's question with a brief explanation and request. "Go to Dr. Richards and tell him to come at once: I've drunk the belladonna mixture by mistake; there's no time to lose." My father was already out of the house! My sister brought me the mustard and I mixed a strong dose with hot water and took it as an emetic; but it didn't work. I went upstairs to my bedroom again and put my fingers down my throat over the bath: I retched and retched but nothing came: plainly the stomach was paralysed. My sister came in crying. "I'm afraid there's no hope, Nita", I said, "the Doctor told me there was enough to kill a dozen men and I've drunk it all fasting; but you've always been good and kind to me, dear, and death is nothing."

She was sobbing terribly, so to give her something to do, I asked her to fetch me a kettle full of hot water; she vanished downstairs to get it and I stood before the glass to make up my accounts with my own soul. I knew now it was the belladonna I had taken, all of it on an empty stomach: no chance; in ten minutes I should be insensible, in a few hours dead: dead! was I afraid? I recognized with pride that I was not one whit afraid or in any doubt. Death is nothing but an eternal sleep, nothing! Yet I wished that I could have had time to prove myself and show what was in me! Was Smith right? Could I indeed have become one of the best heads in the world? Could I have been with the really great ones had I lived? No one could tell now but I made up my mind as at the time of the rattlesnake bite, to do my best to live. All this time I was drinking cold water: now my sister brought the jug of warm water, saying, "It may make you throw up, dear" and I began drinking it in long draughts. Bit by bit I felt it more difficult to think, so I kissed my sister, saying, "I had better get into bed while I can walk, as I'm rather heavy!" And then as I got into bed I said, "I wonder whether I shall be carried out next feet-foremost while they chant the Miserere! Never mind, I've had a great draught of life and I'm ready to go if go I must!"

At this moment Dr. Richards came in: "Now how, how in Goodness' name, man, after our talk and all, how did ye come to take it?" His fussiness and strong Welsh accent made me laugh: "give me the stomach pump, doctor, for I'm full of liquid to the gullet", I cried. I took the tube and pushed it down, sitting up in bed, and he depressed it; but only a brownish stream came: I had absorbed most of the belladonna. That was nearly my last conscious thought, only in myself I determined to keep thinking as long as I could. I heard the Doctor say: "I'll give him opium—a large dose", and I smiled to myself at the thought that the narcotic opium and the stimulant belladonna would alike induce unconsciousness, the one by exciting the heart's action, the other by slackening it....

Many hours afterwards I awoke: it was night, candles were burning and Dr. Richards was leaning over me: "do you know me?" he asked and at once I answered: "Of course I know you, Richards", and I went on jubilant to say: "I'm saved: I've won through. Had I been going to die, I should never have recovered consciousness." To my astonishment his brow wrinkled and he said, "drink this and then go to sleep again quietly: it's all right", and he held a glass of whitish liquid to my lips. I drained the glass and said joyously: "Milk! how funny you should give me milk; that's not prescribed in any of your books." He told me afterwards it was Castor-oil he had given me and I had mistaken it for milk. I somehow felt that my tongue was running away with me even before he laid his hand on my forehead to quiet me saying: "There please! don't talk, rest! please!" and I pretended to obey him; but couldn't make out why he shut me up! I could not recall my words either—why?

A dreadful thought shook me suddenly: had I been talking nonsense? My father's face too appeared to be dreadfully perturbed while I was speaking.

"Could one think sanely and yet talk like a madman? What an appalling fate!" I resolved in that case to use my revolver on myself as soon as I knew that my state was hopeless: that thought gave me peace and I turned at once to compose myself. In a few minutes more I was fast asleep.

The next time I awoke, it was again night and again the Doctor was beside me and my sister: "Do you know me?" he asked again, and again I replied: "Of course I know you and Sis here as well."

"That's great", he cried joyously, "now you'll soon be well again."

"Of course I shall", I cried joyously, "I told you that before: but you seemed hurt; did I wander in my mind?"

"There, there", he cried, "don't excite yourself and you'll soon be well again!"

"Was it a near squeak?" I asked.

"You must know it was", he replied, "you took sixty grains of belladonna fasting and the books give at most quarter of a grain for a dose and declare one grain to be generally fatal. I shall never be able to brag of your case in the medical journals", he went on smiling, "for no one would ever believe that a heart could go on galloping far too fast to count, but certainly two hundred odd times a minute for thirty odd hours without bursting. You've been tested", he concluded, "as no one was ever tested before and have come back safe! But now sleep again", he said, "sleep is Nature's restorative."

Next morning I awoke rested but very weak: the Doctor came in and sponged me in warm water and changed my linen: my nightshirt and a great part of the sheet were quite brown. "Can you make water?" he asked, handing me a bed-dish: I tried and at once succeeded.

"The wonder is complete!!" he cried, "I'll bet, you have cured your lumbago too", and indeed I was completely free of pain.

That evening or the next my father and I had a great, heart-to-heart talk. I told him all my ambitions and he tried to persuade me to take one hundred pounds a year from him to continue my studies. I told him I couldn't, though I was just as grateful. "I'll get work as soon as I am strong", I said; but his unselfish affection shook my very soul and when he told me that my sister, too, had agreed he should make me the allowance, I could only shake my head and thank him. That evening I went to bed early and he came and sat with me: he said that the doctor advised that I should take a long rest. Strange colored lights kept sweeping across my sight every time I shut my eyes: so I asked him to lie beside me and hold my hand. At once he lay down beside me and with his hand in mine, I soon fell asleep and slept like a log till seven next morning. I awoke perfectly well and refreshed and was shocked to see that my father's face was strangely drawn and white and when he tried to get off the bed, he nearly fell. I saw then that he had lain all the night through on the brass edge of the bed rather than risk disturbing me to give him more room. From that time to the end of his noble and unselfish life, some twenty-five years later, I had only praise and admiration for him.

As soon as I began to take note of things, I remarked that Lizzie no longer came near my room. One day I asked my sister what had become of her. To my astonishment my sister broke out in passionate dislike of her: "while you were lying unconscious", she cried, "and the doctor was taking your pulse every few minutes, evidently frightened: he asked me could he get a prescription made up at once: he wanted to inject morphia, he said, to stop or check the racing of your heart. He wrote the prescription and I sent Lizzie with it and told her to be as quick as she could for your life might depend on it. When she didn't come back in ten minutes, I got the Doctor to write it out again and sent Father with it. He brought it back in double-quick time. Hours passed and Lizzie didn't return: she had gone out before ten and didn't get back till it was almost one. I asked her where she had been? Why she hadn't got back sooner? She replied coolly that she had been listening to the Band. I was so shocked and angry I wouldn't keep her another moment. I sent her away at once. Think of it! I have no patience with such heartless brutes!"

Lizzie's callousness seemed to me even stranger than it seemed to my sister. I have often noticed that girls are less considerate of others than even boys, unless their affections are engaged, but I certainly thought I had half won Lizzie at least! However, the fact is so peculiar that I insert it here for what it may be worth.

During my convalescence which lasted three months, Molly went for a visit to some friends: at the time I regretted it; now looking back I have no doubt she went away to free herself from an engagement she thought ill-advised. Missing her I went about with her younger, prettier sister Kathleen who was more sensuous and more affectionate than Molly.

A little later, Molly went to Dresden to stay with an elder married sister: thence she wrote to me to set her free and I consented as a matter of course very willingly. Indeed I had already more real affection for Kathleen than Molly had ever called to life in me.

As I got strong again I came to know a young Oxford man who professed to be astonished at my knowledge of literature and one day he came to me with the news that Grant Allen, the writer, had thrown up his job as Professor of Literature at Brighton College: "why should you not apply for it: it's about two hundred pounds a year and they can do no worse than refuse you."

I wrote to Taine at once, telling him of the position and my illness and asking him to send me a letter of recommendation if he thought I was fit. By return of post I got a letter from him recommending me in the warmest way. This letter I sent on to Dr. Bigge, the Headmaster, together with one from Professor Smith of Lawrence and Dr. Bigge answered by asking me to come to Brighton to see him. Within twenty-four hours I went and was accepted forthwith, though he thought I looked too young to keep discipline. He soon realised that his fears were merely imaginary: I could have kept order in a cage of hyenas.

A long book would not exhaust my year as a Master in Brighton College; but only two or three happenings require notice here as affecting my character and its growth. First of all, I found in every class of thirty lads, five or six of real ability, and in the whole school three or four of astonishing minds, well graced, too in manners and spirit. But six out of ten were both stupid and obstinate and these I left wholly to their own devices.

Dr. Bigge warned me by a report of my work exhibited on the notice-board of the Sixth Form that while some of my scholars displayed great improvement, the vast majority showed none at all. I went to see him immediately and handed him my written resignation to take place at any moment he pleased. "I cannot bother with the fools who don't even wish to learn", I said, "but I'll do anything for the others."

Most of the abler boys liked me, I believe, and a little characteristic incident came to help me. There was a Form-master named Wolverton, an Oxford man and son of a well-known Archdeacon, who sometimes went out with me to the theatre or the roller-skating rink in West Street. One night at the rink he drew my attention to a youth in a straw hat going out accompanied by a woman.

"Look at that", said Wolverton, "there goes So and So in our colors and with a woman! Did you see him?"

"I didn't pay much attention", I replied, "but surely there's nothing unusual in a Sixth Form boy trying his wings outside the nest."

At the next Masters' Meeting, to my horror, Wolverton related the circumstance and ended up by declaring that unless the boy could give the name of the woman, he should be expelled. He called upon me as a witness to the fact.

I got up at once and said that I was far too shortsighted to distinguish the boy at half the distance and I refused to be used in the matter in any way.

Dr. Bigge thought the offence very grave: "the morals of a boy", he declared, "were the most important part of his education: the matter must be probed to the bottom: he thought that on reflection I would not deny that I had seen a College boy that night in colors and in suspicious company."

I thereupon got up and freed my soul; the whole crew seemed to me mere hypocrites.

"In the Doctor's own House", I said, "where I take evening preparation, I could give him a list of boys who are known as lovers, notorious even, and so long as this vice is winked at throughout the school, I shall be no party to persecuting anybody for yielding to legitimate and natural passion." I had hardly got out the last words when Cotteril, the son of the Bishop of Edinburgh, got up and called upon me to free his House from any such odious and unbearable suspicion.

I retorted immediately that there was a pair in his house known as "The Inseparables" and went on to state that my quarrel was with the whole boardinghouse system and not with individual masters who, I was fain to believe, did their best.

The Vice-principal, Dr. Newton, was the only one who even recognized my good motives: he came away from the meeting with me and advised me to consult with his wife. After this I was practically boycotted by the masters: I had dared to say in public what Wolverton and others of them had admitted to me in private a dozen times.

Mrs. Newton, the vice-principal's wife, was one of the leaders of Brighton society: she was what the French call une maitresse femme, and a born leader in any society. She advised me to form girls' classes in literature for the half-holidays each week; was good enough to send out the circulars and lend her drawing-room for my first lectures. In a week I had fifty pupils who paid me half a crown a lesson and I soon found myself drawing ten pounds a week in addition to my pay. I saved every penny and thus came in a year to monetary freedom.

At every crisis in my life I have been helped by good friends who have aided me out of pure kindness at cost of time and trouble to themselves. Smith helped me in Lawrence and Mrs. Newton at Brighton out of bountiful human sympathy.

Before this even I had got to know a man named Harold Hamilton, manager of the London & County Bank, I think, at Brighton. It amused him to see how quickly and regularly my balance grew: soon I confided my plans to him and my purpose: he was all sympathy. I lent him books and his daughter Ada was assiduous at all my lectures.

In the nick of time for me the war broke out between Chili and Peru: Chilian bonds dropped from 90 to 60: I saw Hamilton and assured him that Chili if left alone, could beat all South America: he advised me to wait and see. A little later Bolivia threw in her lot with Peru and Chilian bonds fell to 43 or 44. At once I went to Hamilton and asked him to buy Chilians for all I possessed on a margin of three or four. After much talk he did what I wished on a margin of ten: a fortnight later came the news of the first Chilian victory and Chilians jumped to 60 odd and continued to climb steadily: I sold at over 80 and thus netted from my first five hundred pounds over two thousand pounds and by Christmas was free once more to study with a mind at case. Hamilton told me that he had followed my lead a little later but had made more from a larger investment.

The most important happening at Brighton I must now relate. I have already told in a pen-portrait of Carlyle published by Austin Harrison in the "English Review" some twelve years ago how I went one Sunday morning and called upon my hero, Thomas Carlyle in Chelsea. I told there, too, how on more than one Sunday I used to meet him on his morning walk along the Chelsea embankment, and how once at least he talked to me of his wife and admitted his impotence.

I only gave a summary of a few talks in my portrait of him; for the traits did not call for strengthening by repetition; but here I am inclined to add a few details, for everything about Carlyle at his best, is of enduring interest!

When I told him how I had been affected by reading Emerson's speech to the students of Dartmouth College and how it had in a way forced me to give up my law-practice and go to Europe to study, he broke in excitedly:

"I remember well reading that very page to my wife and saying that nothing like it for pure nobility had been heard since Schiller went silent. It had a great power with it.... And so that started you off and changed your way of life?... I don't wonder ... it was a great Call."

After that Carlyle seemed to like me. At our final parting too, when I was going to Germany to study and he wished me "God speed and Goodspeed! on the way that lies before ye", he spoke again of Emerson and the sorrow he had felt on parting with him, deep, deep sorrow and regret, and he added, laying his hands on my shoulders, "sorrowing most of all that they should see his face no more forever." I remembered the passage and cried:

"Oh, Sir, I should have said that, for mine is the loss, mine the unspeakable misfortune now", and through my tears I saw that his eyes too were full.

He had just given me a letter to Froude, "good, kindly Froude", who, he was sure, would help me in any way of commendation to some literary position "if I have gone, as is most likely", and in due time Froude did help me as I shall tell in the proper place.

My pen-portrait of Carlyle was ferociously attacked by a kinsman, Alexander Carlyle, who evidently believed that I had got my knowledge of Carlyle's weakness from Froude's revelations in 1904. But luckily for me, Sir Charles Jessel remembered a dinner in the Garrick Club given by him in 1886 or 1887, at which both Sir Richard Quain and myself were present. Jessel recalled distinctly that I had that evening told the story of Carlyle's impotence as explaining the sadness of his married life and had then asserted that the confession came to me from Carlyle himself.

At that dinner Sir Richard Quain said that he had been Mrs. Carlyle's physician and that he would tell me later exactly what Mrs. Carlyle had confessed to him. Here is Quain's account as he gave it me that night in a private room at the Garrick. He said:

"I had been a friend of the Carlyles for years: he was a hero to me, one of the wisest and best of men: she was singularly witty and worldly-wise and pleased me even more than the sage. One evening I found her in great pain on the sofa: when I asked her where the pain was, she indicated her lower belly and I guessed at once that it must be some trouble connected with the change of life.

"I begged her to go up to her bedroom and I would come in a quarter of an hour and examine her, assuring her the while that I was sure I could give her almost immediate relief. She went upstairs. In about ten minutes I asked her husband, would he come with me? He replied in his broadest Scotch accent, always a sign of emotion with him:

'I'll have naething to do with it. Ye must just arrange it yerselves'.

"Thereupon I went upstairs and knocked at Mrs. Carlyle's bedroom door: no reply: I tried to enter: the door was locked and unable to get an answer I went downstairs in a huff and flung out of the house.

"I stayed away for a fortnight but when I went back one evening I was horrified to see how ill Mrs. Carlyle looked stretched out on the sofa, and as pale as death. 'You're worse?' I asked.

'Much worse and weaker!' she replied.

'You naughty obstinate creature!' I cried.

'I'm your friend and your doctor and anything but a fool: I'm sure I can cure you in double-quick time and you prefer to suffer. It's stupid of you and worse—Come up now at once and think of me only as your doctor', and I half lifted, half helped her to the door: I supported her up the stairs and at the door of her room, she said:

'Give me ten minutes, Doctor, and I'll be ready. I promise you I won't lock the door again.'

"With that assurance I waited and in ten minutes knocked and went in.

"Mrs. Carlyle was lying on the bed with a woolly-white shawl round her head and face. I thought it absurd affectation in an old married woman, so I resolved on drastic measures: I turned the light full on, then I put my hand under her dress and with one toss threw it right over her head. I pulled her legs apart, dragged her to the edge of the bed and began inserting the speculum in her vulva: I met an obstacle: I looked—and immediately sprang up: 'Why, you're a virgo intacta' (an untouched virgin!) I exclaimed.

She pulled the shawl from her head and said: 'What did you expect?'

'Anything but that', I cried, 'in a woman married these five and twenty years!'

"I soon found the cause of her trouble and cured it or rather did away with it: that night she rested well and was her old gay, mutinous self when I called next day.

"A little later she told me her story.

"After the marriage", she said, "Carlyle was strange and out of sorts, very nervous, he seemed, and irritable. When we reached the house we had supper and about eleven o'clock I said I would go to bed, being rather tired: he nodded and grunted something. I put my hands on his shoulders as I passed him and said "Dear, do you know that you haven't kissed me once, all day—this day of days!" and I bent down and laid my cheek against his. He kissed me; but said: "You, women are always kissing—I'll be up soon!" Forced to be content with that I went upstairs, undressed and got into bed: he hadn't even kissed me of his own accord, the whole day!

"A little later he came up, undressed and got into bed beside me. I expected him to take me in his arms and kiss and caress me.

"'Nothing of the sort, he lay there, jiggling like', ("I guessed what she meant", said Quain, "the poor devil in a blue funk was frigging himself to get a cock-stand.") 'I thought for some time', Mrs. Carlyle went on, 'one moment I wanted to kiss and caress him; the next moment I felt indignant. Suddenly it occurred to me that in all my hopes and imaginings of a first night, I had never got near the reality: silent, the man lay there jiggling, jiggling. Suddenly I burst out laughing: it was all too wretched! too absurd!'

"'At once he got out of bed with the one scornful word 'Woman!' and went into the next room: he never came back to my bed.

"'Yet he's one of the best and noblest men in the world and if he had been more expansive and told me oftener that he loved me, I could easily have forgiven him any bodily weakness; silence is love's worst enemy and after all he never really made me jealous save for a short time with Lady Ashburnham. I suppose I've been as happy with him as I could have been with anyone yet—'

"That's my story", said Quain in conclusion, "and I make you a present of it: even in the Elysian Fields I shall be content to be in the Carlyles' company. They were a great pair!"

Just one scene more. When I told Carlyle how I had made some twenty-five hundred pounds in the year and told him besides how a banker offered me almost the certainty of a great fortune if I would buy with him a certain coal-wharf at Tunbridge Wells (it was Hamilton's pet scheme), he was greatly astonished. "I want to know", I went on, "if you think I'll be able to do good work in literature; if so I'll do my best. Otherwise I ought to make money and not waste time in making myself another second-rate writer."

"No one can tell you that", said Carlyle slowly, "You'll be lucky if you reach the knowledge of it yourself before ye die! I thought my Frederic was great work; yet the other day you said I had buried him under the dozen volumes and you may be right; but have I ever done anything that will live?—"

"Sure", I broke in, heartsore at my gibe, "Sure, your French Revolution must live and the "Heroes and Hero Worship", and "Latter Day Pamphlets" and, and—"

"Enough", he cried, "You're sure?"

"Quite, quite sure", I repeated. Then he said, "You can be equally sure of your own place; for we can all reach the heights we are able to oversee."

AFTERWORD TO THE FIRST VOLUME OF MY LIFE'S STORY.

I had hardly written "Finis" at the end of this book when the faults in it, faults both of omission and commission, rose in swarms and robbed me of my joy in the work.

It will be six or seven years at least before I shall know whether the book is good and life-worthy or not and yet need drives me to publish it at once.

Did not Horace require nine years to judge his work?

I, therefore, want the reader to know my intention; I want to give him the key, so to speak, to this chamber of my soul.

First of all I wished to destroy or, at least, to qualify the universal opinion that love in youth is all romance and idealism. The masters all paint it crowned with roses of illusion: Juliet is only fourteen: Romeo, having lost his love, refuses life: Goethe follows Shakespeare in his Mignon and Marguerite: even the great humorist Heine and the so-called realist, Balzac, adopt the same convention. Yet to me it is absolutely untrue in regard to the male in boyhood and early youth, say from thirteen to twenty: the sex-urge, the lust of the flesh was so overwhelming in me that I was conscious only of desire. When the rattlesnake's poison-bag is full, he strikes at everything that moves, even the blades of grass; the poor brute is blinded and in pain with the overplus. In my youth I was blind, too, through excess of semen.

I often say that I was thirty-five years of age before I saw an ugly woman, a woman that is, whom I didn't desire. In early puberty, all women tempted me; and all girls still more poignantly.

From twenty to twenty-three, I began to distinguish qualities of the mind and heart and soul; to my amazement, I preferred Kate to Lily, though Lily gave me keener sensations: Rose excited me very little yet I knew she was of rarer, finer quality than even Sophy who seemed to me an unequalled bedfellow.

From that time on the charms of spirit, heart and soul, drew me with ever-increasing magnetism, overpowering the pleasures of the senses though plastic beauty exercises as much fascination over me today as it did fifty years ago. I never knew the illusion of love, the rose-mist of passion till I was twenty-seven and I was intoxicated with it for years; but that story will be for my second volume.

Now strange to say, my loves till I left America just taught me as much of the refinements of passion, as is commonly known in these States.

France and Greece made me wise to all that Europe has to teach; that deeper knowledge too is for the second volume in which I shall relate how a French girl surpassed Sophy's art as far as Sophy surpassed Rose's ingenuous yielding.

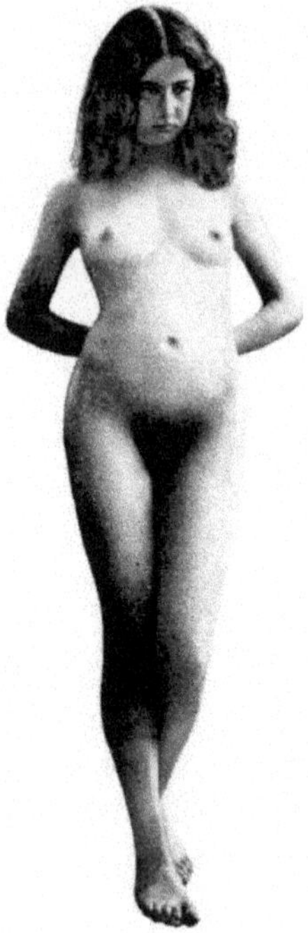

But it was not till I was over forty and had made my second journey round the world that I learned in India and Burmah, all the high mysteries of sense and the profounder artistry of the immemorial East. I hope to tell it all in a third volume, together with my vision of European and world-politics. Then I may tell in a fourth volume of my breakdown in health and how I won it back again and how I found a pearl of women and learned from her what affection really means, the treasures of tenderness, sweet-thoughted-wisdom and self-abnegation that constitute the woman's soul. Vergil may lead Dante through Hell and Purgatory: it is Beatrice alone who can show him Paradise and guide him to the Divine. Having learned the wisdom of women—to absorb and not to reason—having experienced the irresistible might of gentleness and soul-subduing pity, I may tell of my beginnings in literature and art and how I won to the front and worked with my peers and joyed in their achievements, always believing my own to be better. Without this blessed conviction how could I ever have undergone the labor or endured the shame or faced the loneliness of the Garden, or carried the cross of my own Crucifixion; for every artist's life begins in joy and hope and ends in the shrouding shadows of doubt and defeat and the chill of everlasting night.

In these books as in my life, there should be a crescendo of interest and understanding: I shall win the ears of men first and their senses, and later their minds and hearts and finally their souls; for I shall show them all the beautiful things I have discovered in Life's pilgrimage, all the sweet and lovable things too and so encourage and cheer them and those aftercomers, my peers, whose sounding footsteps already I seem to hear, and I shall say as little as may be of defeats and downfalls and disgraces save by way of warning; for it is courage men need most in life, courage and lovingkindness.

Is it not written in the book of Fate that he who gives most receives most and do we not all, if we would tell the truth, win more love than we give: Are we not all debtors to the overflowing bounty of God?

Frank Harris.

The Catskills Mts., this 25th day of August 1922.

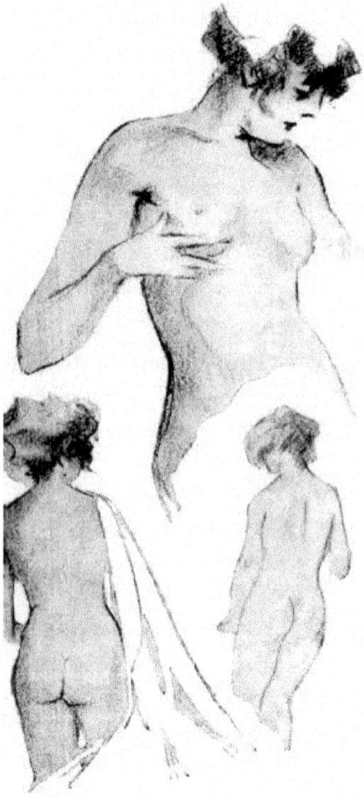

Milton Keynes UK
Ingram Content Group UK Ltd.
UKHW020758200524
442968UK00018B/748

9 789357 967365